The Archaeology of Mothering

The Archaeology of Mothering

An African-American Midwife's Tale

Laurie A. Wilkie

ROUTLEDGE
NEW YORK AND LONDON

Published in 2003 by
Routledge
29 West 35th Street
New York, New York 10001
www.routledge-ny.com

Published in Great Britain by
Routledge
11 New Fetter Lane
London EC4P 4EE
www.routledge.co.uk

Library of Congress Cataloging-in-Publication Data

Wilkie, Laurie A., 1968–
    The archaeology of mothering : an African-American midwife's tale / Laurie A. Wilkie.
        p.   cm.
    ISBN 0-415-94569-0 (Hardcover : alk. paper) – ISBN 0-415-94570-4
(Paperback : alk. paper)
    1. Perryman, Lucrecia.   2. African American midwives—Alabama—
Mobile—Biography.   3. African American mothers—Social conditions—History.
4. Women slaves—United States—Social conditions—History.   5. Motherhood—
United States—History.   I. Title.
RG950.P474W54   2003
618.2′0089′96073—dc21

                                                                    2003006002

To Mom and Alex

Contents

List of Figures

List of Tables

Acknowledgments

I was fortunate to be surrounded by many friends, family members, and colleagues who helped directly and indirectly with this project, and though I am sure I will overlook people here, please know that all input has been greatly appreciated. If it were not for George Shorter's invitation to become involved in this project, and later, his encouragement that we follow through on the excavation in published form, the years of interpretive simmering that went into this project would never have occurred.

The archaeological materials recovered from the Perryman site were housed for a number of years at the Archaeology Laboratory of Louisiana State University, where the washing, cataloging, and analysis of the materials took place. A number of LSU graduate and undergraduate students helped with the materials, and I would particularly like to thank Michelle Fontenot, Meghan Burnett, Karen Martinez-Lopez, Rachel Campo, and Brad Duplantis. Meghan and Brad also did the preliminary illustrations for a number of the artifacts.

Earlier aspects of this prospect received valuable feedback from Barbara Voss, Bonnie Clark, Amy Ramsay, and Robert Schmidt of Berkeley, and I likewise received helpful feedback from Amy Young and Garrett Fessler on earlier aspects of the project. Chats off and on over the years with Maria Franklin have also greatly enriched this project. Margaret Conkey and Rosemary Joyce have mentored me during different aspects of this project, and their insights and support have been invaluable. Rosemary provided invaluable advice into the narrative aspect of this work, and I am most grateful. Rosemary was the first to suggest that Hazel, my fictional interviewer, needed to be more accessible as a person of her own. I am also grateful to Kathy Corbett, who took off her architectural historian hat to read through the narrative portion and provided keen literary perspectives. Any success I have had in making Hazel an important voice in this dialogue owes much to Kathy's urging and support. I tried out different aspects of this work on various undergraduate and graduate students during the project's development, and they always provided me with additional insights and valuable critiques. They have my sincere thanks.

I appreciate the comments and suggestions made by Mary Beaudry, a reviewer for Routledge, and an anonymous reviewer for Routledge; their thoughtful reviews greatly aided the final revisions of the manuscript. Mary, in an act of generosity, made detailed editorial suggestions that tremendously improved the flow and logic of the document. I also thank the funding sources that supported this project. The University of California's Committee on Research first funded this project as a Faculty Mentor Grant that allowed me to work closely with Meg Conkey; later, the Committee on Research granted me a Humanitites Fellowship, which allowed me to take a full year of sabbatical leave. Ultimately, this funding allowed me to complete this work.

Frieda Roberts, the Mobile County assessor, provided great support, and she and her staff on different occasions provided navigational help through the county records. Likewise, I would like to thank the staffs of the Mobile Public Library's Mobile History Room, the staff members of the University of South Alabama Archives and the Mobile Municipal Archive; their help greatly enriched the historical content of this project. I would like to thank Marilyn Culpepper, executive director of the Historic Mobile Preservation Society for permission to reproduce a photograph of Lucrecia Perryman from her organization's William E. Wilson Photographic Archive, as well as for being very gracious and a pleasure to work with.

Likewise, I greatly appreciate Dr. Greg Waselkov of the University of South Alabama for supporting the initial development of this project in his monograph series. Without his urging that George and I write the project up, I would not have been inspired to develop the research in its current form. Likewise, Sonja Kaderly Axsmith, a staff member of the University of South Alabama's Center for Archaeological Studies lent her geneaological expertise to this project, helping George and me to sort out the original lineages for the Perrymans.

I would like to thank Dr. Bill Davidson, former chair of the Department of Geography and Anthropology at LSU, who originally invited me to spend my sabbatical there and made me most welcome, as did his successor, Dr. Craig Colten. I would also like to thank the faculty and graduate students of LSU who provided various kinds of support during the writing process, ranging from provocative debates to ensuring that I was properly plied with caffeine. Of course, the LSU faculty member I owe the most to is my husband, Paul Farnsworth, who is a constant source of physical and intellectual support. Paul not only listened to my ongoing ramblings with great patience, but also allowed me to take over his office and take the "good" printer during my yearlong stay.

Of course, I need to acknowledge my lovely daughter, Alexandra, who ultimately made the current study possible. She has spent her entire life indoctrinating me into the mysteries of motherhood, and patiently copes with me as I stumble. In her company, I have come not only to know those highly romanticized rewards of motherhood, but have also seen the ways that my new status has irrevocably changed the way I am perceived in the world—for the better and worse. I am sometimes less of a scholar to be her mom, and sometimes less of a mom to be a scholar, but she is wonderful at providing me with "daughter-love," and forgives me, for now, my flaws.

Priti Gress, archaeology editor for Routledge, has been wonderful to work with, and I greatly appreciate her support of this project. Salwa Jabado, editorial assistant at Routledge, has also been very supportive and quick to respond to questions and concerns. I would also like to thank Nikki Hirschman, my production editor, and Norma McLemore, who copyedited the manuscript for Routledge. I have enjoyed working with the press.

Lastly, I would like to thank the Butler family of Mobile for supporting my efforts to understand the experiences of their ancestors. I hope they find the current work of value to them. I have come to hold a great deal of respect for their family, and have been enriched by the experience of meeting them. Thank you.

Prologue

Since mothering is a topic that defies neutrality and distance given our particular societal context, I think it important to briefly discuss how I came to engage in this study, and how my thinking first developed. I also want to briefly introduce the reader to my reasoning behind structuring the study as I have done. I have been associated with this project for seven years now—a length of time that in some ways seems embarrassingly long but that has also allowed me to develop several very different subject positions relative to it.

The Perryman materials were excavated in 1994 during the relandscaping and expansion of facilities at Crawford Park in Mobile, Alabama. I was finishing my dissertation in Louisiana at the time, and when invited by a friend and colleague, George Shorter of the University of Southern Alabama, to join him in the salvage excavation of the site, I agreed. At the time, the excavation had to be undertaken quickly, and we did not have any documentary information regarding the archaeological site. The materials were in good preservation and context. Given the paucity of later historical sites excavated in Mobile (and the prevalence of pot-hunting activities in the city), we decided that the site had the potential to shed light on the experiences of families living in late-nineteenth-century Mobile, and, given the opportunity, should be excavated rather than destroyed. It was only as we conducted preliminary archival research that we realized that the site had been occupied by a widowed African-American midwife during the 1880s and 1890s.

Lucrecia Perryman had lived on the property, first with her husband and children. After her husband's death, she turned to midwifery as a means of supporting her family. The small, shallow trash deposit George had found and collected dated to the period of the Perrymans' married life together, while the back-filled well dated to the time of her retirement from midwifery. The vast numbers of medically related artifacts suggested that Perryman had dumped much of her "tool kit" following retirement.

One of my interests during my dissertation research at a Louisiana plantation had been African-American medical practice and the fusion of traditional herbal remedies with patent medicine use (Wilkie 2000a). I was thrilled to have the opportunity to study African-American midwifery through archaeology. Lay midwives commonly supervised births by black and white women in the South. In the northern United States, this was a role commonly held by immigrant women from Italy, Ireland, and eastern Europe. As the end of the nineteenth

century approached, medical school–trained physicians were being produced
in great numbers by growing numbers of new medical schools (Mongeau 1985;
Susie 1988). The medical industry was actively looking for arenas of expansion.
Obstetrics and pediatrics, traditionally falling in the treatment realm of women
health professionals, such as midwives, became ideal arenas for expansion. The
obstacle to such expansion was, of course, the midwife.

The American Medical Association (AMA) began a systematic campaign in
the early twentieth century to shake women's faith in midwives. In the South, in
a state-by-state "informational" campaign, African-American midwives were
portrayed as superstitious, inept, elderly, unsanitary, and generally unhealthy to
newborns (e.g., Baughman 1928; see S. Smith 1995). State legislatures enacted
legislation requiring that midwives be licensed, supervised, and regulated by
the state in which they worked. They were limited as to what medicines or
procedures they could use, and many found that requests for license renewals
were denied, effectively forcing them to retire. Eventually, lay midwifery was
eliminated in the South, and women of all socioeconomic statuses and colors
found the only birth option for them was a physician-directed hospital birth
(Susie 1988). Though the experiences of New England midwife Martha Ballard,
as recorded in her diary, have become well known through the tremendous
work of Laurel Thatcher Ulrich (1991), documents left by midwives are rare.
Although feminist historians became interested in the experiences of African-
American midwives and conducted several oral history projects (e.g., Susie
1988; Logan 1989; S. Smith 1995; Fraser 1998), interviews were with women
whose practices had been shaped by the period of regulation, not those who
came before. Regulation came to Alabama in 1925, 14 years after Lucrecia's
retirement. The Perryman materials, therefore, provided a unique opportunity
to study pre-regulation midwifery practice, particularly a means of studying a
distinct ethnomedical tradition.

I worked on the materials from the site in this vein through 1995 and part of
1996, during which time I was hired to a tenure-track position at the University
of California, Berkeley. While I worked on the midwifery research during my
first semester at Berkeley, I quickly found my attentions distracted by the need
to publish a "tenure book" from the dissertation. By the middle of 1996 and
early 1997, my husband and I were trying to start a family, and slow progress
toward that goal left me with little interest in studying midwifery, so the project
sat untended but not forgotten.

When I was pregnant, I was drawn back to the project, but with my thoughts
filled with images of cherub-faced infants, I found myself more intrigued by
the birthing aspect of midwifery practice. I became fascinated by the ways that
midwives were able to combine traditional and new medical practices and products into the birth experience in ways that would have been reassuring to the
different generations of women attending a particular birth. It was during this
time that I first explored the idea of African-American midwives serving as

generational and gender mediators for their communities (Wilkie 2000b, n.d.). I was also impressed with the autonomy over their bodies that women had during midwife-assisted births, and how many practices from midwifery had become incorporated into what was presented to me in birthing classes as enlightened physician-directed birth. I developed these ideas through October 1997, when the birth of my daughter pretty much slammed the brakes on further writing for a time.

As the "must-publish" tasks necessary to earn tenure became completed, I once again returned to my consideration of the Perryman family in the spring of 2000. George Shorter was by then (and remains) a lab director in the Archaeology Laboratory of the University of Southern Alabama (USA), under the direction of Dr. Gregory Waselkov. Waselkov has had a long-term commitment to making Alabama archaeology accessible to the public, and one successful example of this has been USA's archaeological monograph series, supported by the Alabama Historic Commission, which published volumes on local archaeology directed toward lay audiences. The Perryman site seemed like a perfect addition to the series, and George and I agreed to finally write up the "how many of what was found where" aspect of the site in its entirety (Wilkie and Shorter 2001).

When I sat down to do the pedestrian task of determining minimum numbers of vessels counts for the entire assemblage, I realized that in my previous work, I had ignored the small assemblage dating to the period before Lucrecia was a midwife. In my focus on her life as a midwife, I had ignored Perryman's life as a wife and mother. I had not made this connection despite the great attention I had paid in my other research projects to the literature in history discussing the experiences of African-American women during enslavement (e.g., Giddings 1984; A. Davis 1983; Collins 2000; J. Jones 1985). Motherhood and the roles of mothering had not entered my mind as themes that tied together the archaeology. A review of the existing literature, with only a few exceptions (e.g., Edwards-Ingram 2001; Larsen 1994), demonstrates that I am not alone in failure to "see" motherhood.

I realized that I needed to intellectually regroup and reconsider the ways that I was looking at the materials from this site. The archaeology provided two small glimpses into a long life-history narrative. I realized that I had missed one of the most important sets of contrasts that surely shaped much of Lucrecia Perryman's life experience. She had been a mother during enslavement; she had been a mother after enslavement. I reread transcripts of ex-slave narratives gathered by the WPA's Federal Writer's Project in the 1930s. For the first time I noticed how many women distinguished between the numbers of children they had born in slavery versus freedom (see, e.g., Rawick 1973, 1974a, 1974b, 1977, 1979).

Lucrecia, by my best historical figuring, had 11 children. Five were born during slavery; six were born in freedom. Only three of her slavery-born children made it to adulthood, and only one of those outlived their mother. Five of

Lucrecia's freedom children lived to adulthood; of those, four outlived their mother. While Marshall was alive, Lucrecia Perryman's chosen professions were full-time wife and mother. Only after Marshall's death and the loss of her eldest son's income did Lucrecia reenter the workforce, as a midwife.

Upon reading Patricia Hill Collins's 1994 essay "Shifting the Center: Race, Class, and Feminist Theorizing about Motherhood," I felt that I could perhaps now better understand Lucrecia Perryman's sojourn into midwifery. Once she could no longer support her children as their full-time mother, she turned to motherwork for her community. By working as a midwife, she increased, not diminished, the circle of those she mothered. Only once I delved further into the literature on mothering did I realize that Lucrecia was contending with multiple and conflicting social constructions of what it meant to be a woman and mother throughout her lifetime. Ultimately, even the elimination of lay midwifery was the triumph of one mothering paradigm over another.

Archaeologists who work in the richly recorded past endure a challenge not faced by our brethren who study the deep past. I know the names of most of the people who lived at the site designated 1MB99. I know their kinship relationships to one another. I have traced them through census and legal documents. I have held their death certificates. I have stood at their graves. I have seen some of their faces in photographs. I have spoken to some of their descendants, people who remembered and loved them. This is no abstract past society or culture I am studying; nor are these hypothesized "agents" or "social actors" who once occupied this site. I am dealing with the material culture of an extended family, one whose members I can identify in the documentary record.

In some ways, there is great freedom in identifying who lived in a space at a particular time. I have the luxury of knowing the Perrymans' race, ethnic heritage, socioeconomic class, and financial dealings. I know when they were born, when they married and had children, and, for the most part, when they died. I can, to some degree, reconstruct when particular family members lived on the property. Some archaeologists who focus on sites that lack the aid of texts have been known to accuse people who do research of the sort that I do as "cheating," "having it easy," or, my favorite, "only needing to be able to read a book" to do the archaeology. I do not know if it's particularly easy, but it is certainly engaging.

There are different challenges that go along with studying the recorded past— especially when dealing with named persons. Those annoying little documentary details always threaten to undermine your interpretation. Before we began the archival research for this project, George Shorter and I engaged in free-association interpretation, hypothesizing that the site occupants might be German or Dutch immigrants, given the apparent preference for pharmacies with German and Dutch proprietors in the assemblage, as well as the presence of German malt extracts. In the field one day, we were able to ramble on about reinforcing ethnic identities through patronage of businesses and so on.

Our first trip to the Mobile library to consult the business directories ended that interpretive fancy. There it was, a perfectly good interpretation ruined by overwhelming documentary evidence that the property occupant-owners were African-American. This is not to say that I have privileged the documentary record over the archaeological—instead, I have tried to maintain an active tension between the two, using one source to interrogate, deconstruct, or illuminate the other. My end goal has always been to construct interpretations in which neither the documentary nor the archaeological evidence can be removed without destroying the integrity of the interpretive argument.

This project, as I mentioned, began as a "quick and dirty" salvage excavation that left us with little time to do background research. Only after years of sporadic research were we able to track down a genealogy of the Perrymans that was complete enough to allow us to find potential descendants. In speaking with several of Lucrecia and Marshall Perryman's great-grandchildren, I was astounded—absolutely astounded—to learn that they had known (and in part been raised by) Lucrecia Perryman's eldest daughter, Caroline, who had been born into slavery in 1853. In our national discourses, we often like to exaggerate how much time has filled the gap between slavery and now, how distant it all seems. Yet, how close it feels as you sit with a family telling you stories their great-aunt told them of slavery days. So little time seems to have passed when you realize there are people living today who were raised by people who were enslaved—what is the passage of years compared to the strength of firsthand memories? The experience left me with a new urgency regarding my research and its relevance, but also an appalling sense of responsibility. I have always striven to be responsible in my interpretations, sprinkling my writing with caveats of "maybe," "perhaps" and "possibly." Now, however, the proscription "Do no harm" held greater weight.

Those of us who work with community partners to create research directions and interpretive possibilities together are sometimes accused of constructing archaeological pasts simply to please particular constituent groups. I have had reviewers of articles I have written about community partnering accuse me of pandering to the vocal minority and selling out the validity of my interpretations. The critique seems to be that by considering the interests of descendant groups, I have somehow sullied the purity of the archaeological record. I have never found consulting with descendant groups leading to anything but an expansion of interpretive potential. If anything, I find myself considering a wider range of potential interpretations and presenting those interpretations. I have found that this approach best serves the goal of committing no harm, for I am not attempting to present a single historical narrative, but attempting to understand the range of possibilities suggested by the archaeological materials. I am not an innovator in this respect, but merely trying to follow the example of others (e.g., Franklin 1997; LaRoche and Blakey 1997; Epperson 1999; Potter 1994; Farnsworth 1993).

I have always found maintaining an analytical distance from my subjects my most difficult challenge. I have always been fascinated by how people experienced the times and places in which they lived, and thrilled by the task of searching for small scraps (or sherds) of evidence that might provide clues and insight into past lives. When I undertake documentary research, I tend to start from the beginning, from the earliest reference I can find to my subject, and then work my way forward whenever possible. Sometimes it is necessary, due to the types of documents being used, to jump forward and backward simultaneously through history, or to sample across time lines. There is a fairly rich documentary record associated with the Perrymans. African-American families are often poorly documented in nineteenth- and early-twentieth-century texts and records. While doing research, you become more intimately acquainted with the details of persons' lives. Mary Beaudry is cited as saying that one should study documents over and over until you can hear the voices of the people who wrote them (Deetz 1993), and certainly the need for intimacy with the documentary record cannot be overstated.

I rarely get to hear voices like those of the Perrymans because the record surviving such families is often bureaucratic in nature, written about them but not by them. Still, I become absorbed in the bits and traces, trying to construct a narrative that makes sense, trying to think of other sources that may allow me to elaborate upon or clarify information. I will admit that I often become fond of the people I study or at least develop an empathy toward them. It is always shocking to me to find death certificates for the people I am researching. Clearly, when studying people born in the 1830s, I intellectually realize that they are no longer living; yet, I am always sad to see confirmation of their passing.

I feel it is very important to explicitly recognize this fondness that I have developed for the Perryman family, particularly Lucrecia Perryman, because from an analytical perspective it can be dangerous. While the Perryman family members were the occupants of this site, and their material represents their collective experiences, in a very real way Lucrecia is the common thread that connected them. She was the person who lived at this site for the duration of the Perrymans' ownership, the person who drew other family members back to the site at different times, the person whose occupation is most marked in the archaeology, and the person whose death led to the abandonment of the site. Her personhood and experiences are central to this study.

It has been important, during the course of this project, to remind myself that while I may know details about the Perrymans, I will never know the Perrymans. This is an important distinction, for it is often tempting to think that we, as the purveyors of garbage, have an inside track on knowing what happened in the past. So how does a scholar ensure that she is not romanticizing her subject or ignoring historical details or interpretations that may cast her subject in an unflattering light? Suddenly, I have crossed into the territory of what makes for good biography versus bad biography. What prehistorian of the deep past typically juggles with those issues? And in reality, this study is an archaeological biography of Lucrecia Perryman and her family; it is an archaeology of their lives at two very different periods of experience. I try to offset my desire for the Perrymans to be merely likable or the urge construct them in a particular way by offering as many competing interpretations of documents and materials as possible, although I do indicate why I favor particular avenues of interpretation over others. In writing this piece, I have attempted to maintain a vigilant consciousness over my interpretations and my motivations for such interpretations. I hope that the result is not too tedious.

There is another aspect to this self-reflection that the reader must also share with me. I have worried that the very personal experiences, those of motherhood, that led me to think about the site and its contents in different ways would also threaten to appropriate the story of the site and its occupants. This, of course, has been an issue for feminist research at large. Motherhood has been seen by some as a universal and unifying experience for women, a place of common ground for the feminist movement (e.g., Chodorow 1978; Ruddick 1980), but feminist critiques (e.g., Collins 2000; Spelman 1988; Giddings 1984; Glenn, Chang and Forcey 1994) emphasize that the experiences of white middle-class heterosexual women have been privileged in these discourses. This could not be a study about mothering from my perspective, nor could I allow my experiences of mothering to subvert or cloak these issues as relevant to the Perrymans. No matter how much empathy I might feel for Lucrecia Perryman, I cannot ever *feel* what it was that she experienced as a mother who first bore children during slavery, or later as a wife raising young children with her husband, or finally, as an impoverished widow struggling to support her family. This is not to say that I do not attempt to imagine it—nor is this to suggest that I do not think that the experience of motherhood and nurturing can be a route for forging commonalities between women of diverse experiences.

I have been careful not to superimpose my own experiences with pregnancy, childbirth, or child rearing into my interpretations of the Perrymans' lives. One of the elephants in the room is, of course, the difference in my and Lucrecia's races. I can intellectualize the intersecting oppressions of race, class, and gender that closed in on African-American women like Lucrecia following Emancipation, but I have not experienced this multifronted oppression firsthand. I am very cognizant that this can be perceived as a weakness of my research. Where possible, I have tried to rely upon the words of African-American women and men, be they from oral history accounts, newspaper reports, literary pieces, or scholarly works. This is an example of how archaeologists must rely on descendant groups, broadly defined, in our interpretations.

While on one level this is an archaeology of Lucrecia Perryman and her life, it is also an archaeology of Lucrecia Perryman as a representative for the broader experiences of thousands of other women who shared her experiences. This is an archaeology of African-American mothering, and as such it is also about women who, as both enslaved and free mothers, raised children in a society that did not value them. This is an archaeology of women who juggled competing paradigms of motherhood in the context of a world that defined them, solely based on their ethnoracial assignment, as "bad mothers." This is also an archaeology of African-American women who did motherwork in the form of midwifery. Though once numerous in their calling, these women were driven out of practice. With their demise, understandings of the body and spirit that had been first spun in Africa, woven together in the Diaspora, and tended and mended by following generations were lost. The materiality of Lucrecia's mothering and midwifery has implications for our understanding of these other persons, who did not drop the trash dropped by the Perrymans but who may have constructed their physical world in similar ways. Relative to this broader, less specific population, there are readings of the material culture found at the Perryman site that may be relevant to them but were not part of the Perrymans' reality.

How should one balance these two scales of reality? How to tell both the story of many without obscuring Lucrecia Perryman's unique personhood, and how to tell the story of many without attributing absolutes to the materials of Lucrecia Perryman that she would contest? An archaeologist is never a disinterested party in constructing interpretations of the past, but at what point does one risk crossing the line between rigorous data-driven interpretation and historical fiction? And of course, the follow-up question is, What constitutes good historical fiction? It is this issue that now deserves some brief consideration.

There has been much written of late about narrative and its uses in archaeology. The use of narrative to present archaeological data from a different perspective is not new in archaeology, particularly within historical archaeology. Ascher and Fairbanks (1971) presented their interpretations of African-American life at a Cumberland Island, Georgia, slave cabin in the form of a radio transcript, alternating between archaeological description and excerpts drawn from WPA ex-slave narratives. The resulting paper is haunting, and it effectively draws the reader back to the people who left the objects rather than to the objects themselves by juxtaposing the oral historical and material records. What may be one of the most widely read archaeology books ever, James Deetz's *In Small Things Forgotten* (1977), begins with a series of short narratives providing verbal snapshots of colonial life. These vignettes, combined with Deetz's wonderfully vernacular and accessible prose, immediately grips readers. Similarly, Leland Ferguson's use of interspersed narrative, within his book *Uncommon Ground* (1992), succeeds in making the relevance of the pottery analyses he presents transparent to the reader.

One of the strengths of narrative is its ability to make dry material accessible to non-professionals, as was the intent behind the recent publication of *Tales of the Vasco* (A. Praetzellis, Ziesing, and Praetgellis 1997). This attribute of accessibility, combined with the ease of using this medium to highlight the experiences of oft-ignored past actors such as women and children, has made narrative popular within feminist archaeologies. Janet Spector's *What This Awl Means* (1993) and Ruth Tringham's "Households with Faces" (1991) did much to draw attention to the use of narrative within feminist archaeological interpretation.

Within historical archaeology, alternative approaches to presenting archaeological interpretation were dramatically explored in a session called "Archaeologists as Storytellers" at the 1997 meetings of the Society for Historical Archaeology. Later published as a special issue of the society's journal (Praetzellis and Praetzellis 1998c), these papers spawned a follow-up session as well as a special forum discussion in 2000 (e.g., Gibbs 2000; Little 2000; Majewski 2000). It is in these articles that we see archaeologists begin to grapple more tangibly with the issue of what role narrative or storytelling has to play in historical archaeology. Gibbs's stance is that although narratives have a role to play in public interpretation, archaeologists should also use narratives as a means to build hypotheses (2000).

Although supportive of the use of storytelling as a means of "creating a more equal relationship between documentary and material culture sources" (p. 12) Barbara Little (2000) raises one of the most serious concerns regarding narrative, writing: "We may similarly be concerned about the authority we may lend to certain fictions as some of us try to tell stories in such a way that our private visions of the past become public and laden with the imprimatur of "real" and therefore trustworthy archaeologists" (11). Orser (2001a) has raised similar concerns in his introduction to the volume *Race and the Archaeology of Identity,* worrying that narratives simply become a mechanism for reaffirming current racialized subject positions. The concerns of these scholars are valid and reaffirm the need for narratives to be undertaken self-reflexively. I see narrative as a means for subverting and rising above the context in which we are enmeshed, as a means of consciously attempting to remove oneself from a particular subject position. Still, the question of what constitutes good versus bad narrative remains to be addressed.

In a provocative and beautifully reasoned book, Rosemary Joyce (2002c) has explored the ways that archaeologists create texts, within and outside disciplinary boundaries, using the "conceptual vocabulary and approach" of Mikhail Bakhtin to underscore the monologic nature of many archaeological narratives and to suggest ways for archaeologists to recapture the "multivoicedness" of "the experience of constructing archaeological knowledge" (Joyce 2002b). While archaeologists are increasingly aware that any act of interpretation is a form of storytelling, Joyce clearly illustrates the ways that archaeologists use jargon and resignified terms (collectively falling under Bakhtin's term *heteroglossia*) to create a stratified language hierarchy within the discipline that ultimately serves to undermine the collective experience of archaeological knowledge production. As such, Joyce demonstrates how Bakhtin's dialogic approach, which stipulates that the self is only formed when engaged with an other, provides a means for archaeologists to construct polyphonic (multivocal) narratives.

In regard to the use of fictive narrative in archaeological interpretations, Bakhtin's work emphasizes the idea of answerability—that dialogue is essentially ethical (Joyce 2002b). Joyce and Preucel (2002) write: "Accounts of the past created by archaeologists are utterances, social acts of communication oriented toward an addressee whose evaluation of the utterance is crucial to its realization as a meaningful action" (p. 31). Similarly, according to Bakhtin, we cannot place ourselves in the position of the other, for to do so is to transform them into mere mirrors of ourselves (Joyce 2002c). In writing archaeological fictive narratives, this has important bearing. No matter what empathy we may feel for the subjects of our research, we do not have access to their thoughts, feelings, or motivations, and to impart these characteristics through narrative to someone who once lived is to risk simply creating narratives about ourselves.

Joyce considers this issue relative to the different receptions enjoyed by the fictive narratives of Janet Spector (1991, 1993) and Ruth Tringham (1991), finding that Tringham is more widely critiqued for creating completely fictive but archaeologically plausible characters than Spector is for her story about how a particular artifact came to be lost. Joyce (2002b) writes: "On the surface it should be more problematic to impute motivations, feelings, and thoughts to someone who actually lived, and who cannot speak for themselves. Tringham's practice of making up plausible personifications of the types of person who are implicit in theoretical perspectives can do no violence to the actual thoughts and motivations of someone who was never more than a fictional character" (125).

In his introduction to an edited volume on storytelling in archaeology, Adrian Praetzellis (1998) playfully considered how past people might view this development: "Will the storytellers ever know if the motivations that they have assigned to their characters are authentic? Of course not. Would these people, long dead, approve of what we have to say of them, or for them? Frankly, I have no idea what the New England businessman-attorney Josiah Gallup would think of the words that I have impudently put into his mouth. Fortunately for us storytellers, none of our subjects are in a position to argue with us or to file charges of slander" (2). I understand and attempt to heed the call for archaeologists to engage creatively with their materials, and remain impressed by some of the brilliant work that has resulted from these efforts (e.g., Beaudry 1998; Costello 1998; Praetzellis and Praezellis 1998b). Indeed, I have been known to imbue known historical actors with intention and motivation in fictive narratives (Wilkie 2000a), and find the process of writing such narratives helpful as an interpretive device. I remained concerned about the implications of our work, however, when topics that we explore have explosive debates surrounding them, such as the topic of abortion, which I explore in this work. Archaeologists must deal with uncomfortable topics and topics that stir contemporary passions. Narrative provides another means to fully explore interpretations that are valid for the archaeological materials but may not have been valid for specific sites. With this in mind, let me just briefly outline my intentions behind the structure of this work.

In this work, I have strived to create a multivocal document. Where possible, I have tried to use the words of people who have had life experiences similar to those of the Perryman family. These are stories drawn from ethnographies, published oral histories, and autobiographies. Anger, pain, wistfulness, desire, and determination radiate from these narratives, and it is difficult to imagine fictive characters that could be more poignant. Most powerful for me have always been the WPA ex-slave narratives in which people talk about the violence done against their families, the losses, separations, the never-to-be-known conclusions. These dialogs are devastating in their directness. What has always impressed me as well in these narratives is how joy and pathos are so eloquently intertwined. There is much unhappy material in this work, and I discuss some of the more heartrending circumstances and effects of enslavement. African Americans may have endured physical and mental horrors as enslaved people, but the informants' stories reveal that through humor, love, and cynicism, they endured. Whenever I have been able to find firsthand accounts to describe the circumstances and practices I see the archaeology communicating, I use their words.

I have also included a series of fictive narratives that I have constructed. My intent in including these pieces is to underscore the dialogic and recursive nature of archaeological interpretation and the transformative effect those discourses can have on participants. These narrative interludes fall in the spaces between chapters and should be seen as prefaces to the chapters that follow them. They deal with some of the issues faced by African-American women in their struggle first as enslaved people, then as freed women, to be recognized as "good mothers." Good mothering includes the decision as to whether or not to mother, and in this area, that of birth control and abortion, our current society is divided (Ginsburg 1989; Oakley 1984). The archaeological evidence of these practices, as we will discuss, is present but ambiguous. I include narratives to fill some of the spaces between historical sources—subjects otherwise lost in the documentary record due to the sensitive or dangerous nature of their very existence. I have presented these narratives in the form of interview transcripts, following the form of the WPA ex-slave narratives.

A single interviewer, Hazel Neumann, transcribed all these fictive narratives. She is in many ways an extension of me. The interviews are dated, and I hope they reflect the growth of understanding experienced by the interviewer as she builds greater rapport with her informants. I have chosen this form for several reasons. The narrative allows for the first-person account, yet because they are transcribed from interview notes, I have declined to attempt any representation of dialect, although I have employed some southern idioms in the dialogue (see Foster 1997:5). Interviewers have often used their exaggerated recording of dialects to trivialize and denigrate their informants. I do include turns of phrase or expressions that are common, when appropriate, in oral history transcripts. I also like the narrative format for the inherent ambiguity it holds. I place a young white interviewer in the narratives, imagining what might have been said if interview circumstances had been altered, and dangerous questions asked and answered. The quality of any oral history is shaped by informant and interviewer rapport. As the interviewer continues with a project, she gradually learns what questions to ask and what verbal encouragements to offer. For this reason, I opted to use a single interviewer for the narratives. By maintaining her identity as white, it is my intent to maintain the racial tension inherent in these kinds of dialogs. I also found the narratives a way for me to deal more completely with my own positionality within different feminist discourses.

Let me state from the outset that the persons confronted in the narratives, the author herself, and any biographical information (mainly found in the editor's note in Narrative Interlude I) about her are fictive. I have created a contextual history for Hazel because she represents a too often invisible participant in archaeological dialogue: the interpreter. The intellectual, methodological, and personal biases and insights that each archaeologist brings to her interpretive effort shapes the gaze she bring to constructions of the past. Interpretation is never easy. Nor is it ever final: insight grows over one's career. In creating a history for Hazel, I am trying to personify that part of the dialogue. Hazel's letters to her husband serve to present insight into her response to these materials, her decreasing naiveté as she begins to understand more of the conditions and issues dealt with by her subjects, as well as her increasing concern about what her role is in preserving that past. Hazel's concerns and growth in part mirror my own, but they are emblematic of our discipline's growth pains as well.

I hope that collectively, the narratives communicate the agency of the African-American women in shaping the oral historical record, as well as represent Bakhtin's dialogic approach, with knowledge being produced by actors engaged in communication. These interviews are included to raise possibilities of meaning suggested by the archaeology and to suggest motivations not appropriately attributed to historically known actors without other evidence. The narratives do not necessarily represent the best interpretation for what happened at the Perryman site. The intent of their inclusion is enrichment, not distraction or usurping of attention from the primary focus of this piece, African-American mothering in its various aspects.

It has taken much longer than I would have imagined when George and I first pulled medicine bottles from the Perryman well to brush the dirt from that site off my hands. We archaeologists have seen many calls, in the last decade, for reflexive and reflective archaeologies that consider the multiple subject positions of past actors as well as archaeologists. I am convinced that the woman I was when this site was first excavated was not capable of writing the book now here. That is not to say that this is necessarily a better book, just a very different one. I hope, if nothing more, that this study prompts other archaeologists to challenge archaeologically what it has meant for women in the recent past to navigate through the myriad of societal pressures to mother in particular ways, or to assume the cross-culturally broader role of nurturer/caregiver. I am also hopeful that the extra time these interpretations have spent fermenting have been advantageous, and will lend a fuller flavor to the final work.

1
Why an Archaeology of Mothering?

Introduction: What Is It to Be a Mother?

For my five-year-old daughter, "family" is still a sacred trinity of "mommy," "daddy," and "baby." It will not be long until her social contacts lead her to encounter other kinds of loving, nurturing families. With artificial insemination, DNA testing, surrogate mothers, remarriages, and adoption now common, and cloning seemingly on the horizon, the ways in which families become constructed will become more diverse. As the legal system attempts to sort out who is responsible for paying support for whom and who is a parent, contemporary society is forcefully confronted with the socially constructed nature of the role "parent" (Strathern 1992; Ragoné and Twine 2000; Chase and Rogers 2001).

While the notion that biology does not necessarily a parent make has become more acknowledged by the Western public, there is still a sense that what it is to act as a parent is more universal and essential—or natural. This is particularly true of women known as "mothers." After Andrea Yates drowned her five children one by one in a bathtub, her lawyers offered in her defense that Yates, who clearly suffers from mental illness, must have been unaware of her actions, for no "loving mother" could do such a thing to her children. Such is the psychological power of the Western patriarchal ideology that asserts a women's natural role is to reproduce and mother (Chodorow 1978). The nuclear family consisting of a working father, stay-at-home mother, and children of American society is so much a part of our hegemonic discourse that alternative realities and arrangements can be met with hostility (Gailey 2000; Dalton 2000).

Yet what it is to be a mother or to mother is as much a social construct as other cultural experiences, and as much a performative venture as other social identities. As such, what it is to mother well is constantly shifting and being renegotiated in private and public discourses (Glenn 1994). The ideologies that shape mothering are fluid, situated within changing social, economic, and political realities. Even the feelings that a mother nurtures for her children are socially constructed, routinized and performed. "Mother love," or the natural affection that a woman is believed to hold for her child, is itself a social construction (Lewis 1997). Perhaps this has been most powerfully demonstrated in Nancy Scheper-Hughes's (1992) exploration of what she refers to as "M(Other)" love in the Alto do Cruzeiro of Brazil. Here, mother love was an expensive luxury that could cost a mother all, instead of a few, of her children. Economic conditions were so dire in the area that, Scheper-Hughes found, mothers had to form a protective detachment from their infants and children so that they could endure the death of children. This detachment was so extreme as to allow women to choose infants they determined most likely to be healthy, and to severely neglect those believed destined to die. Placed in dire circumstances, women had to channel their emotions for their children pragmatically. Mary Picone (1998) has observed similar situations in Japan, where infanticide was still practiced with great regularity through the Second World War. Economic circumstances and lack of reliable birth control also led to high rates of abortion. Coexisting with the great demand for abortion were the *mizugo* cults, directed at appeasing the spirits of aborted fetuses.

Parenting, but particularly mothering, becomes the focus of cultural tensions and communal discourse because of the central importance of successful child rearing in any society. Children are a form of natural resource whose successful transformation to adulthood ensures a society's continuation. Childhood "is a primary nexus of mediation between public norms and private life" (Scheper-Hughes and Sargent 1998b:1), and caregivers cannot be separated from those debates. Mothering, then, is both a private and public endeavor, with individuals involved in mothering conscious of multiple scales of responsibility—to her children, her kin, and her broader community (Ruddick 1980).

Research into mothering, how children are nurtured, and motherhood as a socially constituted and negotiated institution have been main themes in feminist thinking. Many women have the experience of mothering; it brings with it differing losses and gains in status, joy, heartbreak, and ambivalence, and for birthgivers it brings a transformative embodied experience. Feminists have explored motherhood from multiple angles and perspectives. One important ongoing site of debate has been whether it is biologically ordained that women should be children's primary caretakers (e.g., Ortner 1972; Chodorow 1978; Abel and Nelson 1990; Holloway and Featherstone 1997; MacCormack and Strathern 1980). Another has focused on the ways maternity is used to oppress women cross-culturally (e.g., Rosaldo and Lamphere 1974; Rich 1976; Bassin and Kaplan 1994). In these analyses, it is motherhood as an institution that is the focus of consideration, as well as the ways that women unwittingly reproduce the institution that devalues them. Indeed, feminists have been unable to agree on whether motherhood is a good or bad for women, though collectively they do resist the paradigm of "essential mothering," which posits that womanhood is defined by the ability to reproduce and raise children (DiQuinzio 1999).

In much of Western society, a normative view of mothering demands self-sacrifice and total attention be paid to children by their mothers. Behavioral and social problems that arise later in a child's life can ultimately be traced to experiences of inferior mothering (Chase and Rogers 2001; Ladd-Taylor and Umansky 1998). Picone (1998:51) observed that poor mothering was used in Japan to explain the behavior of rapists and murderous pedophiles. This is a society where a mere 100 years prior a Japanese moralist proclaimed, "Women were such imperfect beings that mothers should not be in contact with impressionable children" (Picone 1998:50).

"Intensive mothering," as it has been termed by Sharon Hays (1996), is rooted in the rise of industrialism and the separation of the household unit from a role in production among the predominantly white middle classes. Women's labor increasingly became associated with the protection of the household, and control of wealth and the family's symbolic capital became the domain of male workers. Women who worked outside of the home, either out of financial need or for self-fulfillment, were automatically constructed as "bad mothers." The hegemonic discourse surrounding the "cult of true womanhood" excluded many women, and they continued to be excluded by feminist movements, which privileged the experiences of sexism by white middle-class women (Spelman 1988; Collins 1994). In the nineteenth- and early-twentieth-century United States, the cult of true womanhood led women to be equated with their reproductive organs. Proclaimed to be interested only in (and good only for) bearing and raising children, women became the butt of fierce arguments by male pundits that they should not be educated. The energy used to fuel the intellect, it seems, was drained from the womb and ovaries, rendering educated women infertile and prone to mental diseases (Bullough and Voght 1984).

It was in part the entrenched notion of the "unthinking" mother that led Sara Ruddick (1980, 1994) to theorize mothering, and in particular, "maternal thought" as a community-oriented way of being that characterized mothers' cultural participation. But what is it to mother? Ruddick (1994:33) perceives mothering as a form of caring work that exists in response to the needs of children. To see a child's need for protection is to mother. "There is nothing inevitable about maternal response: many people, including some birthgivers, do not recognize children as 'demanding'; some, including some birthgivers, respond to children's demands with indifference, assault, or active neglect; some, including many birthgivers, are unable to respond because they themselves are victims of violence or neglect." Ruddick's work on maternal thinking has been influential in the field, but it has also been used to illustrate that feminism continues to take as its focus the experiences of white middle-class women (A. Davis 1983; Giddings 1984; Spelman 1988; Collins 2000). Spelman (1988:15) has observed, "One's gender identity is not related to one's racial and class identity as the parts of pop-bead necklaces are related, separable and insertable in other 'strands' with different racial and class 'parts'"—in other words, it is misguided to conceive of a universal woman's experience.

Collins (1994, 2000) has called for feminists to consider the full diversity of women's mothering experiences, and to recognize that

> women of color have performed motherwork that challenges social constructions of work and family as separate spheres, of male and female gender roles as similarly dichotomized, and of the search for autonomy as the guiding human

> question . . . 'motherwork' goes beyond ensuring the survival of one's own bi-
> ological children or those of one's family. This type of motherwork recognizes
> that individual survival, empowerment, and identity require group survival em-
> powerment, and identity. (1994:47)

It is through the exploration of difference that we can begin to understand how social constructions of motherhood create divergent opportunities and experiences of women of differing sexual orientations, races, ethnicities and socioeconomic classes. Recent work focusing on difference in mothering experience (e.g. Glenn et al. 1994; Scheper-Hughes and Sargent 1998b; Ladd-Taylor and Umansky 1998; Ragoné and Twine 2000; Strathern 1992) has demonstrated the rich potential for this research. It is the work of these feminists that has most influenced this archaeology of mothering, and I join Maria Franklin (2001) in recognizing the need for historical archaeologists to incorporate black feminist perspectives into our research.

Archaeology is, in many ways, a brilliant forum in which to explore mothering and motherwork. Ideologies regarding normative expectations for childrearing and nurturing are likely to be reified through a number of material media, such as ritual performance, public art, or household goods. The performative practice of parenting would be part of a routinized experience and extractable from household contexts. Although material culture has not been the focus of most studies of mothering, I will quickly refer to several that suggest the great potential that exists in this area. Ruth Schwartz Cowan (1983) in her study of household gadgets, has demonstrated how money-saving devices designed to lighten the workloads of full-time homemakers and mothers actually increased the amount of time necessary to conduct housework. More recently, Linda Layne (2000) has written about the ways that grieving parents use a baby's belongings to comfort themselves following a miscarriage, stillbirth, or infant's death. Rima Apple's (1997) study of scientific mothering was drawn, in part, from a study of advertising cards. Archaeology contains great potential for understanding the experiences of caregivers and parents, and particularly motherhood as it has been constructed in the recent past.

Mothering and Archaeology

Surely, the discipline of archaeology, with recent research focusing on women, children, gender, sex, and sexuality (e.g., Gero and Conkey 1991; Gilchrist 1994, 1999; Joyce 2000; Meskell 1999; Schmidt and Voss 2000; Sofaer-Derevenski 2000) has mothering and motherhood covered under its ever-widening post-processual umbrella? Do we really need an archaeology of something else? One would think that mothering, certainly a socially constructed and gendered activity cross-culturally, with its definite sexual and reproductive dimensions and associations with children, would be a focus within one of the numerous recently edited volumes associated with these topics. That in fact is not the case, however. In established texts relating to gender and archaeology (e.g., Gero and Conkey 1991; Wright 1996; Seifert 1991; Nelson 1997), women produce pottery, textiles, and lithics, they pound acorns, and they commune with awls. Mothering is generally absent, unless you include mother goddesses.

The term "mother" is not even commonly found in the indices of texts on gender in archaeology. To demonstrate how obscure the term is, neither Roberta Gilchrist's recent and seemingly comprehensive text *Gender and Archaeology* (1999) nor Joanna Sofaer-Derevenski's edited volume *Children and Material Culture* (2000) include it. I should also add, quickly, that I am throwing stones at myself here as well. When putting together the index for my previous book (Wilkie 2000a), which focuses on intergenerational dynamics in several households, including mother-child relationships, I never considered that someone might want to look up the topic of "mother" or "mothering" in my index. Nor did I explicitly explore mothering and motherhood in the study.

The absence of mothering from archaeological discourse is surprising. Archaeologies of gender and sexuality are becoming more common in the field, although they still lag behind such popular topics as warfare, subsistence, political and economic systems, and cannibalism. Much of gendered archaeology comes from second- or third-wave feminist theorizing, but somehow archaeology has not yet embraced the feminist histories, sociologies, and anthropologies related to mothering. A number of important feminist studies have explored motherhood since the late 1970s (e.g., Rich 1976; Chodorow 1978; Ruddick 1980; Ryan 1981; Scheper-Hughes 1992; Glenn et al. 1994), and in the last five years or so we have seen a burgeoning publication base dealing with motherhood in the social sciences (e.g., Ladd-Taylor and Umansky 1998; DiQuinzio 1999; Ragoné and Twine 2000; Chase and Rogers 2001). Archaeology has been notoriously slow in keeping up with theoretical and topical trends shaping other disciplines, so perhaps our time lag here is not as surprising as it seems to me. Particularly within historical archaeology, however, theoretical orientations that favor a focus on capitalism, consumerism, and consumption over family, gender, and social networks seem to have led to the squelching of issues related to mothering and motherhood.

I do not wish to give the impression that the archaeological literature is completely lacking in research that addresses aspects of motherhood or mothering. In part, parenting can be inferred from recent studies focusing on children (e.g., Sofaer-Derevenski 1994, 2000). The topic can also be gleaned from works on other topics. Elisabeth Beausang has recently published an article on the mechanics of becoming a mother (childbirth) in prehistory. In this piece, Beausang (2000:73–74) considers mothering to be a constituted as both norms (cultural expectations) and praxis. She focuses her attention predominantly on mothering that takes place during a child's infancy, since at this time the child is most likely to be dependent upon a female for its nurturing, thus justifying the gender implications of a term like "mothering." Lynn Meskell has written about birthing beds in ancient Egypt (2000), and Rosemary Joyce (2000) has discussed childbirth in Mesoamerica as a female complement to the male experience of warfare. Though none of these works deal explicitly with what happens after the transformative experience of birth, that they deal with birth at all is noteworthy.

Perhaps more surprising than the dearth of prehistoric archaeology dealing with mothers and mothering (or to be gender neutral, nurturing) is the same lack of attention the subject receives in American historical or post-medieval archaeologies. Archaeologists who work in recent time periods routinely work at the household level and often have access to documents that define the biological and fictive kinship relationships between members of a household. The much-utilized Federal Population Census in the United States is an excellent example of such a resource. Not only can archaeologists in these circumstances potentially identify specific persons who may have lived at particular sites, but we may also be able to pinpoint deposits to specific times in those persons' lives. At a time when issues of identity and difference are of such interest in archaeology (e.g., Meskell 1999; Joyce 2000; Hodder et al. 1995; S. Jones 1997; Orser 2001a; Delle, Mrozowski, and Paynter 2000), it is surprising that archaeologies of the recent past have not explored more extensively the changes of status and practice that came with marriage and mothering. What publications have dealt explicitly with mothering and motherhood are scant and deserve a brief review.

A published essay by Ywone Edwards-Ingram (2001) and her forthcoming dissertation, which focuses on African-American medical practices during enslavement, are the only other work in historical archaeology of which I am aware to explicitly consider how mothers and mothering were affected by slavery. Edwards-Ingram's study provides an overview of medicinal practices related to reproduction and childrearing, synthesizing ethnohistoric and archaeological data drawn from the American South and the Caribbean. Her study provides insights into the ways that enslaved mothers contested the constraints on their mothering and how they worked to incorporate African healing traditions into their children's lives.

The other explicit study of mothering I have found in historical archaeology was published in 1994 in an article by Eric Larsen called "A Boarding House Madonna: Beyond the Aesthetics of a Portrait Created through Medicine Bottles." Drawing upon four bottles—a nursing bottle, a bottle for a whooping cough cure, and two castoria bottles—recovered from a nineteenth-century Harper's Ferry boarding house, Larsen suggested that the medicines could be associated with "good mothering" practices of the period. The article is unusual in that Larsen attempts to distinguish, although not explicitly, between the dominant ideology governing motherhood versus the practice of mothering found in the boarding house. This piece stands alone as an attempt at an archaeology of mothering. Ultimately, the article could have been strengthened by greater attention to the positioning of working-class women relative to the cult of true womanhood. That said, it is a remarkable contribution.

Diane DiZerga Wall (1991, 1994, 2000) can be credited with bringing the first detailed attention in historical archaeology to the separation of the domestic and industrial spheres of daily life in American society. Though Wall discusses, briefly, the effects of the development of the domestic sphere on child-rearing practices, the focus of her archaeological analysis lies elsewhere—mainly on the strategies employed by middle-class homemakers to jockey for social prestige among themselves through entertaining.

Rebecca Claney (1996) offers a provocative analysis that interprets the ubiquitous "Rebecca at the Well" teapot of mid-nineteenth-century American society to be a material reification of the cult of true womanhood and values of motherhood. Fitts (1999), in a discussion of gentility and Victorian values, notes the importance of child rearing to maintaining class status across generational lines, a point also found in Praetzellis and Praetzellis (1992).

In her study of prostitution, Julia Costello (2000) makes brief mention of mothering in the sex industry. Costello uses multiple first-person oral history narratives from a New Orleans red-light district, Storyville, juxtaposed with historical photographs and artifact illustrations to present a possible view of life inside an early-twentieth-century Los Angeles bordello and to bring the possible meanings of artifacts found there to the fore. In the text is one photograph that illustrates several medical appliances recovered from the site, including a glass breast pump. Costello includes a narrative from the perspective of two adults who had been born to prostitutes. The narrative is brusque and unapologetic. While both individuals refer to the reality of prostitutes getting pregnant, neither refers to what it was like to be raised or mothered in that context. Apart from the photograph of the breast pump, the article gives few clues as to what other artifacts might have been recovered related to mothering or child care. Costello shied away from engaging more politically charged issues, such as what kind of mothers the prostitutes were, whether their mothering challenged or reified socially held notions of motherhood at the time, and, most controversially, what they did to avoid motherhood. While the subject of her text was sexuality as studied through archaeology, her decision to keep separate the personas of "woman the sexual object" and "woman the mother" mimics the Victorian attitudes toward women that she is in part exploring.

Victor Buchli and Gavin Lucas (2000a, 2000b) conducted a fascinating archaeological study in 1997 of a British Council flat that had been occupied by a single mother and her children. The family had suddenly fled the apartment, leaving behind almost all of their material possessions. Buchli and Lucas studied the abandoned site to probe what kinds of information could be gleaned regarding the nature of social relations within the household. Though their study is not explicitly about mothering, it explores the pressures this woman faced as she juggled an ongoing relationship with the children's father, a heroin addict undergoing methadone treatments with responsibilities to her children. The circumstances leading to the woman's flight suggest that she felt compelled to trade the security of subsidized housing for another (perhaps physical) security for herself and her children.

In contrast to the stresses that apparently led her to abandon her home and possessions, the apartment was arranged in ways that suggested the woman was trying to create what she perceived to be a normative lifestyle for her children. A room was dedicated to the children's play and rest, and children's toys were found throughout the two-bedroom home. Representations of normative family life, such as wallpaper bearing the image of a smiling Flintstone family, were used to decorate the children's spaces (Buchli and Lucas 2000). The artifacts from the site suggested that although the father of the children did not live with them there, he was a frequent visitor, in Buchli and Lucas's view, as indicated by the presence of lingerie, birth control devices, his methadone prescription, male-associated artifacts, and abandoned documents at the site.

Buchli and Lucas point out that by fleeing the flat, and therefore, in the eyes of the British housing authority, making herself intentionally homeless, this woman became ineligible for future governmental support. The woman was trying to create for her children a normative family life while also dealing with the break down of a (possibly abusive) relationship. The study is an outstanding illustration of how archaeology can explore provocative (and socially relevant) issues related to social constructions and realities of motherhood.

Motherhood has also been addressed to a limited degree within historical bioarchaeology. In 1985, in an analysis of human remains recovered from an eighteenth-century Barbadian cemetery, Robert Corraccini and his colleagues argued that high incidences of enamel hypoplasia in enslaved populations might be related to systemic stress undergone by individuals as children during the period of weaning from breast milk. This interpretation was later challenged by Michael Blakey and his collaborators (1994) in their analysis of human remains from several American mainland cemeteries. Though still under study and not yet published, research on the recovery of a young woman buried with her newborn child at New York's African Burial Ground has already yielded perhaps the most emotive images of motherhood from bioarchaeology. The infant is nestled in the mother's arm, a powerful image of the powerlessness of a mother's love in the face of enslavement's brutality.

It is in the arena of the study of race and racism that the neglect of motherhood by archaeologists is most troubling to me. Other social sciences have not been so remiss. Historians have published a number of important works on the ways racism differentially shapes social constructions of womanhood, which in turn determine the rights of motherhood (e.g., White 1985; A. Davis 1983, 1998; Collins 1994, 2000; Fox-Genovese 1988; Giddings 1984; Gaspar and Hine 1996). In particular, black feminists (Collins 2000; A. Davis 1983; Roberts 1997; Spelman 1988) have powerfully demonstrated that black women continue to be oppressed and condemned by stereotypes dating to slavery. They further contend that the history of race relations in the United States can be seen as a struggle to control black women's bodies and reproduction.

The slave economies of the pre-abolition North and the antebellum South were dependent upon African-American women producing healthy offspring and assuring that enslaved parents had little to no control over those children. Enslaved women were subjected to marriages arranged by planters, rape, high infant mortality rates, and the sudden separation by sale or inheritance from their families (see chapter 3). Even a very quick review of oral histories gathered in the 1930s and '40s from former slaves demonstrates how the instability of family life and the loss of control over child care and rearing clung to the memories of African-American women long after the end of slavery. Toni Morrison's book *Beloved* (1987), perhaps more than any other text, evokes the special horrors of enslavement that were endured by women. Perhaps because archaeologists are typically white and middle class, they have been reluctant to dwell on any kind of violence endured by enslaved people (see Farnsworth 2000 for a fuller discussion) and certainly have not looked at the unique effects that enslavement had on parenting.

After Emancipation, family life was an arena in which African Americans immediately sought to gain control. Herbert Gutman, in a classic work (1976), documented African Americans' rush to legally marry after the end of slavery. Jacqueline Jones (1985) and Paula Giddings (1984) have also investigated how African-American women sought to redefine their roles in the eyes of society following Emancipation by establishing themselves as full-time mothers and homemakers. Other scholars, such as Trudier Harris (1982) and Childress (1986), have written about the conflicts endured by African-American women employed to care for white women's children, at the cost of limited time with their own families. My point is not to provide a complete review of the vast literature produced by historians, sociologists, anthropologists, and others on this topic, but instead to emphasize that despite the visibility of this issue in other disciplines, archaeologists have not dealt with this topic.

African-American archaeology has dealt with issues of generalized racism and responses to racism (e.g., Epperson 1997; Orser 2001b; Wilkie 2000a); African continuities and ethnicity (e.g., Armstrong 1990; L. Ferguson 1992; Deetz 1993); African-American resistance during enslavement (Leone 1995); economic and power hierarchies of the plantation (e.g., Otto 1984; Orser 1987, 1988); the pursuit of wealth and affluence by African-Americans following enslavement (Mullins 1999a); and the role of the African-American community and scholars in the practice of archaeology (e.g., Franklin 1997; LaRoche and Blakey 1997). Increasingly, archaeologies of the African-American experience have been influenced by the works of Mark Leone (1995) and Charles Orser (1996) who have independently argued that historical archaeology must be an archaeology of capitalism and that its interpretations must engage with global contexts. Analyses that strive to focus on the economic struggles and achievements of African-Americans, as demonstrated through archaeology, have provided much-needed insights into the ways that African-American families created spaces for themselves within class-based economic systems (e.g., Delle 1997; Mullins 1999; Orser 1988).

Yet, these studies simultaneously fail to engage and, in fact, obscure from analytical view other kinds of social discourses and ideologies that existed and were also powerful in replicating societal inequalities and systems of oppression. Ideologies regarding proper "mothering" may have sprung from the middle class at particular times in history, but they are enmeshed with discourses on race, gender, and power as well. Hegemonic discourses asserted that only women of a certain color and class were natural and good mothers. Motherhood and proper child rearing were seen within the politically engaged African-American community as a means of racial uplift and movement toward equality.

Perhaps this would be a time to return to the first question I posed. Do we need an archaeology of mothering? For prehistoric periods, I would argue, we need to challenge notions of parenting and child care that may subconsciously shape archaeological interpretations. The organization of child care and supervision would have been an ongoing consideration in any society, and it therefore deserves our consideration as much as do other prehistoric economic activities. Further, it seems that these issues are essential to any consideration of past gender systems. It may be that once we turn our attention more fully to the issue of parenting, we will be able to explore how members of different cultural groups dealt with cultural norms and demands regarding child care and nurturing. It is fascinating that the topic of mothering, or more broadly, parenting, has received little attention from archaeologists working in the deeper past, those remote time period that offer no texts to aid us. This is the case even at a time when women and children as independent actors are the focus of increased archaeological study (e.g., Moore and Scott 1997; Sofaer-Derevenski 2000). Perhaps we find mothering and the potential associations with the oppression of women because of the constraints of child care, as experienced in Western society, to be distasteful or less interesting than archaeologies of female empowerment.

Certainly, the mechanics of reproduction (conception, pregnancy, and birth) have traditionally required participation of a female body. We can safely assume that birthgivers have been a human universal phenomenon (aside from the very recent past). What happens to the baby once it is out of the uterus and clear of the birth canal is quite a different situation. From ethnography we know that child rearing is approached in diverse ways across the human spectrum (Scheper-Hughes 1992; Ortner 1996; Glenn et al. 1994). To study mothering per se rather than parenting or child rearing in prehistoric situations seems to me to potentially graft certain expectations or biases on the prehistoric past.

That said, we cannot assume, like Beausang (2000) that mothering practices are best studied archaeologically from a narrow range of potential activities such as birth or breastfeeding. Certainly, to problematize the notion of mother, and to ask the question of how families were arranged is an issue currently grappled with in prehistoric archaeology by anyone engaged in household archaeological research (e.g., Joyce and Gillespie 2000; Allison 1999; Wilk 1997; Mehrer 1995).

While I would suggest that "parenting" and, if contextually appropriate, "mothering" are necessary categories of analysis for prehistoric archaeology, I would just as strongly argue that an archaeology of mothering is essential for archaeologies of the recent and text-aided pasts. Particularly with the advent of the modern era, "mother," rather than "parent" or "father," is a politically and socially loaded term (Hays 1996). "Good mothers," "bad mothers," "welfare mothers," "mommy-track mothers," "stay-at-home moms," "soccer moms," and "mother love" are just a few examples of symbolically laden terms generated in specific social historical contexts that generate strong reactions and associations in contemporary discourses. With the exception of "deadbeat dads" in American society, there is no comparable male-associated parental label, although there is a movement to study fatherhood (Lupton and Barclay 1997). The politically charged nature of the term "mother," while certainly a product of the last several hundred years or so of history, at least in the United States, is exactly why archaeologists of the recent past should not ignore the issue of "mothering" in their work. What constitutes "motherhood" at any given time, and particularly proper and improper forms of it, is socially constructed, fluid, and changing. Anyone who has had a child has probably at one time or another engaged in intergenerational debates regarding proper child-rearing practice, demonstrating how quickly attitudes can shift in this arena. I want to briefly introduce the historically constructed paradigms of motherhood and mothering that will be explored further in this work.

Historians have explored different mothering ideologies that have shaped U.S. history. "Republican mothering" ideologies shaped mothering of the late eighteenth and early nineteenth centuries in the United States (Blackwell 1992). "Intensive mothering" of the Victorian period accompanied the separation of domestic and public spheres (Hays 1996; Lewis 1997), and "scientific mothering" accompanied the growth of mass-produced goods and advertising, and physician-dominated women's health care (Apple 1997). These are just a few of the competing mothering ideologies that shaped expectations of child care and were embedded within broader social debates and political agendas. At the least, the ability to participate in and perform the proper mothering behavior had implications for acceptance into or recognition of acceptance into a particular social class. At the opposite extreme, failure or inability to comply could cost children their health and education, and could cost women the right to raise their children (Ladd-Taylor and Umansky 1998) or, with the implementation of mandatory sterilization in the United States in the early twentieth century, even their right to bear children at all (Roberts 1997; Noll 1998). Minority women and women of the lower classes continuously found themselves used as examples of "bad mothers" as they attempted to juggle the financial realities of their families and societal prescriptions on mothering (Glenn et al. 1994; Ladd-Taylor and Umansky 1998; Ragoné and Twine 2000; Chase and Rogers 2001).

Middle-class women may have been constrained by mothering ideologies of their time, but they also were known to use their sacred status as mothers to their advantage. The assumed moral superiority of mothers during the Victorian period was used by women to generate political clout for themselves—fueling the abolitionist, women's suffrage, and temperance movements (A. Davis 1983).

For women raising children, mothering is simultaneously practice, image, and ideology. It may be privately undertaken, often within the realm of the home, but it is publicly scrutinized. A child's cleanliness, manners, maturity, dress, playthings, temperament, and behavior, among many other things, are constantly judged by outsiders, and if found lacking, blame is often laid at the feet of the mother (Ladd-Taylor and Umansky 1998). Archaeology is well suited to studying mothering practices, for we are students of the way things are done, the way things are presented, and why things are thought to be done the way they are. We can work at a microscalar level, focusing our research on the household and thus looking at the ways that mothering ideologies shaped mothering practice and presentation. It also allows us to explore how mothers contested boundaries placed upon them through mothering roles. In this study, for instance, I will demonstrate through historical archaeology how mothering ideologies of the white middle class were actively appropriated by one African-American family as a way of contesting racialized notions of black womanhood that were entrenched in the nineteenth and early twentieth centuries.

This work will explore the experiences of the Perryman family. Marshall and Lucrecia Perryman, following Emancipation, settled in Mobile, Alabama, first purchasing land there in 1866. Lucrecia brought at least three children with her to the marriage. During the (at least) 18 years of their marriage, they added five additional children to their family. Following Marshall's death in 1884, Lucrecia found it necessary to leave full-time care of her children to enter the workforce. She was called to the vocation of midwifery. Lucrecia remained a midwife until 1911, retiring to full-time rearing of children orphaned by her daughter's death. It will be my contention that midwifery was not a random career choice for Perryman, but a field in which she could apply her vast mothering experiences to educate younger generations of black women.

Archaeological materials recovered from the Perryman house site offer two windows into the Perrymans' lives. The first deposit provides a view of family life in the Perryman household before the death of Marshall. While this is the smaller of the assemblages, through a combination of archaeological and documentary sources we can see how the elder Perrymans were actively pursuing opportunities not available to African-American families during enslavement. The second deposit dates to the time of Lucrecia's retirement from midwifery and allows us a rare glimpse into the material culture and practice of pre-regulation African-American midwifery.

Through a consideration of these materials, we can see not only the ways that Lucrecia appropriated the materiality of white middle-class motherhood, but also the ways that she incorporated that materiality into her midwifery practice. We also see how changing ideologies of motherhood that occurred over the course of her career were creatively juggled and incorporated into her midwifery practice. It is my assertion that Lucrecia's appropriation of white middle-class mothering was not merely ambitious emulation, but was a conscious and intentional politicized action of a woman who had borne five children during slavery.

In chapter 2, I introduce the documentary history of the Perryman family during their time in Mobile. I attempt to situate their experiences into broader issues that dominated the periods in which they lived. I take the opportunity in chapter 3 to consider what it was to mother during enslavement, and to explore the legacy of enslavement through the experiences of following generations of African-American women.

It is in chapter 4 that I begin to explore the politicization of mothering in the African-American community following Emancipation. I will consider how values of domesticity and mothering related to the cult of true womanhood are expressed in the household goods and practices of the Perryman family. It is my assertion that for Lucrecia Perryman, the vocation of midwifery was an extension of her mothering for her family, what Patricia Hill Collins has dubbed "motherwork." Through her work as a midwife, Perryman was able to teach mothering across generations, serving as both a conduit for the transmission of cultural practice rooted in an African past as well as for innovation.

In chapter 5, I investigate how the archaeology supports this claim. Although Christian doctrine has increasingly asserted that motherhood is the natural state of women, generations of women have known the opposite to be true. The contested realms of birth control and abortion, and the midwife's role in these arenas, are the focus of chapter 6.

Chapter 7 builds upon the notion of midwifery as motherwork as it pertained to scientific mothering and movements for racial uplift. Motherhood and domesticity did not escape the nineteenth- and twentieth-century marches toward professionalism, scientism, and modernity. Prescriptive literature increasingly demanded that women become scientists of the household, and the ideology of scientific mothering took hold. Lucrecia Perryman, based on the archaeological materials, supported scientific mothering as a means of racial uplift and introduced its principles to her clients. Ironically, it was the adoption of scientific mothering principles by African-American women, particularly among the elite and middle class, combined with growing pressure and antagonism from the medical industry, that drove African-American midwives out of their practices.

In the final chapter, chapter 8, I return to the question I originally posed: Why do we need an archaeology of mothering? It is in this chapter that I explore what an archaeology that focuses on mothering has revealed about the experiences of freed African-American women that might be obscured through other analytical lenses.

2
The Perryman Family of Mobile

Families continually change in composition. Marriages, births, and adoptions can add new members, while deaths, relocations, and alienations can remove members. Archaeology cannot always catch the changing tides of families' experiences. Our stories, by the nature of our research, are often place-specific and time-bound. In urban historical archaeology, we are often documenting brief episodes in a family's long-term experiences, as if we are looking in a window, or staying with them for a few months before moving on. The spatial and temporal aspect of the materials we study becomes the subject of our fascination and attention, to the point where we risk developing archaeological tunnel vision. It is important that we recognize that we are not studying a family so much as a family at a particular place and time.

Often, we cannot tie our materials to a particular family, but rather to a neighborhood or community. Or, perhaps, the people associated with our materials stayed for too short a time at our site to have left a mark on the historical record—the only testimony to their stay being the garbage they have left behind. Bonnie Gums's (1998:22) study of an African-American neighborhood in Mobile graphically demonstrates this problem. At one address she found there to have been at least 23 different heads of household listed over a period of 64 years, with no information available for 20 years of that period. What kind of an archaeological record was left during these short, fleeting occupations? In our interpretations of archaeological materials, sometimes we think only in terms of site occupants, not families or boarders or other kinds of households. In those circumstances, the social relationships between those cohabiting in a location remain unclear to us, and though we are loath to admit it, we are robbed of certain interpretive insights.

I mention these circumstances merely to acknowledge that terms like "family" and "household" are loaded terms that denote certain kinds of relationships between cohabiting persons and that these relationships can be rendered, to some degree, static in the archaeological record. The kinds of documents available to us regarding the Perryman family are also periodic, mainly drawn from county, city, and federal records that were typically compiled annually or once a decade. From this combination of small portals into the family's experiences, I weave the historical archaeological narrative. The weave remains a loose one, with many gaps and holes.

The Perryman family appears out of the mists of a poorly documented slavery past in 1869, when Marshall Perryman purchased a plot of land in Mobile, Alabama. From this point on, it is possible to trace the family through historical records such as the federal population census, the Mobile city directory, land transfers and other court records, through cemetery and vital statistics records (such as death and marriage certificates). While these documentary sources are often incomplete and sometimes contradictory, they do at least provide a partial sketch of the family's experiences. Sometimes, these records provide tantalizing clues into the experiences of the family before 1869, but attempts to follow leads to other kinds of documentary evidence have been thwarted by the nature of slavery-period records related to African Americans. The history of Lucrecia and Marshall Perryman's early adult lives—their lives before settling in Mobile—is murky, inferred, and frustratingly intriguing.

The Perrymans' Early Years

When Marshall and Lucrecia's life together began is vaguely hinted at in the documentary record. According to the 1870 census, Marshall and Lucrecia Perryman's first child was born in 1866. Based on the father's place of birth indicated by that same census, we learn that Lucrecia's older children had a biological father other than Marshall. Lucrecia's last child by this unknown individual was born in 1862. Therefore, sometime between 1862 and 1866, Marshall and Lucrecia began a life and family together. By 1869, they are known to have been living in Mobile on a parcel of land Marshall bought. They remained there for the rest of their lives. For Marshall, this was to be only 15 years; for Lucrecia, 68 years. She would live out her years on the first piece of property her husband bought in Mobile, living in the house that they built together. Here she would raise her children and many of her grandchildren.

Where the couple met, the time and circumstances of their first meeting, are lost to us. Census records and vague family recollections provide some clues, but no answers. I will go through the available historical data related to the family in some detail. Some of the evidence is contradictory. We are often tempted to privilege the "authority" of the historical record over alternative ways of knowing, such as archaeology and oral history—after all, I am not aware of history ever being seriously accused of being archaeology's handmaiden (Noel-Hume 1969). It is important to remember that historical interpretations are just as constructed as archaeological ones. I am presenting the historical evidence in detail so that my interpretation of that evidence is open to review. The kinds of history that archaeologists engage in are often akin to the work done by genealogists—very microscalar in their scopes. I am fortunate that a number of social historians (e.g., Amos 1985; Ewert 2001; Nordmann 1990; Scribner 2001) have studied the aggregated experiences of Mobile families through time, and I use their work to situate the experiences of the Perrymans.

The Documentary Sources

Census records are notoriously problematic for historical research. Enumerators often missed houses, asked neighbors to provide information about families other than their own, made assumptions about racial identity, age, and literacy (among other things), and were generally sloppy in their work. Conducted every 10 years, just as now, the census has provided information that varies greatly from decade to decade. The earliest censuses (until 1850) recorded only the heads of household (typically the male head) and lumped together by age and sex the remaining persons living at an address. In 1850, the non-slave population was listed individually under the head of household. In 1850 and 1860, as a result of reform and abolition movements in the northern United States, special slave returns were gathered. As a clear demonstration of the dehumanizing nature of enslavement, while individuals are listed in this census by color, age, sex, and infirmity, their names do not appear. It is only beginning in 1870 that formerly enslaved people are among the named people found in the census.

Problems with the census do not end, of course, in 1870. Different kinds of information were collected during different censuses. Literacy is not recorded until 1870. Beginning in 1880, individuals were asked about the location of their parents' birth. The vast majority of the 1890 census returns were destroyed in the 1906 San Francisco earthquake and fire, leaving a large gap in the record. While immensely useful, the census is also immensely flawed. It is necessary when using census data to do so critically and to challenge the information contained within other historical sources where possible.

Supplementing information about the Perryman family from the census are Mobile city directories. Compiled every year or two, seemingly dependent on the publisher at the time, the city directories provide a listing of Mobile's occupants (or at least heads of households and renters), their color, occupation, and address. The Perrymans lived on property just outside the incorporated boundaries of the city of Mobile. As a result, they are not consistently listed in the city directory, even though other historical sources demonstrate that their occupation was continuous. It seems that only the family's proximity to Magnolia Cemetery, an important Mobile landmark, ensured that they were included as often as they were in the directory. Even then, it appears that there is little agreement as to how their address should be described. To someone unfamiliar with the area, it would appear from the directories that the Perryman family shifted between different houses on three different streets. Still, the directories are particularly helpful for the periods of time between censuses.

Assorted other sources were also used to construct this narrative of the Perryman family history. As landholders, the Perrymans were the subject of a greater number of court documents than a non-land-holding family would have been. Title transfers, court affidavits, and Marshall Perryman's will and probate were also recovered and served to clarify relationships among members of the families. Some city of Mobile tax records were also found for the family. A surprising number of death certificates were available through the Alabama Center for Health Statistics. Marshall Perryman also purchased a burial plot for his family at Magnolia Cemetery. Although incomplete for early internments, these records helped clarify kinship relationships and birth and death dates for some members of the Perryman family. Finally, descendants of the Perrymans were also able to provide some family history. In all, I found a relatively rich public documentary record associated with this family.

Before Mobile

Much of what can be inferred about the Perryman's pre-Mobile history is drawn from census records. Lucrecia's journey from her place of birth to Mobile is more completely documented than Marshall's, in some ways, simply because she was a mother. Her children's respective places of birth are listed in the census, and provide us with some indication of where she was at the times of their different births.

The 1870 census lists Lucrecia's age as 34, placing her date of birth at 1836. In this particular census, her place of birth is listed as New York, but this is the only instance in which this location is named as such. In each of the other census records, she is listed as having been born in North Carolina. In the 1880 census, the information on Lucrecia's age is consistent. She is described as 44 years of age, again suggesting an 1836 date of birth. A mere 20 years later, however, her age is listed as 75, with her date of birth explicitly being listed as 1825. In 1910, she has aged even more rapidly, with her age listed as 91 years old. At the time of her death, Lucrecia's Mobile death certificate lists her age as 80 years (MCDC 1917). This age would coincide with an 1836 birthdate. As I'll discuss later, there are several reasons why it may have been advantageous for Lucretia to exaggerate her age in her later years, including enhancing her prestige as a midwife.

Census records from 1880 and 1900 identify both of Lucrecia's parents as having been born in North Carolina. Only the 1910 census contradicts this information, listing Lucrecia's father as born in North Carolina and her mother in Maryland. Two of Lucrecia's great-grandchildren remember her daughter Caroline stating that she and her mother had been slaves in "the Carolinas." They had no memory of any particular place name being mentioned, nor any mention of earlier husbands or other family members from that time in their lives.

Lucrecia had had at least three living children before she and Marshall had their first. Caroline, Sarah (also listed as Sallie or Sally in different records), and Frank were born to Lucrecia and an unknown man (Figure 2.1). Caroline was the eldest, having been born in 1855 in North Carolina. Her recollections of "slave times" as told to Lucrecia's great grandchildren are the only source that confirms that at least Lucrecia and her children had been born into enslavement. Two of Caroline's stories made strong impressions on her great-nieces and -nephew,

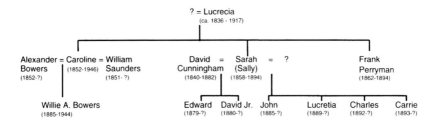

Figure 2.1 Lucrecia Perryman's family tree

all of whom are now past 80. First, they recalled Caroline saying that during slave times, her mother had to be stern with her children. The other story relates that after Emancipation, Lucrecia did not like to cut her hair or have others cut it, for it reminded her of slavery times, when slaves were forced to have their hair cut short. She preferred to wear her hair in long plaits. In the three photographs that have been located of Lucrecia Perryman, her hair is long and pulled back from her face in one, and in the others, bundled high under a cloth wrap. I am particularly fond of this story, for it speaks to me of a woman who insisted on regaining control and possession of her body after the horrors of enslavement—a woman who rebelled against even the memory of enslavement.

The federal population census consistently lists Caroline's birthplace as North Carolina. Her parents are consistently listed as from North Carolina. Her sister, Sarah (Sally) was born four years later, 1859, in Missouri. Frank, the youngest of the three, was born in 1862, in Louisiana. His death certificate specifies that his place of birth was New Orleans. Unlike their sister Caroline, who lived into her nineties, neither Sarah nor Frank reached old age, and they appear in only two surviving censuses. In the 1880 census, only Caroline is described as a stepchild of Marshall Perryman (the head of household). Sarah and Frank are described as his daughter and son. This contradicts other information in the same census that describes Caroline, Sarah, and Frank as each having North Carolina–born parents, whereas the younger children are listed as having a North Carolina–born mother and a Jamaica-born father. As I will discuss further in a moment, Marshall is listed in this census as having been born in Jamaica. In his will, Marshall does specify that Frank is his stepson, but makes no similar distinction for Sarah or Caroline (Probate Court of Mobile County [PCMC] 1884). In a 1936 court affidavit, Caroline self-identifies as the stepdaughter of Marshall Perryman (PCMC 1936).

The relationship between Marshall and the children is important to note for several reasons. Foremost, Frank's conception provides a date after which (a terminus post quem of sorts, to use an archaeological term) Marshall and Lucrecia became involved. Second, we cannot assume, simply because each of them has a North Carolina heritage (through their parents), that they knew one another in that state. There is nothing to suggest that Marshall ever lived in Missouri or Louisiana. A search of marriage records in Mobile and New Orleans failed to locate a marriage license for Marshall and Lucrecia Perryman. This is not necessarily proof that the two did not marry in one of these places, for records of African-American marriages (or any marriages for that matter) are not complete. Persons marrying in churches, unless there was legal incentive, such as inheritance issues, did not necessarily register their marriages with the state. Finally, the kinship relations between Marshall and the different children had implications for the inheritance of Marshall's estate after his death.

We can only speculate as to what led to Lucrecia's relocation first to Missouri and then to New Orleans. Missouri had been admitted to the United States as a slave-holding state as a result of the 1820 Missouri Compromise, which maintained the balance of slave-holding to free states by creating the state of Maine to balance the admission of Missouri (McPherson 1982). Prior to the compromise, slaveholders and anti-slavery proponents engaged in attempts to outnumber one another in the territory. On August 30, 1861, General John C. Fremont, commander of the Western Department, proclaimed martial law in Missouri and freed the slaves of every Confederate in the state. Abraham Lincoln modified the edict on September 11, 1861, to conform to the Confiscation Act of August 6, 1861, which confiscated only those slaves who had been employed directly in the aid of the Confederate forces (building dams, etc.) (McPherson 1982:41). It is interesting to consider whether these events in Missouri are somehow related to Frank's being born in 1862 in Louisiana. Although occupied early in the Civil War (Gill 1997), New Orleans remained a fiercely Confederate stronghold in its sympathies. Without some further clue, such as a name of an enslaver or some other sort of family story, we face a historical dead end. Lucrecia's descendants did not recall any mention of Lucrecia having a first husband, of Caroline ever having a last name other than Perryman, or her married names, and had never heard Caroline mention living anywhere but the Carolinas during slavery. All we know for certain is that Lucrecia would have found herself and her young family moving ever deeper in the South as slavery came to a close. For an enslaved woman raised in the Carolinas, the specter of being sold down the river by the never ceasing bands of speculators that traveled through that state would have been an ever-present threat and could have made the reality more terrifying.

Marshall's past is even more clouded than Lucrecia's. Marshall is recorded in the 1870 census as having been born in Alabama in 1839; his mother, Livonia, who lived with the Perrymans at the time, is listed as having been born in North Carolina in 1815. The 1880 census provides contradictory information. Marshall's place of birth is listed as "Jamaica," and his parents' birthplaces are both listed as North Carolina. Marshall's date of birth is also different, now being listed as 1830. His mother, now listed as L. Lavinia Goode, is also older than would be expected, based on the 1870 census. Her birthdate is now listed as 1805, but still North Carolina. Contradictions in census records are commonplace—particularly for African-American families, who have historically been undercounted and less thoroughly documented than white families in the census (Blassingame 1979). Often, it is possible to clarify these kinds of inconsistencies by triangulating information with other documents. Unfortunately, Marshall Perryman died in 1884. Although there is a death certificate for him entered with the county, it is incomplete and does not include information such as his age at death, or how long he had resided in the area before his death (MCDC 1884). Marshall's mother also died between the 1880 and 1900 censuses, but no death certificates filed under Goode or Perryman have been found for her, nor does she appear in the Magnolia Cemetery records or in city sexton records.

The reference to Marshall's being born in Jamaica is fascinating for its implications, if that was indeed his birthplace. It is unfortunate that it is mentioned in only one census. By the time of the 1900 census, Marshall had been dead for 15 years. The entry for Walter, Perryman's youngest child, lists his father's birthplace as North Carolina, yet another contradiction. One possibility that could account for North Carolinian–born slaves giving birth to a son in Jamaica would be if Marshall's parents had been enslaved to one of the many British loyalists who had lived in North Carolina (Troxler 1976). In return for their loyalty to the British government during the American Revolution, the loyalists were rewarded with money and sometimes with land grants in other British plantation colonies, such as Bermuda, the Bahamas, Barbados, and Jamaica.

Most of the loyalists left for the British Caribbean during the period of 1785 through the 1790s. It is possible that Marshall's North Carolina–born parents were taken to Jamaica with their loyalist owner as children. At the time Marshall was born, around 1830, the abolition movement in Britain was gaining force (Craton and Saunders 1992), and it was clear that slavery would be eliminated in the near future. Prior to the abolition of British slavery in 1835, many loyalists sold their British holdings and returned with their slaves to the United States, where slavery appeared to be an institution with an endless future. It also was not uncommon for planters to have multiple plantation holdings in the American South and Caribbean, and to shift enslaved people among locations. Again, how this might relate to Marshall is merely speculation.

There is one other facet to this enigma worth considering. In both the 1870 and 1880 censuses, each of the Perrymans is listed under the category of race as "mulatto." The exception is Lavinia Goode, who in each census is listed as "black." While the listing of race is one of the most subjective of the census categories, usually decided by the enumerator (rather than a self-identification), it is interesting that two separate enumerators made the same classification decision. This raises the question of whether Perryman is the surname of Marshall's father.

Perryman was not a common name in antebellum Mobile, its incidence limited to a single family. Milton T. Perryman, a native of South Carolina, first appears in the census records for Mobile in 1850. He is listed in the 1860 census as a 60-year-old merchant with real estate holdings valued at $10,000 and a personal estate valued at $150,000. Perryman's wife, Johanna Haines Saunders, hailed from New Bern, North Carolina (H. Thompson 1974). The couple had married in 1818 in Edgefield, South Carolina (Langdon 1990:85), where they resided with Mumford Perryman (father of Milton) until at least 1820 (FPC 1820). After 1820, it has not been possible to trace Milton Perryman again until the 1850 census. He does not appear in any of the census indices for the southern states in 1830 or 1840. Likewise, his father, Mumford, has not been located. A review of published probate records and cemetery data from Edgefield County, his last known address, also failed to confirm whether or not he died during this period. It is certainly possible that the Perrymans were residing outside of the country. The Milton Perryman family was in Mobile by 1845, when their daughter was recorded as being born in that city. Certainly, we cannot discount the possibility that there is a connection, be it ownership or otherwise, between these Perrymans and Marshall Perryman. The name is not a common one in the South, and after Emancipation, Marshall's is the only African-American family to bear the name.

Milton Perryman held 24 people in slavery, including one 60-year-old and two 45-year-old black women. Certainly, these women fall within the reported age ranges for Marshall's mother, Lavinia. The demographics of the slave-holdings do not represent a natural population curve, for 20 of the 24 enslaved people are described as female. Three mulattoes, described as "fugitives from slavery" are included in the list; they are an 18-year-old female, a 35-year-old female, and a 25-year-old male. In 1860, Marshall would have been, based on the competing census records, between 21 and 30 years of age. Whether these individuals were in fact fugitives or released with their owner's permission is open to debate. Only 84 slaves were manumitted in Mobile between 1818 and 1845. A review of these records failed to identify any Perrymans or Goodes (PCMC-manumissions). In 1805, the Alabama legislature had determined that manumissions were illegal unless the owner could demonstrate that the slave in question had performed a meritorious act for the owner or the territory (Nordmann 1990:34). The law was changed in 1834 to allow judges to man-umit slaves. Any manumitted slave had to leave the state within 12 months (Nordmann 1990:35). In his dissertation on the freed black population of Mobile, Nordmann observed that enslaved people who were able to raise the value of their person would often be allowed to purchase themselves from own-ers who allowed them to go free without legally manumitting them (Nordmann 1990:34). Milton lived in Mobile until his death in 1871 (H. Thompson 1974). His death predates Marshall's final large land purchase. Unfortunately, the county has no will on file for him.

Eli S. Perryman, son of Milton, by 1860 had established his own household in Mobile, next to that of his parents. The younger Perryman is recorded as having been born in Alabama in 1829. His real estate is valued at $20,000, and his personal property at $40,000. Like his father, his occupation was that of merchant, and he was the owner of 21 enslaved people. His slave population was much younger than his father's, with the oldest being a 35-year-old female. Twelve of his 21 slaves were described as female. There are three mulattoes in the younger Perryman's population, a 32-year-old woman, a 20-year-old woman, and a 35-year-old woman. Unlike his father's slaves, none of Eli's enslaved people are described as fugitives from slavery.

I hope it is clear why I have digressed and spent some amount of ink discussing the white Perrymans of Mobile. While I do not have any "smoking gun," documentarily speaking, to link the two families, certainly we must consider the possibility that Marshall Perryman's name was derived from the white Perrymans of Mobile. The connections of the family back to the Carolinas fits with the background of Marshall Perryman. Likewise, the white Perrymans had significant slave-holdings, and certainly each of their slave populations included individuals who, based on their age, race, and sex, could be Marshall and his mother. Finally, since the white Perrymans were merchants, the labors in which their enslaved people were engaged would have prepared them for similar work after Emancipation. Marshall's only documented employment after freedom was for the grocery and portage business of Mobile merchant William B. Vail.

Vail shared ownership of five enslaved people with his brother as part of an inheritance from his father, but none of the people listed come close to matching Lavinia Goode or Marshall Perryman, suggesting that the two were not enslaved by Vail, thus eliminating one possible explanation for Vail's apparent concern for Perryman. Vail becomes a sort of legal protector for Perryman, signing as an agent for him in financial matters as early as 1869. As we will explore later, it is probably because of Vail's representation of Perryman that the family was able to maintain ownership of their land immediately following Marshall's death. Vail was a Mobile native who generationally was an age mate of Marshall Perryman. As a fellow grocer whose business was located a short distance from the Perrymans', Vail would have known the Milton Perryman family. Was the protective relationship that Vail had with Marshall Perryman that of a man taking care of a family friend's illegitimate son? Such practices were not uncommon in the Old South (Nordmann 1990; Alexander 1991). This is a question that should at least be pondered, if unanswerable. Mixed racial heritage often provided a route for entrée into land ownership and into the middle class that was not available to all African Americans. As I will discuss shortly, Marshall Perryman acquired the family's landholdings from several very prominent white Mobile residents, all former slaveholders. This circumstance, again, seems rather odd for an African-American man who had no other connection to this society.

Let us focus now on other aspects of Marshall's pre-Emancipation family life for a moment. There is only one suggestion from the documentary record that Marshall had children other than those born to him and Lucrecia. In his will, he mentions a daughter, "Brice Perryman, now married to Henry Jefferson." I have not been able to locate any records in Mobile that relate to a Henry and Brice Jefferson, and for now, the identity of this woman remains a mystery. "Brice" does not seem to be a nickname for any of the other known Perryman children, nor is Jefferson a surname encountered during any of the genealogical research into the family in Mobile. There was a Henry (age 35) and Florida (age 33) Jefferson living on Texas Street near Broad Street in the 1880 census. This intersection is about seven blocks from the property of Marshall and Lucrecia. A Henry and Elizabeth Jefferson are recorded in 1884, in the Mobile city directory as living at George and Elmira. Elizabeth Jefferson died in 1893, but her death certificate does not list the name of her father. No land transactions exist in the county records to suggest that the parcel of land left to Brice Jefferson ever came to her possession. Like so many other details of the family's history, further information about this otherwise unknown daughter remains elusive.

The Perrymans in Mobile: Married Life

Once the Perrymans settled in Mobile, their lives come into better historical resolution. Although their first child, daughter Emma, was born in 1866 in Alabama, it is not clear whether she was born in Mobile.

During the antebellum period, Mobile was an important port city. By 1840, Mobile ranked second only to New Orleans as a cotton exporter. By 1860, the city was home to 30,000 people (Amos 1985:20). The Perryman family may have been drawn to the area by work opportunities. Following the Civil War, African-American labor was reportedly hard to find in the city (Fleming 1911:445). Recently freed people took advantage of wages set by the Freedmen's Bureau (Table 2.1; after Fleming 1911:422) and invested their earnings in savings and land. The Mobile branch of the Freeman's bank had 3,260 depositors in 1870, who had deposited an average of $165 to the bank, for a total holding of $539,534.30. At least $50,000 of this money was invested in land ownership (Fleming 1911:454).

The Perrymans joined in the effort to acquire land. The earliest reference to the family living in Mobile is found in Mobile County probate records of 1869. Marshall Perryman is recorded as buying a piece of land from Charles W. Gazzam

Table 2.1 Wages Set by Freedmen's Bureau (after Fleming 1911:422).

	18 to 40 Years Old	14 to 18 Years Old; 40 to 55 Years Old	12 to 14 Years Old
Men	$25.00	$20.00	$15.00
Women	$18.00	$14.00	$10.00

and his wife, Clementine. The 62-year-old Gazzam, a native of England, was a longtime Mobile resident, living in the area by 1850. He resided elsewhere in the Eighth Ward, and he was the co-proprieter of a local foundry, B. F. Skaats and Company, and president of the Mobile First National Bank until 1868 (Amos 1985:212; C. Mathews 1941:14). In the 1860 census his personal estate was estimated to be $60,000. It is interesting that Gazzam, a former slaveholder himself, was willing to sell land to an African American. The parcel was described as

> beginning at the South east corner of a three acre lot of John Seed as now owner and occupied by him east of Ann Street and running thence southwardly parallel with Ann Street one hundred and eighty one feet six inches to a point on the northern margin of a new street to be laid out twenty feet wide next month adjoining the west end of Magnolia Cemetery owned by the City of Mobile thence westwardly parallel with said Cemetery lot along the "western" margin of said next street to a point which will give the lot hereby conveyed a full width of fifty five feet in a perpendicular line to Ann Street, thence northwestwardly [sic] parallel with Ann Street, one hundred and eighty six feet and six inches to John Seeds Southern boundary line and thence along said last mentioned line fifty five feet to the place of beginning. (PCMC 1869:502)

The total purchase price for the parcel was $200. Perryman paid $50 for the property, and worked out a payment schedule for the remainder and interest. Payments of $50 were to be made to Gazzam by Perryman on the first of each May for the next four years. The final $50 was the interest payment (PCMC 1870). The conveyance record makes no mention of existing structures on the property, and given its location on the outskirts of Mobile (Figure 2.2), it is likely that the Perrymans erected the first structure there. The land seems like an unlikely location to live. The small lot was surrounded by the larger landholdings of their neighbors. Some families might have been uncomfortable living on a plot of land facing such a large cemetery.

In 1870, the population census did not specify a street address for the family. This is common in the census for unincorporated areas. Marshall was listed at this time as working for a grocer (probably W. B. Vail), Lucrecia (listed as Christiana) was employed as a laundress, and Livinia Goode was listed as "keeping house." Presumably Marshall's mother cared for the children—Caroline, now 15; Sallie, 11; Frank, 8; Emma, 4; and Rachel, 1—when Lucrecia was working. Though it cannot be confirmed, it seems likely that the family was living on the Ann Street lot. Emma was the first of Lucrecia and Marshall's children together, and was listed as having been born in Alabama, as was her young sister, Rachel. African Americans living in Mobile were quick to take advantage of educational opportunities offered through the auspices of the Freedmen's Bureau. In 1870, Caroline, Sarah (listed as Sallie), and Frank were described as having been attending school, placing them among 16,097 African-American students. These numbers would increase rapidly, with 54,595 African-American students enrolled in Mobile schools only five years later (Fleming 1911:634).

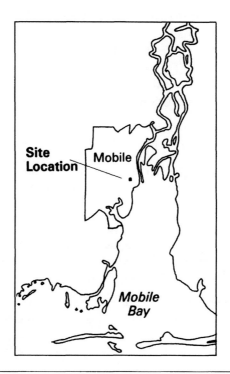

Figure 2.2 Site location

In 1870, according to the census, neighboring families to the Perrymans included Jonathon (John) Seed, a white gardener from England, and his five children; the Bush brothers, Henry and Joseph, who were from France and worked as a drayman and gardener, respectively; C. Hainsworth, a white Alabamian dairyman; and Artemis Hansberry, a black gardener with an estate valued at $1,200, and his wife, Emira. Intriguingly, Emira is also listed as working as a laundress—perhaps she and Lucrecia worked together. Though sparsely populated, the area was home to a population from diverse racial and geographic backgrounds (FPC 1870) (Figure 2.3).

The Perryman family's presence in Mobile was documented for the first time in the Mobile city directory in 1871. Marshall's occupation is listed as a "colored porter," working for the William B. Vail drayage company. Vail's business was located in the waterfront area of the city, about three miles away from the family residence. Marshall's address was listed as east and south of Ann Street, confirming the family's occupation of their land holding. Marshall would continue to work for Vail until his death. Lucrecia does not appear in the city directory, but whether she was no longer employed outside of the home is unclear, since women were often left out of the directories.

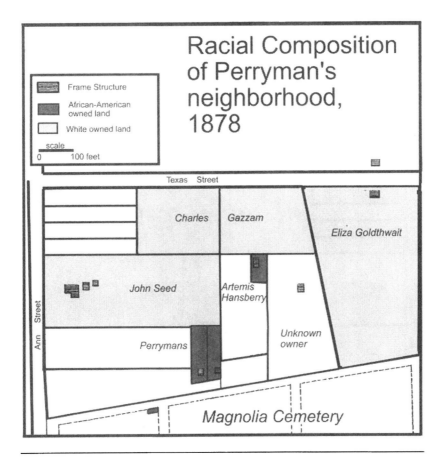

Figure 2.3   Racial backgrounds of Perryman's neighbors, 1878 (after Hopkins 1878)

The economic fortunes of the family seem to have been good, for in 1873, Marshall Perryman purchased a second lot from C. W. Gazzam. On this occasion, however, he paid for the lot with $250 "cash in hand." This second lot adjoined the first he had purchased on the western property line. The conveyance describes the original lot (1861) as the Perrymans' residence. The second lot was fifty feet wide with a depth of 200 feet on the boundary with John Seed's holdings (PCMC 1873).

A map of Mobile produced by G. M. Hopkins in 1878 provides the only doc-ument showing the location of structures on the Perryman properties (Fig-ure 2.4). Situated in the southern quarter of the parcels are two small wood frame structures, one on each lot. It is impossible to know whether the houses faced to-ward or away from the cemetery. According to family memory, Marshall, Lucrecia, and their growing family occupied the original home, and Caroline and her

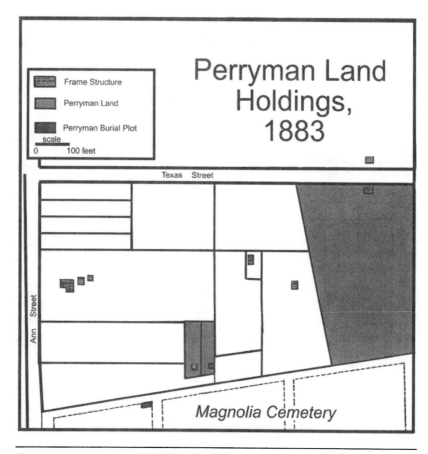

Figure 2.4 Perryman family's landholdings and structures, 1883

husband lived in the second house. Caroline would have been 18 years of age in 1873, and perhaps her marriage inspired the purchase of the second parcel of land. By 1878, Frank Perryman was also working for William B. Vail.

Based on the 1878 map, the Perrymans would have had few immediate neighbors at this time. Jonathon (listed as John) Seed still held the property behind the Perrymans, and his house and outbuildings faced Ann Street. Seed was a widower at the time, living with his four daughters and son. The Hansberry family owned and resided on the property immediately east of the Perrymans', and Eliza Goldthwait owned a large parcel to the east of these, on which she had one structure. Her residence faced Texas Street. Depending upon the ground cover, these structures were close enough to be visible to one another, but the area would have had a rural feeling to it.

Eastward, beyond the Goldthwait parcel, there was greater development along Texas Street, with closely spaced, small housing clustering along the street. Based

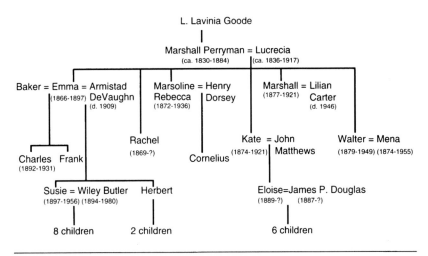

Figure 2.5 Marshall and Lucrecia Perryman's family tree

on the 1880 census, houses along Texas Street were occupied by racially diverse families, but more African-American than white families. In contrast, Ann Street was the location of increasingly exclusive housing, including the homes of real estate agents, futures brokers, bankers, and merchants. The rural areas outside of Mobile had become popular suburbs as early as 1858, when the first mule-drawn omnibus was begun to provide service to the areas of Summerville and Spring Hill (Amos 1985:70). The gradual gentrification of the neighborhood would ultimately cost the Perrymans much of their landholdings. During this time, however, there is no indication that the growing white suburban population located to their east was positively or negatively affecting the value of the Perrymans' land.

Beginning in 1870, Marshall Perryman appears in the real estate tax records for the city of Mobile, with W. B. Vail as his agent. From 1870 to 1874, Perryman's lands are valued at $200, and he was charged annually a $50 assessor's fee. Marshall missed his payment in 1871, but in 1873 paid his accumulated taxes in full. In 1879, reflecting the purchase of additional land, the value of the property had increased to $400. The taxes due that year appear to be $24. During his lifetime, Marshall was able to keep the real estate taxes on their property paid in full, a circumstance that also helped the family keep the land after his death (Mobile Municipal Archive [MMA] 1870–1925).

At the time of the 1880 census, the Perryman family had continued to grow, by birth and marriage (Figure 2.5). Two of Lucrecia's older children had married, and Lucrecia had become a grandmother. Emma and her sister M. Rebecca, 8, now attended school. Caroline and her husband, 28-year-old Alexander Bowers, were living with the rest of the Perrymans. One cannot help but wonder what the elder Perrymans thought of their son-in-law, who held no occupation. Family members suggest that Bowers holds little esteem in the descendants' collective memory.

Sarah's (listed as Sallie) husband may have been viewed as the better addition to the family. Her husband, Dave Cunningham, worked as a waiter at one of the hotels in Mobile's downtown. The couple resided in a rental property in the Third Ward near his place of employment with their infant son, Edward. Cunningham was a 38-year-old native of Alabama who had worked since at least 1870 as a waiter. The Cunninghams' marriage, although it would produce two sons, Edward and young David, was not to be long-lived. Cunningham died from unknown circumstances in 1882 and was buried in the Perryman family plot in Magnolia Cemetery (Magnolia Cemetery Records n.d.).

Despite Sarah's departure, there was no shortage of children living in the Perryman compound. Frank, now 18, continued to live with his parents. Emma, now 14, had a houseful of younger siblings. The Perrymans added four children to their household between the 1870 and 1880 census: M. Rebecca (also known as Marsoline); Kate, 6; the couple's first son, Marshall, Jr., 3; and the baby of the family, Walter, who was one month old at the time of the census. Walter would be the Perrymans' last child. Lucrecia was 44 years old at the time of Walter's birth. There was a 25-year span in age between her youngest and eldest children. Marshall's mother was still living with the family but has no occupation listed. Lucrecia was now described as "keeping house."

The decade of the 1870s had not brought all joy to the Perryman household. Rachel Perryman, Marshall and Lucrecia's second-eldest child, does not appear in the census. Rachel would have been 11 years old at the time of the 1880 census, and therefore, not likely to be living on her own elsewhere. She is not one of the individuals listed as buried in the Magnolia Cemetery plot, but records before 1900 were poorly kept for the cemetery. Marshall Perryman had already purchased Lot 29 of Square 25 in Magnolia Cemetery before his own death in 1884, but cemetery records do not indicate when he purchased it, only that he is still, even today, considered the owner. His burial is not recorded, nor is that of his mother or Rachel. David Cunningham is the earliest confirmed burial in the lot, but only because a headstone is associated with his grave. No other trace of Rachel has been found in the historical record, and it can only be assumed that she passed away. The Perryman cemetery plot is located on the border of the cemetery, within easy viewing distance from the family home. Even in death, the Perryman family remained in close proximity to one another, and too soon, the plot would become final resting place to more family members.

Marshall purchased his last parcel of land in 1881. By this time, he may have been feeling the first effects of the "consumption" (pulmonary tuberculosis) that would kill him in three years' time. For his last purchase, Marshall acquired the parcel that had been owned by Eliza Goldthwait. Goldthwait was a well-to-do widow of a local judge, who by May 1880 was living on her Government Street property. She had been born in North Carolina to North and a South

Carolinians. In the antebellum period, she supported herself by renting the labor of her 17 enslaved people (Amos 1985:88). This piece of property dwarfed the earlier two purchased by the family. It measured approximately 200 by 640 feet, or around 2.9 acres. Marshall purchased the property for a down payment of $200 and a promise of two additional annual payments of $100 (PCMC 1881). The last payment would have occurred a year before Marshall's death.

Marshall died May 14, 1884. His death certificate indicates that he had been ill for about two years prior to his death, and his doctor visited during the prior week (MCDC 1884). Marshall clearly realized that his illness would soon be fatal on May 12, 1884, when he gathered together William Vail, his employer of 13 years, to record his will, and his neighbors Artemis, now going by the name William, Hansberry and Jonathon Seed to serve as witnesses.

It is remarkable to find African-American wills for this period. Disenfranchised from property ownership, few persons had any need for a will. By the mid-1880s, Reconstruction had ended, and African Americans were enduring retaliation from the newly restored white southern power structure. Violence against African Americans took physical, political, and economic forms (Litwack 1979, 1999). African-American families who had built landholdings for themselves during Reconstruction, as the Perrymans had, too often found themselves cheated, robbed, or otherwise dispossessed of their acquired wealth. Writing in 1911, W. E. B. Du Bois commented on this situation,

> Few people realize how difficult it is in the South for the poor man to save who wants to. Usually in the country districts there are but two methods open to him: To hoard his money or to hand it over to some white friend. There have been numberless cases where such white friends and patrons have taken care of the money of their Negro clients and acted as bankers, with the result that the coloured man has been able to keep his saving secure and accumulate. However, in an unfortunately large number of other cases the colored man has been cheated. (30)

Perryman's will represents not only a testimony to how he wished to dispose of his property, but also to the trust he placed in the men left to oversee it. Perryman stated, "I hereby appoint my friend, W. B. Vail, of Mobile, to be executor of this my will and I expressly relieve him from giving bond as such executor." That he chose to refer to Vail as his friend, rather than employer, struck an interesting note with me.

Although Marshall's age at death is not certain, he was most likely between 45 and 54 years of age. Vail would have been 42 at the time of Marshall's death. As of 1880, Vail was a bachelor, living with his widowed mother and two younger stepsiblings. His occupation was listed as a wholesale and retail grocer. His mother had been born in North Carolina, while his father was a native of Alabama. Also living in the Vail household were a mulatto couple, who worked as cook and servant for the family, and their three children. Vail seems to have built his business after the Civil War, for he is described in the 1860 census merely as a "clerk," with personal property valued at $3,000. His brother is assessed as having personal property of equal value, and it is likely that this sum represents their inheritance from their father. According to the 1860 census, the brothers had inherited five slaves, ranging in age from 16 to 80, from their father. It is likely that these individuals represent the extent of the brothers' worth. Vail served in the Confederate army's Alabama Third Infantry, Company E (Hewett 1996:416), and returned after the war to Mobile.

Marshall Perryman's trust in his employer was well founded. Vail followed the estate through probate and ensured that Perryman's wishes were respected. At a time when so many African-American families who had established some financial security and wealth for themselves during Reconstruction found that security taken away, it is difficult not to wonder at the Perrymans' ability to retain their property. Portions of the land purchased by Perryman still remain in possession of several of his descendants. He and Lucrecia indeed left an important material legacy for their children.

The will itself provides some further insight into Marshall Perryman and his relationships with his family members. His will first specifies that his debts and funeral expenses be paid from his estate. Second, he leaves "to my Stepson Frank Perryman, a lot of land to be taken from the east side of my land [sic] fronting on Texas Street—heretofore conveyed to me by deed of Mrs. Eliza Goldthwaite, the said land hereby revised to my step son to have a front of fifty feet on Texas Street with a depth southwardly of two hundred feet." Adjacent to the lot left to Frank, an equal-sized lot was left to Brice, the wife of Henry Jefferson. Adjacent to that property, a 50 foot by 100 lot was granted to Caroline. Sarah (listed as Ellen) received a lot of the same size. The remainder of the estate was left by Marshall, "to my beloved wife Crissy to have and to hold during the term of her natural life and after her death to go absolutely to my children, Emma, Rebecca, Katie, Marshall and Walter, and my stepson Frank Perryman share and share alike."

Marshall left land to his children and stepchildren. He seems to have held Frank in special esteem, leaving him land both immediately and in the event of his mother's death. Frank would have been a very young child when Lucrecia and Marshall married. With the exception of Frank, the Perrymans would remain a family of daughters—the Perrymans' first four children together were girls—until the birth of young Marshall in 1877. Marshall would never know either of his biological sons as more than very young children. Frank had worked with his father at W. B. Vail for five years, and it is likely that part of his wages supported the family's ability to purchase property.

As deep as Marshall's affection for his stepson may have been, however, one aspect of the will suggests that Marshall sensed the potential for weakness in the man. His will went on to specify:

> It is my desire however that if it should be deemed advisable by my wife and my stepson Frank Perryman to sell my two lots on Delaware Street conveyed to

me by Mr. C. W. Gazzam [these were the "home lots"] and wife then *with the written consent of my executor herein after named* [emphasis added] my said wife to be deemed the absolute owner of said lots so as to make good title thereto in fee simple provided however the proceeds of said lots to be paid over to my said executor and to be paid out so much thereof as may be necessary in building a suitable house upon my land lying west of the lots above devised to my children. (PCMC 1884:591)

The stipulation that any sale of the home place be overseen by Vail protected Lucrecia from having the land sold out from under her by her son.

The years following Marshall's death were surely difficult, emotionally and financially, for the family. Frank Perryman continued to work for W. B. Vail, being promoted from a driver to a porter, the position once held by his stepfather (MCD 1885). No occupation is listed for Lucrecia during this time, but she would have been responsible for the care of several young children. Caroline could have provided some aid with child care, although in 1885 she gave birth to her only living child, a son named Willie. After 1887, however, Frank was no longer listed as working at Vail and Co. This could be an oversight of the directory, but this seems less likely since Marshall and Frank had been missed by the directory only once since 1873. Instead, the lack of job listing may hint at larger problems within the family.

On February 25, 1889, Frank Perryman was recorded as selling his inheritance property to one Joseph MacKrone for a sum of $125 (PCMC 1889). The 1889 document clearly describes the land left to Frank in his stepfather's will, a parcel of land taken from the original Goldthwaite tract. It appears, however, that Frank may have misled MacKrone into thinking he was purchasing the land with Lucrecia's house on it as well as the Texas Street property. Based on the legal documents, MacKrone was not literate, signing the court documents with an "X." On February 24, 1891, a quit claim was filed from MacKrone [*sic*] to Lucrecia Perryman. Lucrecia paid a sum of $25 for MacKrone to release any claim to the home lots and reasserting MacKrone's ownership of the land Frank had inherited (PCMC 1891).

Frank, meanwhile, had moved to Chicago. While there, he contracted a pulmonary infection, probably tuberculosis. He returned to Mobile in late 1893 and died in his mother's home in February of 1894, only 31 years old (MCDC 1894a). He was buried in Magnolia Cemetery; his grave marker still stands.

Whatever the circumstances of the relationship between Frank and his mother in his last years, his return home brought more grief with it. Sarah Cunningham, now a widow and a mother to six young children, fell ill with the same disease that had killed Frank. Six months after her brother died, Sarah died (MCDC 1894b). She was buried in Magnolia Cemetery, next to her husband. Her young children stayed with Lucrecia. Of the three children Lucrecia had carried from enslavement, only her daughter Caroline still lived.

Caroline's life was not without its problems. After two decades of marriage to Alexander Bowers, Caroline sued for and was granted a divorce (USA 1994).

While it has not been possible to locate any records further documenting the case, Caroline must have been enduring some form of dire hardship for a divorce to be granted. Only five divorces were granted in the city of Mobile that year. Even descendants who had clear memories of Caroline could not remember her ever mentioning her first husband, although it was known to them that her son was not blood kin to her second husband.

It is in 1892 that the first evidence of Lucrecia's return to the workforce is found. In the city directory of that year she is listed as "a nurse." She does not appear again in the directory until 1897, now described as a "sick nurse." In 1899, 1900, and 1901, she is described as "midwife," then again as a nurse in 1904, 1905, and 1907. The terms "nurse" and "midwife" seem to have been interchangeable. In the 1900 census, the same time that she was listed as a midwife in the Mobile city directory, her occupation is described as "nurse." Lucrecia's descendants described her as a nurse who cared for pregnant women, delivered babies, and cared for infants and children.

In the 1899, 1900, and 1901 city directories, midwives were listed under a distinct subheading in the business section of the directory. The numbers of midwives varies greatly across the years, suggesting that more midwives practiced than were listed. Midwives depended on word-of-mouth and repeat customers for much of their business. In 1899, 12 women were listed as midwives. One of the women is described as "Creole," seven as "colored," and four (including Lucrecia) do not have a race listed, indicating they were believed to be white. In 1900, the number of midwives listed had risen to 29—of these, 24 of the women were "colored." Lucrecia was now described as colored. The following year's directory included 36 midwives. Again, the majority of the women, 29 of them, were African-American. This is typical of midwifery throughout the American South (Fraser 1998). African-American midwives served white and black clientele alike, but with the growing popularity of hospital births during the late nineteenth and early twentieth centuries, white women increasingly opted to have their children under the supervision of a physician in a hospital.

In the 1901 directory, six pairs of women working as midwives share the same last names, suggesting that women were training younger relatives in midwifery. This was a common practice, extending back through the antebellum period. Apprenticeship to an older midwife was the only means of entering the field. Lucrecia does not appear to have been trained by a relative, nor does she appear to have trained any of her children or grandchildren in the trade. Given the changing attitudes toward African-American midwives that coincided with shifting mothering ideologies in the early twentieth century, midwifery as a vocation may have no longer appeared to have a future. While we cannot know who trained Lucrecia, the directories do provide interesting possibilities. In the 1899 directory, two black women were listed as having residences on Texas Street and working as midwives. Sarah Taylor, who lived at 961 Texas, appeared only in the 1899 directory. Orrie Harris relocated after 1899 from 855 Texas to

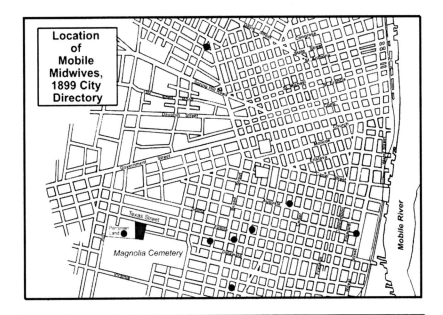

Figure 2.6   The distribution of Mobile's midwives in 1899

965 Church. Each of these women lived near the Perryman property. It was typical of older midwives to train their replacements as they neared retirement, and to leave their practice to their apprentices. In the 1900 and 1901 directories, Lucrecia was the only African-American midwife serving that part of the city (Figures 2.6, 2.7).

At the time when Lucrecia entered midwifery, significant African-American populations still lived in the area of her home. By the time of her retirement, around 1910 or 1911, the Ann and Texas Street areas had become more white and middle class in their demographics. It may well be that the community no longer required a midwife. For most of the city, the Mobile City Hospital, run by the Sisters of Charity, served the health needs of the city's populace, providing care for black and white patients on alternating days (Scribner 2001:163).

The beginning of the twentieth century brought profound changes for African-American residents. In 1901, Jim Crow laws were officially adopted in Alabama. The first segregation law was passed in Mobile in 1902. Segregation, which had already existed in Mobile from the 1870s, became a legal way of life. Segregation of the city's streetcars led to a boycott of the system, which lasted for two months. Racial violence, including a lynching, occurred (Scribner 2001:169). The city had grown in population. The city of 30,000 the Perrymans first called home was home to 40,000 people in 1900, and would grow to 60,000 by 1920 (Scribner 2001:155). The rural areas of Mobile County saw a population

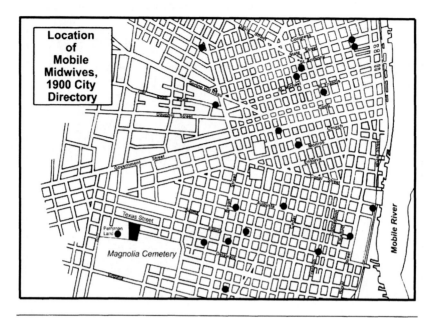

Figure 2.7   The distribution of Mobile's midwives in 1900

increase of 41 percent during that same period, reflecting increased suburban-
ization. Yet, despite the overall growth of the city, African Americans began to
leave the city in search of better opportunities. The city shifted from a port
town to a railroad town as timber increasingly vied with cotton as the city's
most important export (Scribner 2001).

The Perryman properties remained the focus of much activity and family
life. Although by 1900 only two of Lucrecia and Marshall's children, Caroline
and Walter, still lived with their mother, the two original houses were filled with
Perryman grandchildren.

Throughout this time, Caroline remained at home, caring for the five children
of her deceased sister Sally. In 1897, she remarried. Her new husband, William
Saunders, was a 45-year-old mulatto carpenter who had been born in Virginia.
The pair remained together until Saunders's death. The couple had no children,
but raised together many of her siblings' children. She was affectionately known
to her descendants as "Mama Caroline." Raising her sisters' children was no small
task. In 1900, the youngest child, Carrie, who went by the surname Perryman,
was only 7 years old. Charley was 8, and Lucretia, 11. The eldest two, David and
John, were 20 and 15, respectively. David, by 1901, was working as a porter.

Although fewer of Lucrecia's children were living on the home lot, as time passed, many of the children and grandchildren returned to live with her for varying
lengths of time. Kate Perryman, then working as a laundress, returned briefly
in 1905 to live with her mother (Table 2.2). Edward, the oldest Cunningham

Table 2.2 Occupants of Perryman Land through Time

Year	Known Occupants (Represents the minimum number of people living on property in any given year)
1870	Lavinia Goode
	Marshall Perryman
	Lucrecia Perryman
	Caroline Perryman
	Sally Perryman
	Frank Perryman
	Emma Perryman
	Rachel Perryman
1880	Lavinia Goode
	Marshall Perryman
	Lucrecia Perryman
	Caroline Perryman
	Bowers
	Alec Bowers
	Frank Perryman
	Emma Perryman
	M. Rebecca Perryman
	Kate Perryman
	Marshall Perryman Jr.
	Walter Perryman
1900	Lucrecia Perryman
	Walter Perryman
	Caroline Bowers
	Saunders
	William Saunders
	Willie Bowers
	Dave Cunningham
	John Cunningham
	Lucretia Cunningham
	Carrie Cunningham
	Charles Baker
1901	Lucrecia Perryman
	Dave Cunningham
1904	Lucrecia Perryman
	Kate Perryman
1907	Lucrecia Perryman
	Edward Cunningham
1910	Lucrecia Perryman
	Lucretia Adris
	Carrie Perryman
	Katie Matthews
	Eloise Douglas
	James P. Douglas
	Theresa Douglas
	Katie L. Douglas
	Baker Perryman
1913	Lucrecia Perryman
	Carrie Perryman
1914	Lucrecia Perryman
	Walter Perryman

child, lived at Magnolia Lane, the designation given to the Perryman's road, from 1907 to 1909, along with his brother, David. The pair worked as pressers at a local cleaners' operation. Their younger half-sisters, Carrie (a stenographer) and Lucretia Perryman, lived with their grandmother in 1913. Walter returned again to the home lot in 1914, while working as a gardener. Caroline continued to live in the house next to her mother's until Lucrecia's death, only then relocating to a new house on the Perryman parcel.

As children became adults and married, several of them took claim of the parcels left to them by their father. By 1904, young Marshall Perryman was working as a gardener, and living in a house at the "head of Frye." Frye Street was built through the middle of the original Goldthwaite tract and appears on the 1911 Sanborn Fire Insurance map. After leaving his mother's home, Walter Perryman lived on Elmira Street before settling in 1911 at 1914 Texas Street, on what was by that time known as the Perryman Parcel. Emma Perryman Baker DeVaughn settled with her husband and young children on one of the lots in the early 1900s as well, according to family members. A number of these parcels are still owned by Perryman descendants.

After 1908, there is no evidence to suggest that Lucrecia was still working. The 1910 census lists no occupation for her. Whether this is conclusive or not, given the overall seeming random nature of the family's inclusion in the city directories after 1900, is open to debate. Around 1910 or 1911, however, the well located on the home lot property was backfilled with a large assemblage of trash that included, among many other household goods, a wide range of materials that seem to have been related to Lucrecia's midwife practice.

Carol Stack and Linda Burton (1994) have created a term, *kinscription,* to describe work that individuals are conscripted to do in service of the family good. Certainly, Frank Perryman's support of his mother and siblings after his stepfather's death is an example of such kinscription. The stresses of these obligations may have been too great for Frank and may explain why he fled to Chicago. After 1908, the city directory suggests that Lucrecia often had the company of at least one relative in her home. It could be that her family was ensuring that she was taken care of as she approached old age. Lucrecia lived until February 4, 1917, dying at 1 P.M. Her cause of death was listed as "arterioscleroses, artereal insufficiency," with influenza a contributing factor. According to the death certificate, she had been ill for the year prior to her death. She was interred in Magnolia Cemetery, in Lot 129, square 5, laid to rest with her husband and at least three of her children.

Following Lucrecia's death, the home property was seized by the city of Mobile to pay back taxes. The family had not paid property taxes since Marshall's death, and the accumulation, combined with the gentrification of the surrounding neighborhood, placed the family with an impossible debt burden (Table 2.3). The parcels of land first purchased for $400 from Charles Gazzam by Marshall Perryman were valued at $1,620 in 1916 (MMA 1881–1908). Caroline and her husband moved to one of the other lots of land owned by the family.

Table 2.3 Perryman Property Value (Municipal Tax Books, Mobile)

Year	Assessed Value of Property
1870	$200.20
1871	$200.00
1872	$200.00
1873	$200.00
1874	$200.00
1879	$400.00
1880	$400.00
1886	$200.00*
1898	$300.00
1899	$600.00
1905	$800.00
1906	$1000.00
1917	$1320.00
1921	$1620.00

*Property is back to original two lots, children have inherited the rest.

It appears that the siblings agreed to follow the conditions of Marshall Perryman's will, that the land be divided amongst the surviving family members. In 1922, they had the Goldthwait parcel surveyed and divided into lots and officially recorded as "Perryman Place." The surviving heirs at this point were Susie Butler DeVaughn, the daughter of the deceased Emma, and her husband, Wiley; Walter Perryman and his wife, Mena; Eloise Douglas, the daughter of the deceased Kate, and her husband, James; Caroline Saunders; Marsoline Dorsey (M. Rebecca); and Lillie Perryman, the widow of young Marshall Perryman (PCMC 1922). After this point, the chains of title for portions of the property become difficult to trace. It appears that Walter attempted to engineer the sale of large portions of the property away from other family members as a means of paying his accumulated back property taxes. It is recorded in 1923 that Walter and Marshall Perryman both ultimately lost their landholdings to pay their accumulated property taxes. Walter sold his property in 1923 to a John Radcliffe and his wife for the sum of $125 (PCMC 1923). Radcliffe also purchased the former holdings of John Seed and Charles Gazzam. Radcliffe sold these properties as a package to the city of Mobile in 1925 for a sum of $18,000 (PCMC 1925). This is the property that became Crawford Park, a white-only recreational area in a nearly all-white neighborhood (Alabama State Planning Commission 1941).

The Archaeological Site

This narrative was intended to provide what is known about the broader rhythms and events that marked the lives of Marshall and Lucretia Perryman, and their

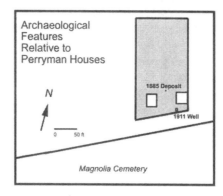

Figure 2.8 Location of archaeological features on the Perryman property

descendants, as associated with a particular place. With the grading of the Perrymans' property to create a city park, the equivalent archaeological record, the midden of their day-to-day activities, was lost. Instead, the archaeological remains from the site were limited to two major subsurface features (Figure 2.8). In contrast to a continuous midden, the two features contain materials that were deposited during a brief span of time, at particular moments in the family's history. The advantage of such deposits is that they allow for a consideration of how changing family circumstances are reflected in their material life. Such comparisons are more difficult to make in situations in which deposits were continuously created.

The first feature was a small trash pit, designated Feature 3, which was located in the area between the Bowers and Perryman houses. Based on glass artifacts recovered from the feature, the most likely time for the deposition of these materials was sometime around 1885. Though admittedly a small sample, consisting of 102 glass fragments (representing a minimum of 44 vessels) and 150 ceramic sherds (a minimum of 9 vessels), this assemblage provides insight into an important time in the family's history.

This assemblage corresponds to the period immediately after Marshall Perryman's death. The materials included in this deposit represent some of the patterns and priorities that characterized life in the Perryman household during Marshall and Lucrecia's married life. Both of the households on the home lot at this time were composed of families with young children. Caroline and Lucrecia were both employed as mothers full time, and their material lives would be representative of their homemaking and child rearing.

The second feature was a large back-filled well located in front of Marshall and Lucrecia's house. The well contained artifacts to depths of at least 130 cm (Figure 2.9). The materials recovered from Feature 1, the well, represent a later

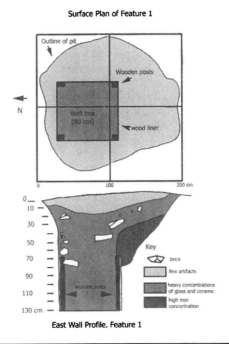

Figure 2.9   Profile and plan view of the Perryman well

period in the Perryman family history. A vast number of easily datable artifacts were recovered. Nearly a third of the bottles represented in this feature,
158 specimens, were recovered whole from the well. A minimum of 68 bottles
representing 10 local companies were also recovered (Table 2.4). Based upon
dates derived from Mobile city directories, most of these products would have
been available from the late 1890s through the first decade of the twentieth
century. A Coca-Cola bottle made in Mobile no earlier than 1909 represents the
latest of these firms. Similarly, a Stein soda bottle must have been manufactured
between 1909 and 1910.

Products of a number of national and international bottle manufacturers and
bottlers, identified by their base marks (Toulouse 1971), were recovered from
the feature. Only one, Roth and Company of San Francisco, manufactured its
product prior to 1900. The other 14 companies produced wares through the
late nineteenth to early twentieth centuries. Several American Bottling Company
marks recovered from the well provide a TPQ (terminus post quem, or the date
when the most recent artifact was first manufactured) of 1905.

The well was excavated in a combination of natural and arbitrary levels. A
dark silty sand containing a few artifacts capped the deposit. Underlying this
layer was a rich uniform deposit that extended to at least a depth of 130 cm.

Table 2.4 Local Companies Represented among the Artifacts

Company	Known Dates of Operation (Based on review of city directories from 1885 to 1925)	Number Found
D. Palliser Soda Works	1885–1899	3
West Ward Drug Store	1890–1903	1
E. Carre Soda Works	1891–1920	14
Dave S. Bauer Brothers Druggists	1893–1907	2
Bienville Pharmacy	1895–1910	2
G. Van Antwerp (and Son) Apothecaries	1895–1925+	27
J. G. Hulsbusch Druggist	1898–1906	1
Phoenix Bottle Works	1898–1912	7
D. Palliser's Sons, Soda Works	1900–1918	3
Mobile Bottling Plant, Coca-Cola	1909–1925+	1
Stein's Bottle Works	1909–1910	7
A. J. Hamilton, Druggist, Mobile	Unknown	1
J. N. Hamilton, Druggist, Mobile	Unknown	1
Spring Hill, Alabama, Bottling Works	Unknown	1
Choctow Soda Works	Unknown	2

This deposit was excavated in 10-cm levels. When the above-mentioned glass marks are considered according to the archaeological level from which they were recovered, there is no evidence of chronological differentiation among the levels. During analysis, the reconstruction of vessels from fragments found throughout the feature indicated that the deposit represents a single episode of refuse disposal. A consideration of ceramic manufacturers' marks further supports this contention (Table 2.5). The majority of ceramics were produced during the 1890s–1910 period. A single "Alfred Colley" mark, dating between 1904 and 1914, provides the narrowest time bracket for the origin of the ceramic materials.

Considering all the evidence, the well feature seems to represent a single, large-scale dumping episode dating around 1909 or shortly thereafter. The accumulated materials recovered from the well represent daily activities of the Perryman family from the 1890s until circa 1910, corresponding not only to the period after Marshall's death, but to the time during which Lucrecia worked as a midwife. Several converging factors could have contributed to the backfilling of the well. Based on Sanborn maps of the area, water was not piped to area around Magnolia Cemetery until between 1904 and 1924. Open wells were a hazard, particularly to households with small children. The advent of piped water to

Table 2.5 Glass Manufacture Dates

Feature 3

Company	Embossing	Date Range	Number Found at Feature
D. Palliser Soda Works	D. Palliser cor. Dauphin and Bayou, Mobile, ALA (on base, Pat APR 13th 1875 Arthur Christin)	At least 1885–1899	1
Fellows Chemists	LLOWS CHEMISTS		1
Durkee	Durkee		
Parker Brothers	Parker Bro. Worcestershire Sauce		2
Conrad's Soda			2
Hunyadi Janos	Saxlehner Hunyadi Janos Bitterquelle	1863–1900 (Toulouse 1971:257)	2
Roth and Videane	R & Co.	1879–1888	1.

Feature 1

Mark	Manufacturer	Date Range	Number in Level
IGCO	Illinois Glass Company, Alton, IL	1880–1900 (Toulouse 1971:264)	7
NB	North British Bottle Manufacturing Co., LTD., Shettleston, Scotland	1903–1937 (Toulouse 1971:377)	5
AB	Adolphus Busch Glass Manufacturing Co., Belleville, IL	1904–1907 (Toulouse 1971:26)	3
Root	Root Glass Co., Terre Haute, IN	1901–1932	4
ABGMCO	Adolphus Busch Glass Manufacturing Co., Belleville, IL	1886–1928 (Toulouse 1971:26)	3
WT & Co.	Whitall-Tatum Company, Milleville, NJ	1858–1935 (Toulouse 1971:544)	8
CLGCO	Carr-Lowrey Glass Co., Baltimore, MD	1889–1920 (Toulouse 1971:134)	5

(*continued*)

Table 2.5 (*Continued*)

Mark	Manufacturer	Date Range	Number in Level
		Feature 1	
P	Pierce Glass Co., St. Marys. PA	1905–1917 (Toulouse 1971:412).	1
ABCo	American Bottle Company, Chicago, IL	1905–1916 (Toulouse 1971:30)	2
SB & GCo	Streator Bottle and Glass Co., Streator, IL	1881–1905 (Toulouse 1971:461)	3
J.K.& S.	John Kilner and Sons, Wakefield, Yorkshire, England	1844–c. 1920 (Toulouse 1971:279–280)	3
R & Co	Roth and Co., San Francisco, CA	1879–1888 (Toulouse 1971:438)	1
CS&COLD	Cannington, Shaw and Co., St. Helens, Lancastershire, England	1875–1913 (Toulouse 1971:147–148)	2
B & Co. LD	Bagley and Co., Knottingley, Yorshire, England	1871–1899 (Toulouse 1971:77)	1
LGCO	Louisville Glass Works, Louisville, KY	1856–1900 (Toulouse 1971:323)	1
MB&GCo	Massillon Bottle and Glass Co., Massillon, OH	1900–1904 (Toulouse 1971:348).	2

the property may have necessitated the filling of the well. The well was filled around the time Lucrecia (according to city directories) retired from midwifery. Lucrecia Perryman's grandsons Edward and David Cunningham also appear to have moved from her property to their own residences around this same time. So this period corresponds to several important changes in the family's history. Perhaps Lucrecia, following her retirement, filled the well as part of a household cleanup.

The 1910 census lists a number of individuals living at the property. In addition to Lucrecia, there was her daughter Kate and Kate's husband, John Matthews; Eloise Douglas (Kate's daughter) and her husband, James P. Douglas, with their children Theresa and Kate; and Lucrecia's grandchildren who have taken the Perryman surname, Lucretia, Carrie, and Baker. Perhaps the cleanup effort was undertaken to accommodate the additional family members moving to the property and to dispose of some unwanted possessions accumulating from the departure of others.

These two deposits allow us to explore the multiple ideologies of African-American mothering that the women of the Perryman family encountered during differing life circumstances, against a rapidly changing sociopolitical and economic backdrop. At the time of Marshall's death, the Perryman and Bowers households were organized in a way that many African-American families of the time considered ideal—the women were working outside the public realm, focusing their time and attentions on raising their children and caring for matters of the household. The school-age Perryman children were consistently listed as attending school throughout this period (and following). Black feminist Maria Stewart, speaking in the early 1830s, had urged black women to aid in the uplift of the race by encouraging a love of education in their children (Richardson 1987), and this theme was reinforced in a number of other versus—church, popular literature, and clubs.

After surviving the conditions of enslavement, many African-American men and women found this household labor arrangement to be mutually agreeable. To have authority over one's children was a new and empowering situation for black women. Seclusion from the workforce protected African-American women from the day-to-day harassment and, often, sexual abuse that accompanied the kinds of labor available to them, namely, domestic service (Giddings 1984; J. Jones 1985). During slavery, African-American men were often powerless to prevent the sexual terrorization of the female kin. The Perrymans and Bowerses were fortunate to be in an economic situation that allowed them to pursue this household arrangement. Given Alexander Bowers's apparent lack of regular employment, it is likely that Lucrecia and Carolyn were able to remain out of the work force mainly through the labors of Marshall and Frank Perryman. In the archaeological materials from this time period, it is possible to study the materiality of their domesticity and mothering and, in doing so, to probe how these mothers engaged dominant mothering ideologies.

Following the death of Marshall Perryman, and the possible abandonment by, and eventual death of, Frank Perryman, the economic circumstances of the Perryman families changed substantially. Before her own death, Sarah Cunningham had been widowed, leaving her to raise two small children on her own. She returned to the family compound, residing, apparently, with her parents. Lucrecia had several young children herself, but none as young as Carolyn's son or Sarah's children. As a woman who had endured enslavement as an adult, she knew, to paraphrase the words of Harriet Jacobs, the particular burdens slavery held for women (Jacobs 2000). She would have been doubly loath to see her daughters enter the workforce—unwilling to see them separated from their young children, and unwilling to see them subjected to the physical and psychological tyrannies of domestic service. Following Sarah's death, Carolyn's ability to stay home became an economic necessity—someone had to care for the children full time.

Lucrecia's choice in work, however, did not turn her away from mothering, but instead expanded the network of individuals whom she mothered. As a midwife, Lucrecia was engaged in what Patricia Hill Collins has dubbed "motherwork," or mothering done for the good of the racial or ethnic community (1994). Her calling to midwifery is not surprising given growing political activism among African-American women at the time. Racial uplift was increasingly touted as the duty of middle-class black women. As a landholder, Lucrecia was better situated economically than many of her fellow black Mobilians, and she may have felt inspired to work for her race as well as herself. Midwifery provided an important avenue for instilling notions of health care, beauty, ethics, and values into new generations of African-American women. It was in this role that Lucrecia would confront mothering ideologies in new ways.

Birth was a multigenerational event, tying mothers and daughters. The circumstances of Lucrecia's life allowed her to bridge the experiential gap that existed between women who had been mothers during enslavement and the young women born to them after freedom. In her capacity as midwife, Lucrecia served as what I will refer to as a generational mediator for the community of African-American women. Through her practice she would come to combine innovation and tradition, ensuring that the rich traditions of diverse African pasts remained a part of African-American women's experiences. She would use the rich tradition of African-American midwifery, as it had survived slavery, to interpret and put into practice for her patients new ideologies of motherhood that arose in dominant discourses. Accordingly, Lucrecia was part of the black feminist movements that sought to redefine views of black motherhood that continued to shape women's experiences in the late nineteenth and early twentieth centuries. The archaeological materials from the well site provide dramatic insights into the ways that Lucrecia combated dominant ideologies of black womanhood through her medical practice.

While the archaeological materials from the Perryman compound provide an excellent opportunity to explore African-American mothering in a variety of ways, the materials are less informative for understanding how African-American masculinity and fatherhood were constructed in oppositional and complementary ways to African-American femininity and motherhood. The times at which these particular deposits were created coincide with periods in the family's experiences when the materialities of masculinity would be least visible.

The archaeological portrait painted by materials dating to one time may have little to do with the experiences of a family a mere year later. This is certainly true in the case of the Perryman family. Because our first archaeological portrait dates to the period immediately following Marshall Perryman's death— a transformative event in the family's history—The materials from this time are literally the debris of happier, more secure times, discarded at a time of transition. These materials provide a filtered glimpse of the life the Perrymans lived before 1885.

At the time of the first deposit, Marshall had passed away, as had Sarah's husband David Cunningham. Frank's position in the household is unclear; his relocation to Chicago may reflect a frustration not only with the economic realities of black labor opportunities in Mobile, but also a frustration with his ongoing position as eldest son. At the time of his stepfather's death, he would have been old enough to work, but still young enough for his mother to see him as under her authority. Alexander Bowers was not regularly listed as a resident of the household; in the census, he was described as living in Marshall Perryman's household rather than being listed as a head of his own. The eventual divorce of the Bowerses underscores that there were problems in this relationship that could not be resolved.

The filling of the well also corresponded to a time when adult men were not regular residents of the property. Those who were living sporadically on the property were Lucrecia's youngest son, Walter, who drifted between a number of short-term laboring positions, and her grandsons Edward and David Cunningham, who worked in semi-skilled positions downtown, where they also often resided. The nature of the deposit, which seems to be the result of a cleaning episode following Lucrecia's retirement, again, lends little insight into ideologies of masculinity, except for ways that masculinity articulated with midwifery practice.

I point out these shortcomings of the archaeological record because I want to make clear that this is not an archaeology of matriarchy. The myth of African-American matriarchs is a controlling image of black womanhood originating in slavery and coming to the fore of United States economic and social-political policy in the era of the New Deal and beyond (Giddings 1984; Collins 2000). The critical period of 1869–1884, when Lucrecia and Marshall were living together as husband and wife, and parents, is invisible to us in the archaeological record. The ways that they may have negotiated the construction of their post-Emancipation identities relative to one another and society through material culture are not available to us. Certainly, the documentary record suggests that theirs was a loving relationship, with Marshall treating Lucrecia's older children as his own, differentiating their status as stepchildren only in legal documents, and in the case of the daughters, not even then. It does not seem a stretch from the documentary record to suggest that Marshall saw himself as a provider and protector of his family. Certainly, the steps he took to ensure that his estate would pass to his family after his death demonstrate this. The documentary record seems to indicate that in their relationship, Lucrecia and Marshall were able to establish a balance in their home that suited them. This was no small task in the context of a time when political and economic gains made by African-American men during Reconstruction were systematically being stripped away (Litwack 1999).

Just as evidence of the balance achieved by Marshall and Lucrecia is lost to us in the material record, so is the discord that must have come to characterize the end of Carolyn and Alexander Bowers's marriage. After 1890, African-American men found themselves increasingly disenfranchised from political and economic opportunities. That the women of their families were often the main breadwinners because of their expanded opportunities in domestic and semi-skilled positions created ongoing tensions within the black community and black families (Giddings 1984). African-American women, who had been partners of equal standing within their households since the time of enslavement (Davis 1983), saw that equality erode during the aftermath of physical and sociopolitical violence against African-American men in the late nineteenth and early twentieth centuries, when they were increasingly called upon by religious and political leaders to be submissive to their husbands (Giddings 1984). Many marriages were unable to survive the effects of living in a violent, racist society. Under what circumstances the Bowerses' marriage was dissolved remains unknown to us.

Although Lucrecia Perryman and Caroline Bowers, the two women central to this archaeological narrative, should not be seen as matriarchs (with all the negative connotations that conjures), their strength and determination should be recognized. They managed to raise not only their own children but the children of their kinsmen while engaged in maintaining land acquired by their family. They raised children who were educated at a time when education for black children was still blocked by the white establishment, and education for black girls increasingly eyed suspiciously by a segment of black leadership (Giddings 1984). In the following chapters, I will elaborate upon the ways that the experiences of the Perryman women articulated with and were influenced by competing ideologies of mothering and sociopolitical movements.

Narrative Interlude I

Editor's Note: The WPA period interviews of Hazel Neumann were discovered in 1981 among the papers of the Turnerville, Mississippi, Public Library's History Room. The collection is accompanied by several letters from Hazel to her husband, Peter Neumann. Peter Neumann, of course, was a well-known faculty member in the English Department of the University of Mississippi. The papers were donated to the Turnerville library by the couple's son and daughter, Joseph Neumann and Angelina Neumann-Bassman.

These narratives, collected as part of the Federal Writer's Project Ex-Slave Narratives, were apparently never filed with the state project coordinator, and these interviews are not among the materials in the National Archive. The Mississippi narratives, like those of neighboring Louisiana, have long been notable to scholars for both the talent of the writers working for these states and the scattered and incomplete nature of the collections. The letter accompanying the narratives suggests that Neumann withheld the materials to protect her sources. While much of the subject matter is mundane, some narratives touch upon issues that would have been as volatile in Neumann's times as they are today.

The National Archive does include 25 other interviews believed to have been conducted by Neumann. Like so many of the Mississippi narratives, they are not signed by the interviewer, but scholars such as Mosley (1967) and Bertrand (1978) have convincingly attributed the narratives to Neumann. These other narratives have been published elsewhere.

Given Neumann's later success as a southern short story writer, the discovery of these narratives provides an exciting opportunity to explore the development of her writing style. It is clear from the differences in styles used to present these narratives that Neumann was exploring approaches to presentation, and we can begin to see, even in these seven short selections, the early development of her writer's voice. The dialog is rough, and the prose less than commanding, but they undeniably contain some of the focus on language and rhythm that was so distinctive in Neumann's later writing.

Neumann was a recently married woman of 22 when these interviews were conducted. She had completed her undergraduate studies the previous year at Tulane University in New Orleans. Based upon correspondence housed in the Neumann Papers collection at Oxford, she applied to the writer's program to "experience other worlds" from her own—something she felt compelled to do as an aspiring writer. Peter Neumann seems to have encouraged his wife's pursuits, and, based on examples found in the Oxford archive, the two exchanged numerous letters during their four-month separation. Hazel Neumann left the Writer's Project after her pregnancy became noticeable to her supervisors.

Neumann returned to live with her husband in Oxford following her time with the Writer's Project. Her first published short story, "Lost Loves," appeared in the *Oxford Literary Journal* in 1939. Although of short duration, the experience with the ex-slave narrative project clearly influenced her later works. We can see from a reading of her later short stories, particularly "What a Woman Bears" (1952) and "Cook's Diary" (1960), the influences these interview experiences exerted later in her career. It is tempting to attribute the lead characters in each of these works to women encountered in the narratives.

These narratives also have historical relevance for the insights they provide into African-American life in Mississippi during and after slavery. (Exerpted from Donald Greenblatt, editor, *A Southern Writer Revealed: The Collected Works of Hazel Neumann.* 1986.)

Georgia Thompson

Matthews Quarters Road, 2 miles west of Turnerville, Mississippi
Interview Date: May 5, 1937
Interviewed by: Hazel Neumann

Miss Georgia Thompson lives in a small white-washed house on a quiet dirt road. Her cabin is one of a line of buildings that once housed the slave population of Great Oak plantation. Only a few of the houses are still lived in, and several have collapsed. Georgia's house is tidy and her yard swept. A few flower pots decorate the porch. She motions me into her home, where I catch the rich aroma of simmering stew. Georgia was born in 1850, making her 87 years old. Despite a milkiness to her eyes suggesting the onset of cataracts, she is very alert. Once we are settled on the porch in a pair of old but reliable rocking chairs, she begins to answer my questions.

"If you want to hear about slavery times, you would have been better to talk to my mama. She died last year. It was the consumption that killed her. She was 105 years old. Yes, ma'am, she sure could tell you stories. I don't remember so much of those times, myself. I was just a young girl when the Yankees came through. Seems like times were hard before they came, and they stayed hard after they went. Yes, I was born on this plantation. No, ma'am, I'd rather not talk about ol' massa, best not to speak poorly of the dead."

I ask again if her owner was really that unkind,[*] and she looks at me sternly over her glasses.

"Here, let me show you something." She walks with great vigor to an old chiffarobe and pulls a small red cloth bundle from the back of a creaking drawer.

"My mother had two daughters," she tells me. "Me and a younger one, her name was Carolina, we were both named after the states we were born. Carolina was mama's miracle baby, born in 1854, just after my daddy died. All she had left in the world of him was us two children. Carolina was a pretty baby, and she was so sweet. I remember helping mama care for her. Always smiling and laughing. She was like a little piece of spring. When she was four years old, the young massa married a widow woman with a young daughter. She saw Carolina and decided she had to have her as a playmate slave for her daughter. You know, one she could raise to be a house servant. Ol' massa decided to give my sister to the newlyweds as a present. My mama begged and pleaded to keep Carolina. I've never seen a woman so distraught. It didn't matter. She was taken away. We later heard she had soon been sold to another family after the young miss decided she wasn't fair-skinned enough to be a fashionable attendant. We don't know

[*] Interviewer's note: I've been told by other interviewers that most ex-slaves profess their great and humble love for their former masters, so at first I thought she was "pulling my leg."

what happened to her. Mama would ask everyone who came to the plantation, asked everyone she ever met. My mama had a piece of Carolina's baby hair. She took it to a conjurer."

She paused here to watch my reaction.

"Yes, she took it to a conjurer who made a 'bring back' charm for her. He told mama if she kept it fed and safe, it would draw Carolina back to us. She kept this till her death, and when she was sick, dying, she asked me to keep it, so I could tell Carolina about how she never gave up looking for her. How much she loved her. I thought about burying it with her, so Carolina would be drawn to mama's grave. But I couldn't do it: what if she did come back and I wasn't there to tell her?"

Now her eyes look clearer and she shook her head angrily. "The thing is, my mama grieved for this child the rest of her life. Carolina was so little, she probably never even remembered there was a mama somewhere else, looking for her. She might still be alive, she might live in the next town, but has no idea someone's looking for her. I've prayed that she's dead. At least that way my mama is with her now. Tell me now ol' massa couldn't be that bad." I had no answer, and hurriedly ended the interview. On the way out of the plantation I saw the old cemetery where Miss Thompson's mother is buried.

May 5, 1937

My Dearest, sweet, beloved, husband (I must be missing you),

I hope you are well and not missing me too terribly, though I suppose you had little say in the matter ultimately. You have learned that when I decide to do something, it is a difficult thing to turn me from the task! My health is good, the problems I had experienced before have ended, and I have a new sense of vigor and energy. I am settling into my new post. Turnerville is much as Oxford would be if there was not a university—small, agricultural, poor, and seemingly unconnected to the rest of the world in any kind of clear way. The people are cautious of outsiders, but generally friendly. While I am very excited about this undertaking, I am not sure that I am really of the right temperment to do this well. I had an interview go quite poorly this morning (I am not quite up to discussing it, but it has had me musing all night). I clearly have a certain set of expectations about what the South was like before the war, and it is clear those expectations are going to stand in the way of my work if I cannot dismiss them. Living in the glow of your academic life I have felt myself to be quite worldly, but perhaps the effect has been quite the opposite. I hate to be enigmatic, but it would be easier if you were here to speak with. I am tired, I will write more later.

Your devoted, beloved, sweet wife,
Hazel

3

African-American Mothering
and Enslavement

The image of children being ripped away from their mothers, an all-too-common occurrence, was successfully manipulated by abolitionists to help end human enslavement. Abolitionists realized that for middle-class white women, whose social and ideological and political role was increasingly constructed as "mother," no other aspect of slavery, not even the physical brutality endured by women, would be as powerful. The anguish of mothers separated from children is a theme found throughout the famous abolitionist narratives, such as *Twelve Years a Slave by Solomon Northup* (1968), Frederick Douglass's autobiography (2001), and particularly *Incidents in the Life of a Slave Girl,* a narrative that focuses solely on the efforts of an enslaved woman to rescue her children from bondage while escaping the lecherous advances of an evil enslaver (Jacobs 2000). Harriet Beecher Stowe, in her melodramatic *Uncle Tom's Cabin,* played upon the sentimental views held by Christian mothers in the character of Eliza, to astonishing effect.

Although white women were able to accept black mothers as mirrors of themselves on paper, reality was often different. The wronged Christian mother slave was just one of several archetypes of black womanhood constructed and perpetuated by white society. To understand how enslavement influenced black attitudes toward and approaches to motherhood, it is necessary to consider the diverse ideologies and realities of black womanhood and mothering during slavery. Fortunately, there is a burgeoning literature related to these issues, and I will build on already well established bodies of thought and research (e.g., Collins 2000; Giddings 1984; A. Davis 1983; Gaspar and Hine 1996; Bush 1990).

In this chapter, I want to present and contrast three faces of motherhood: the ideologies of black womanhood and motherhood constructed as opposing binaries to the cult of true womanhood; the experienced realities of reproduction and mothering for African-American women during enslavement; and finally, the ideologies of black womanhood and motherhood that characterized the African-American community during and as a result of enslavement. Obviously, these are areas of consideration that warrant tremendous research outside the scope of this study. My intent is not to present a comprehensive survey of these topics, especially when others have done so in elegant and sophisticated ways (e.g., Collins 2000; A. Davis 1983; Giddings 1984; Fox-Genovese 1988; White 1985) but to provide a review of the broader experiences and practices that ultimately shaped the performance of motherhood and mothering within the Perryman household.

Oppressive Ideologies

While the cult of true womanhood and the confinement of women to the realm of the domestic characterized the experiences of white middle-class women during the nineteenth century, the experiences of black women were radically different. The cult of true womanhood emphasized moral purity, modesty, innocence, submissiveness, and domesticity as virtues for white women to aspire to as wives and mothers (Perkins 1983). As other researchers have exhaustively demonstrated (e.g., Collins 2000; A. Davis 1983; Fox-Genovese 1988), the mythology of white women's virtue and natural maternal endowments was dependent upon the mythology of an equally unvirtuous and neglectful black womanhood. The inhumane treatment of black women, including sexual harassment and rape, the separation of mothers and children, brutal workloads and punishments, could be justified by white society only if black women were defined as "other." How can a woman who by the nature of her race is sexually promiscuous be raped? Why should women who are promiscuous and take multiple partners anyway be allowed to choose and live with a husband and their children?

For Patricia Hill Collins (2000), three persuasive stereotypes of black women constructed during slavery continue to shape social discourse today and to influence perceptions of black womanhood and mothering. Collins argues that the objectification of black women is especially crucial to the maintenance of white supremacy, because black women exist at the intersection of multiple binary oppressions—being black, being female, and, all too often, being poor. Building upon Cheryl Gilkes identification of "mammy" and the "bad black woman," Collins also recognizes the "matriarch" and "jezebel" (who, she argues, also exists in today's social consciousness as "hoochie mama").

The mammy is probably one of the most publicly recognized stereotypes emerging from slavery. Collins suggests that the mammy image serves to "buttress the ideology of the cult of true womanhood, one in which sexuality and fertility are severed" (2000:74). Mammy, as an asexual caregiver, is presented as devoted and loyal to the white children she cares for. Her love for her charges serves to mask the exploitive nature of the work she provides—the low salary and the unreasonable work hours demanded of her. Ultimately, the long work hours take her from her own family. The glamorization of "mammy" inspired an angry 1912 editorial by W. E. B. Du Bois titled "The Black Mother," which said in part,

> The people of America, and especially the people of the Southern states, have felt so keen an appreciation of the qualities of motherhood in the Negro that they have proposed erecting a statue in the national capital to the black mammy. The black nurse of slavery days may receive the tribute of enduring bronze from

the master class. . . . Let us hope that the black mammy, for whom so many sentimental tears have been shed, has disappeared from American life. She existed
under a false social system that deprived her of husband and child. . . . Let the
present-day mammies suckle their own children. Let them walk in the sunshine
with their own toddling boys and girls and put their own sleepy little brothers
and sisters to bed ... let the colored mother of today build her own statue, and
let it be the four walls of her own unsullied home. (1970:101)

Du Bois recognized mammy, as did others, as a haunt intended to subvert the
attempts of African-American women to reclaim their maternal rights.

Sau-Ling Wong (1994) refers to the "mammy" as representive of "diverted
mothering." Diverted mothering occurs when otherwise stigmatized groups
are put into the role of "ideological caregiver" for members of the dominant
social group—typically white middle- and upper-class families. Wong writes:
"Yet upon reflection, one discovers that the superficial concession of white
emotional and spiritual dependence does not alter the economic dependence
of the caregivers of color. It is the latter that makes the former possible, while
the former justifies the continuation for the latter, in an arrangement I have
elsewhere called a 'psycho-spiritual plantation system'" (82). While minority
women have been cast into the role of diverted caregiver, this role does not
provide any respect or elevation of status or treatment in employers' minds.
"Mammy" is emotive, seen as reacting with blind, protective instinct where her
charges are concerned. She is not seen as a reasoned person, and ultimately is
seen as, little more than a child herself (Collins 2000).

Researchers have dramatically illustrated the contrasting impressions that
African American domestics and their employers have of their relationship (e.g.,
Rollins 1985; Tucker 1988). While domestics resent the imposition of their employment on their home lives, and employers' insulting gestures of paternalism
(for instance the "gift" of badly worn cast-off clothing and other household
items), employers interviewed would express shock and surprise when a "loyal"
servant suddenly left their employ. For the employer, the relationship was often
perceived as a fictive kinship relationship, again, the assumption being that the
work provided was done out of love, not for compensation. As Angela Davis
observed (1983:97), for many white employers, servants were seen as extensions
of themselves.

Intimately entwined with the image of the mammy is her stereotypic opposite, the jezebel. By the 1730s, the stereotype of the black woman as "a purely
lascivious creature ... governed by her erotic desires [whose] sexual prowess
led men to wanton passion," was entrenched in the American South (Roberts
1997:10–11). Collins (2000) writes that this image of a deviant black female
sexuality is central to the controlling images of black womanhood, because
"efforts to control Black women's sexuality lie at the heart of Black women's oppression" (81). The image of the jezebel justified planters' expectations of high
fertility from slave women and provided them with an excuse for their sexual

terrorism of enslaved women (A. Davis 1983). As Paula Giddings (1984) so aptly described it, "the White wife was hoisted on a pedestal so high that she was beyond the sensual reach of her own husband"(43); the elevated position of white women ensured that black women would occupy positions of mistress, whore, and breeder. Thus, as Collins (2000) explains, both the mammy and the jezebel are controlling images that are inextricably tied to the economic exploitation of black women in the plantation system. The jezebel also stands in contradiction to constructions of white women's sexuality. The jezebel is portrayed as a sexual aggressor, serving as a foil to the passive, almost asexual status designated to the white women in the cult of true womanhood (82–83). Roberts (1997) elaborates on the effects that the jezebel stereotype has had on other racist constructions of black family life. She notes (11) that Phillip A. Bruce's 1889 book, *The Plantation Negro as a Freeman,* claimed that the supposed need of black men to rape white women arose from the sexual promiscuity of black women. Ultimately, the sexual depravity of black women, and their unnatural mothering, led to the unstable nature of the black family, in Bruce's opinion (12). The negligent black mother image is solidified in what has become known as the "matriarch."

The matriarch is as readily familiar in social dialogues as the mammy and jezebel. The image of the strong black woman who rules her husband and family is firmly entrenched in the American psyche. High incidences of female-headed households had been seen within the black intellectual community as a result of racial oppression and poverty (A. Davis 1983). Regina Kunzel (1994) has demonstrated how during the 1940s and 1950s, black single mothers were increasingly seen as products of pathological cultural dysfunction. While single white mothers were treated as persons suffering from uniquely individual psychological neuroses that led them to seek fulfillment of their need to mother outside of matrimony, black women were symptoms of a broad pathology. Based on a review of writings by social workers dating from the 1920s to the 1950s, Kunzel concludes that most social workers who studied single black mothers attributed the cause of this condition to be the "constitutional hypersexuality and immorality believed to be characteristic of the race" (315). Because these women were also constructed as assertive and domineering (again, qualities opposing those of white women), black women were perceived as being unable to coexist in a "normal" nuclear family arrangement.

While clearly established in the mind of the public and policy makers long before this time, the "matriarchy thesis" was brought sharply to the forefront of policy discussions as a result of the infamous 1965 Moynihan report, "The Negro Family: The Case for National Action." In this report, black women who were not behaving as middle-class white housewives were supposed to act were leading to social problems in black civil society. Moynihan contended that the continued higher education attainments of black women and their greater representation in professional and semi-professional jobs had left black men dispirited. As a result, black women made unattractive marriage partners, thus leading to the dissolution of black families and high out-of-wedlock birthrates (Giddings 1984:326). In short, black women were presented as neglectful mothers and unusually masculine in their behavior, which in turn supposedly threatened the masculinity of black males (Collins 2000:75). The solution proposed by the Moynihan report was for black women to become subservient to black men, to repair damage done to the black family (Giddings 1984:328). Ironically, Moynihan called for black women, who had historically been subjected to controlling images constructed to stand in opposition to (and therefore define) white womanhood, were now again being punished for not being seen as women in the same vein as white women. Just as "mammy" serves to divert attention from unjust labor practice, the "matriarch"—not unequal funding of education, lack of affordable child care, or other effects of racism—is to blame for problems in African-American communities.

The stereotypes created to justify the continued oppression of black women have continued to haunt African Americans, shaping political and economic policies in the United States to the present (Roberts 1997). In the words of Angela Davis (1983), "One of racism's salient historical features has always been the assumption that white men—especially those who wield economic power—possess an incontestable right of access to Black women's bodies." During slavery, access to black women's bodies also meant access to the produce of those bodies. For enslaved women, the only role of mother that was encouraged was that of biological producer.

While the controlling images of black womanhood discussed above shaped the experiences of mothering for enslaved women and the generations that followed them, these are images imposed from outside of the African-American community. African-American woman struggled with and acted against these stereotypes, but they also balanced images of "mother" and "motherhood" that were constructed and held within the African-American community during and beyond enslavement.

To Mother under Enslavement

Women were encouraged to bear children, but were not granted the right to raise them. White interference marked every facet of black mothering, be it the timing of feedings, the ability to keep an infant or young child with one during work, the right to care for a sick child, or even the ability to protect a child from punishment or sale. How then, did mothers negotiate the traps and obstacles of raising children to maximize their control? The documentary record provides some insights, although typically from the planter's perspective. Firsthand accounts of slave mothering are best drawn from slave narratives and former-slave narratives, such as those collected by the WPA. Archaeological excavations centering on quarter buildings, as well as bioarchaeological analyses of human remains, also contribute to our understanding of mothering during enslavement.

Given the constraints placed on child rearing and the uncertainty of life under enslavement, many women chose to avoid becoming mothers. Birth control and abortion provided means of resisting planter attempts to control African-American reproduction while also saving the next generation from a lifetime of hardship (L. Ross 1997). Ellen Craft, who, along with her husband, made a famous flight to freedom in 1849, could not bear the thought of even being married, let alone having a child under enslavement. Her husband explained:

> My wife was torn from her mother's embrace in childhood, and taken to a distant part of the country. She had seen so many other children separated from their parents in this cruel manner, that the mere thought of her ever becoming the mother of a child, to linger out a miserable existence under the wretched system of American slavery, appeared to fill her very soul with horror. (Quoted in Loewenberg and Bogin 1976:106)

There were of course, other reasons to avoid having children. Childbirth was a time of extreme danger for women. Even among middle- and upper-class white women, who received extensive medical care and attention during their pregnancies, births, and recovery periods, death in childbirth was common (Faust 1996; McMillen 1990). Though some African-American women were allowed to use midwives on the plantation to supervise their births, in many cases European doctors or plantation mistresses were called to attend slave births.

The increasing use of intrusive birthing techniques, such as the liberal use of forceps, made women more vulnerable to life-altering injuries related to childbirth. Poorly managed births and postpartum infection could also lead to sterility. Many women were rendered invalids as the result of fistulas (Leavitt 1986). In her study of children's experiences during enslavement, Marie Jenkins Schwartz (2000) found that permanent disability resulting from the complications of pregnancy were common among enslaved women. African-American midwifery traditions emphasized patience and non-intrusive techniques such as massage, particular birth positions, and moving the laboring mother (Susie 1988). White doctors' techniques would have been perceived (rightfully so) as dangerous and foreign. Given the personal risks that existed, enduring a pregnancy that could end in death, just to produce another enslaved child, may have made birth control a very desirable option to enslaved African-American women.

The other stark reality, however, is that birth control was not always in the hands of enslaved people. Cornelia Andrews, who had been enslaved in North Carolina, recalled that some men were castrated on the plantation where she lived. "Yo knows dey ain't let no little runty nigger have no chilluns. Naw sir, dey ain't, dey operate on dem lak dey does de male hog so's dat dey can't have no runty chilluns" (quoted in Rawick 1974a:31). Castration remained a torture employed by the Klan following Emancipation. Onnie Logan (1989) recalled that such men got "fat and chubby" following an attack by the Klan. "They did that a lot, honey. They did that a lot. I had a couple of cousins to be castrated. It didn't cause that much stir cause the black people was always the underdog anyway" (37).

When birth occurred, there were also reports of infanticide among enslaved women. Most often, women were accused of intentionally "lying over" or smothering their infants (A. Davis 1983; White 1985). Barbara Bush (1996) has suggested that the high rate of tetanus-related infant deaths in the Caribbean among enslaved populations may have been the result of infanticide practices. She notes that according to many West African belief systems, the infants' soul is not firmly rooted in the body until the ninth day, so a baby that dies before that time may not have been fully human yet. Bush hypothesizes that Obeah men and other herbalists on the plantations could have provided poisons that mimicked tetanus or were undetectable to release children from a future of enslavement.

Nancy Scheper-Hughes's (1992) research into mother love and child death in Brazil powerfully demonstrates how women in desperate circumstances can justify a triaging of child care, reserving resources of nourishment and care for children they see as most likely to survive. Blakey, Leslie, and Reidy (1994), in their analyses of skeletal material from enslaved African-American populations, have claimed that they are the most nutritionally deficient and labor-abused populations ever studied skeletally. In a complementary study, Richard Steckel (1996) has found that based on recorded height data for enslaved children from 1820 to 1860, "the slums in Lagos, Nigeria, and urban areas of Bangladesh provided environments for growth superior to those faced by slave children" (48). Given that, it would be surprising if infanticide were not a part of enslaved women's experiences.

More recently, scholars have suspected that high incidences of infant mortality for certain women could have been related to SIDS (sudden infant death syndrome) and that poor prenatal care could be as important a contributor to high mortality rates as infanticide (Steckel 1996; White 1985:88). That said, there are notable examples of women killing their children, such as the case of Margaret Garner, a fugitive from slavery who killed her daughter and attempted to kill herself to avoid capture (A. Davis 1983:21). In general, as we will discuss, however, there is much evidence to suggest that enslaved mothers were very invested in their children and sought opportunities that would ensure their survival.

More than one angry ex-slave proclaimed that black women were used as no more than brood mares during slavery. Cicely Cawthon, of Stephens County, Georgia, described it in this way, "They was keerful, just as keerful of you as a breed sow, if you was going to have chillun, but they'd sell you off if you didn't have any" (quoted in Rawick 1977:181). Willie McCullough concurred: "Some of the slave women were looked upon by the slave owners as a stock raiser looks upon his brood sows, that is from the standpoint of production. If a slave woman had children fast she was considered very valuable because slaves were valuable property" (quoted in Rawick 1974b:77). Clara Jones recalled, "I can't tell yo' much 'bout our courtin' cause hit went on fer years an' de Marster wanted us ter git married so's dat I'd have chilluns. When de slaves on de McGee place got married de marster always said dat dere duty wus ter have a houseful of chilluns for him" (quoted in Rawick 1974b:32). One cannot help but wonder if delaying marriage was a way for the couple to start a family in their own time. Jones went on to have 11 children.

Planters' desire to cultivate a strong and productive slave population could lead to what can only be described as selective breeding, with women forced to endure rape and pregnancies by men they did not know or care for. Willie McCullough explained; "Mother tole me that when she became a woman at the age of sixteen years her marster went to a slave owner near by and got a six-foot nigger man, almost an entire stranger to her, and told her she must marry him. Her marster read a paper to them, told them they were man and wife and told this negro he could take her to a certain cabin and go to bed. This was done without getting her consent or even asking her about it. Grandmother said that several different men were put to her just about the same as if she had been a cow or sow" (quoted in Rawick 1974a:78). Jacob Manson recalled a similar arrangement on other Georgia plantations: "A lot of de slave owners had certain strong healthy slave men to serve de slave women. Ginerally dey give one man four women an' dat man better not have nuthin' to do wid de udder women an' de women better not have nuthin to do wid udder men" (quoted in Rawick 1974b:98).

Other planters, while not actively selecting mates, did limit potential marriage partners to those individuals living on the same plantation (e.g., Rawick 1973, 1974a, 1974b, 1977). Marriages between people with different owners did occur, and were met with various degrees of cooperation from enslavers. Hannah Plummer's father was a stonecutter. By hiring his time out and paying his owner, he was able to live with his wife and daughter at their place (Rawick 1974a:178). Other couples attempted to persuade one owner or the other to purchase their spouse and children. Still more couples dealt with long absences from one another and the constant threat that one or the other would be sold away from the area, as happened to Sally Brown's uncle. "My uncle wuz married but he wuz owned by another. He wuz 'lowed to visit his wife on Wednesday and Saturday; that wuz the earliest time he could git off. He went on Wednesday and when he went back on Saturday his wife had been bought by the speculator and he never did know where she was" (quoted in Rawick 1979b:97). Mary Childs's father had to get a pass twice a week to see his wife and 10 children (Rawick 1979b:198). For women, marriages abroad also meant that they were responsible for raising children without the full-time help and support of a spouse.

Pregnancy-related complications caused by poor nutrition, heavy workloads, and unsanitary living conditions were not uncommon for enslaved women.

Women were encouraged to endure continual pregnancies. Frequent and numerous births ravaged women's bodies. One planter observed, "Constant child-bearing, and the life of labor, exposure, and privation which they lead ages them prematurely" (quoted in Schwartz 2000:24). Dropped, or prolapsed, uteruses were common even among very young women, the result of bodies with too many demands placed upon them. A prolapse of the uterus is marked by the uterus slumping into the top of the vaginal canal when the ligaments that formerly supported in it place have become stretched beyond repair. Multiple pregnancies with little recovery time are a primary cause of the condition. In her review of the Touro Hospital records from New Orleans, Bankole (1998:65) found that the enslaved women admitted for prolapsed uteruses from 1855 to 1860 were only between 19 and 24 years of age. The most common treatment of the time for the condition was to fit a patient with a truss or a pessary. Pessaries, which came in a variety of shapes, such as eggs, rings, or phallic-looking rods, were worn in the vaginal tract to support the top of the uterus. The condition and treatment were both uncomfortable—particularly during and following pregnancies.

Because they were more likely to develop pregnancy-related complications, enslaved women also found themselves the object of "scientific" experimentation for early obstetricians. J. Marion Sims is particularly notorious for his sadistic experimentation on the bodies of enslaved women. Vesico-vaginal fistulas, or tears between the vaginal and rectal track, became all too frequent side effects of forceps deliveries. The tears lead to tremendous discomfort and a loss of control over defecation and urination, rendering the women invalids. Sims, through experimentation on black women whom he had purchased, developed a technique for closing the fistulas (Wertz and Wertz 1979:101). "This procedure involved the patient being placed in a knee-elbow position. Air pressure was used to dialate the vagina and a forerunner to the speculum was used. Anarcha [one of the enslaved women] suffered through thirty procedures before the closure of the fistula" (Bankole 1998:103). The procedures were performed during the 1850s and were conducted without the benefit of anesthesia. The suffering experienced by his laboratory subjects is unimaginable, but ultimately earned Sims international recognition and a bronze statue in New York's Central Park (Wertz and Wertz 1979:101). In Louisiana, medical schools experimented with the development of cesarian sections exclusively on enslaved women (Bankole 1998:105).

Pregnancy, although valued by enslavers, did not always bring women relief from the worst and hardest labors demanded of them. Planters were suspicious that women exaggerated the symptoms of pregnancy to escape work, and even questioned the diagnosis of pregnancy. On some plantations women were subjected to cervical exams to determine whether they exhibited the softening of the cervix associated with pregnancy (Schwartz 2000:29). Women were often expected to work at some task (including field labor) until the time of their delivery. Steckel (1996:51–55), in a review of plantation manuals from the South, found that pregnant women had little or no reduction in work loads before the fifth month of their pregnancy. If their pregnancy corresponded to peak times in labor demands, such as the harvest, they could expect no work relief until the time of delivery. The time of confinement following delivery varied, but was typically no longer than a few weeks. Steckel (1996) found on cotton plantations that women could be back in the field within two weeks. Pregnancy did not save women from brutal physical punishments either. Henry Cheaten remembered witnessing a particularly barbaric punishment. "I seen him beat my Auntie who was big wid a chile, an' dat man dug a roun' hole in de groun' an' put her stummick in it, an' beat an' beat her for a half hour straight till de baby come out raight dere in de hole" (quoted in Rawick 1973:66). In Jamaica, one planter reported that "white overseers and bookkeepers kick black women in the belly from one end of Jamaica to the other, harming the women and their unborn children" (quoted in Bush 1996:197).

Childbirth was attended by the plantation mistress, a white physician, or most commonly, an older woman from the quarters. These elders provided assistance in birth as well as other medical care for children and families. Dellie Lewis remembered that her grandmother, a midwife, "useta gib women cloves and whiskey to ease the pain. She also gib em dried watermelon seeds to get rid of the grabel of the kidneys [kidney stones]. For night sweat Grandmammy would put an axe under de bed of de sick pusson wid de blade straight up" (quoted in Rawick 1973:256). Caroline Ates had similar memories, "There wuz nigger women on the plantation that wuz sorter nurses an' if anybody got sick they'd tend ter 'em" (Rawick 1977b:27). As I will discuss further in a later chapter, these African-American midwives played an important role in ensuring mother and infant health, as well as serving as a conduit for cultural traditions.

Women who did decide to have children faced an uncertain future. While scholars like Herbert Gutman (1976) and Anne Patton Malone (1994) have focused on the importance and stability of slave families despite the circumstances of enslavement, the reality was that an economic hardship or estate division in the owner's family could lead to the arbitrary separation from families from one another. The routines of everyday life provided them with little autonomy over their families. Women had little to no control over their schedules, often being separated from young children, even those still suckling, for long parts of the day.

Poor nutrition and housing and demanding work schedules took a toll on the overall health of the enslaved populations, and this toll was heaviest among young children. Epidemics of yellow fever, cholera, small pox, and measles would sweep through quarters, killing young children and infants (e.g., Webb 1983; Sheridan 1985). On the island of Grenada, one slaveholding doctor estimated that among his enslaved population, one out of every three infants died within a month of birth; and only about that same proportion of those who survived infancy could be expected to live to the age of 10 years old. While this plantation seems to have suffered an especially high mortality rate for Grenada as a whole, 18.1 percent of children born in 1820 died within a year, a proportion that increased to 24.9 percent in 1830 (Sheridan 1985:237). Steckel (1996:53) found on cotton plantations in the American South that children born in September–November had an average probability of death of 40.6 percent, versus a 10.5 percent probability of death for children born in other months. The highest mortality rates coincide with the cotton harvest, and greatest demands on women's labor, and may have led to decreased birth weights. African-American mothers had to be prepared for the real possibility that death could easily separate her from a child. Adding to the cruelty, the high mortality rate among African-American infants was often attributed to the poor mothering skills of enslaved women (King 1996:149).

Collective mothering and parenting became the norm on most plantations. Martha Allen, a formerly enslaved North Carolinian, recalled, "De cook nussed de babies while she cooked, so dat de mammies could work in the fiel's an' all de mammies done quz stick de babies in de kitchen on dere way ter de fields" (quoted in Rawick 1974:14). A similar arrangement existed on the Alabama plantation where Henry Barnes was raised. "Dere was a ol' 'omen what kep all de li'l niggers, whilst dey mammies was in de fiel'. Dis ol' 'omen cooked fer de lil uns an fed 'm all day, an dey mammies tuk 'em at night" (quoted in Rawick 1973:22). Tillman Bradshaw experienced a similar situation during his youth on a Georgia plantation. There, an older woman referred to as "Granny" would care for the small children during the day and feed them meals of bread, milk, greens, dumplings, and meat skin (Rawick 1977b:91). The ratios of caregivers to cared for were often appalling. On one plantation, in East Feliciana, Louisiana, a 60-year-old enslaved woman, assisted by a few girls, was said to have been responsible for the care of 30 babies (King 1996:152). Older children were also left in the position of caregiver, with children as young as 10 being solely responsible for an infant's care (King 1996). Workdays for the adults could extend as long as 12 or 13 hours, leaving little time for parents to interact with children (Schwartz 2000:53).

For breast-feeding mothers, the daylong separation from a nursing child would have been physically and emotionally difficult to bear. The narratives provide some evidence that women collectively attempted to thwart planter control over their nursing. Ank Bishop lived on a plantation where child care was the responsibility of one woman. "All de women on Lady Liza's place had to go to de field ev'y day an dem what had suckerlin' babies would come in 'bout 9 o'clock in de mawnin' an' when de bell ring at twelve an' suckerling 'em. One woman tended to all of em in one house. Her name was Ellie Larkin, an' dey call her 'Mammy Larkin.' She all time sent me down in de fiel' for to git 'em come suckle de chillen, 'coze dat made it hard on her when dey gets hungry an' cry" (quoted in Rawick 1979a:36). Mammy Larkin used the excuse of being frustrated by the cries of hungry babies to justify giving mothers additional nursing time with their children. Bishop's recollection is useful because he outlines both what the planter ordained should be done versus actual practice.

Other women attempted to take their children with them in the field. Sara Colquitt recalled, "I worked in the fields everyday from before daylight to almost plump dark. I usta take my littlest baby wid me. I had two chilluns, and I'd tie it up to a tree limb to keep off de ants and bugs whilst I hoed and worked the furrow" (quoted in Rawick 1973:87). Other women were able to leave their children with trusted relatives. Fannie Moore remembered, "My granny she cook for us chillens while our mammy away in de fiel. Dey wasn't much cookin to do. Jes make co'n pone and bring in de milk" (quoted in Rawick 1974b:129).

Nursing seems to have been an arena in which African-American women strove to exert as much influence over their infant's rearing as possible. Some evidence of this has been derived from archaeology. The possibility that the incidence of tooth enamel defects during childhood in the skeletal populations of enslaved persons could be related to nutritional stress at the time of weaning was first proposed by Corruccini, Handler, and Jacobi (1985). They suggested that the transition from a more nutritionally balanced diet of breast milk to the cornmeal-based, low-protein diet typical of slave rations led to physical stress, evidenced in part by disruptions in the formation of tooth enamel. These disruptions, called enamel development defects, can take the form of pits and grooves in the enamel surface. Because the developmental sequence for secondary tooth formation is known, it is possible, from the position of the defects on the tooth, to determine at what age the stress was experienced. Corruccini et al. estimated that weaning took place between the ages of two and four years. This would correspond with weaning practices in West Africa.

More recently, Michael Blakey et al. (1994) have questioned the weaning hypothesis. These authors state that based upon plantation records in the American south, it was rare for planters to allow nursing to take place beyond the first year. Based on a typical birth spacing of two years, also derived from documentary records, they asserted that it was unlikely that the women were still breast-feeding beyond a year due to the ovulation suppression afforded by nursing. In their analysis of 27 African-American skeletons from slavery contexts, they found that enamel development defects occur between 1.5 and 4.5 years of age in that population, later than would have been suggested by the documentary data. It is their conclusion that the defects cannot be tied to weaning stress. Though they may indeed be correct in their assertion that a connection cannot be definitively made between weaning and dental defects, Blakey et al. have fallen into a trap common for those working with documents: the tendency to privilege documents as somehow being a more reliable form of knowing than other approaches to the past. What the documents actually tell us is what the planters *thought* was happening in terms of breast-feeding practices. That the physical data might contradict the documentary evidence is intriguing and deserves some further consideration.

In the prescriptive literature today, how much breast-feeding can be used as birth control is open to some debate. What is agreed is that for ovulation to be suppressed, breast-feeding must be the only source of nutrition for the child and must be done with great regularity. Once breast milk is no longer the primary source of nutrition, the ovulation suppression benefits are reduced. It is clear from the documentary record that planters interfered with breast-feeding practices by determining when women could breast-feed during the day and by separating mothers and infants for long periods of time. Planters often viewed women's desire to nurse until the child was older as a way of avoiding work, and discouraged late weaning (Bush 1996:203). While planters may have denied mothers opportunities during the workday to breast-feed an older child, this would not have prevented the woman from breast-feeding in the evening. The nursing body adjusts to the demands of the feeding routine, making only the amount of milk required. Therefore, a woman could continue to provide night and morning feedings to a child long after midday feedings had been forcibly stopped. In this way, a child could continue to receive the important supplemental nutrition provided by breast milk until weaning was necessitated by the arrival of another child. This would push the weaning age back to age two if a two-year interval between births occurred, or potentially later, thus corresponding to the onset of the dental enamel defects. The negative side effect would be the loss of the ovulation suppression provided by full-time nursing, and increased chance of a new pregnancy. Similarly, if breast-feeding continues during pregnancy, there is increased risk of miscarriage for women prone to miscarriage.

What Blakey et al.'s data may suggest is that mothers refused to comply with planters' policies regarding nursing and were able to protect their children from the horrible impacts of poor nutrition for a little longer. Certainly, whether or not these data represent mothers' resistance to planter interference deserves further consideration before the weaning hypothesis is dismissed based on historical documents created by the planter.

Planter interference marked every aspect of mothering during enslavement. Intimate matters such as health care, nursing, ritual protection (the use of apotropaic devices like protective necklaces or beads), and discipline were meddled in, as was every matter of daily life. Sally Murphy remembered that mothers with young children had to present them once a week to the plantation mistress for inspection (Rawick 1973:295). According to Schwartz (2000:85–86) this was a common Sunday ritual in the South. Children were scrubbed and presented in their finest (this being a relative term) clothing. It was a time for mothers to demonstrate their proficiency in caring for their children as a means of denying planters an opportunity to claim otherwise.

Archaeology provides some further insights into the ways that African-American families, particularly mothers, attempted to ameliorate the conditions of enslavement for their children. Zooarchaeological evidence recovered from cabins in Virginia, Louisiana, South Carolina, Georgia, and other places (e.g., Wilkie 2000a; Scott 2001; Franklin 1997; Deetz 1993) demonstrates that it was normal practice for families to supplement their meager rations by hunting, fishing, foraging, and tending to small provisioning grounds. Louisa Adams remembered her father's important contributions to their diet: "My old daddy partly raised his chilluns on game. He caught rabbits, coons an' possums. He would work all day and hunt at night" (quoted in Rawick 1974b:3). Archaeological excavations have demonstrated that her father's night work was part of many enslaved families' struggle to raise healthy children. Ethnobotanical evidence indicates that in addition to acquiring more plant foods for their families, medicinal plants were also gathered and used (Franklin 1997; Groover and Baumgnn 1996). For children, who were often provided with small rations that contained little protein, these additional foods could have meant the difference between living and dying. In the absence of reliable medical care, African healing systems provided parents with some control over the maintenance of their children's health.

Families also beseeched the spiritual realms for protection for the children. Religious objects including pierced coins, hand amulets, glass beads, engraved spoons, and pots marked with cosmograms have been recovered from archaeological sites throughout the American South and Caribbean (e.g., Edwards-Ingram 2001; Caback, Groover, and Wagers 1995; Franklin 1997; Brown and Cooper 1990; Orser 1994; Wilkie 1997; Yentsch 1994). Pierced coins have been recorded ethnographically as being used as birth coins. Presented to an infant shortly after birth, the coin was worn around the neck and intended to protect the child from harm and illness. Beads are regularly recovered from African-American sites during and beyond the period of enslavement. In West Africa, beads are used to communicate multiple meanings and functions, ranging from gender or age status, ethnic identity, or religious affiliation or status (e.g., Foster 1997). At least one ex-slave narrative suggests that one use of beads was the protection of children. "In them days all darkies wore beads. Babies wore beads around their necks. You wouldn't see a baby without beads. They was made of glass and looked like diamonds. They had 'em in different colors too, white, blue, and red, little plaited strings of beads. When their necks got bigger, they wore another kind, on 'till they got grown. They trimmed hats with beads, ladies and chillun too" (Cicely Cawthon, quoted in Rawick 1977:186). In the uncertain world of enslavement we can see a mother's a plea to supernatural forces for protection of her child.

Parents also had to raise their children to deal with the social conditions particular to enslavement, including dealing with white overseers and planters, living with continual threats of violence, and finding ways to protest and navigate around the oppressions of enslavement. Through this, they lived with the constant threat of separation. Even in plantations where the sale of enslaved people was uncommon, deaths, marriages, or financial changes in the planter family could sunder an enslaved family with little warning. Mary Barbour's mother had 16 children, and as soon as the children reached the age of three, they were sold. Her mother and father ultimately responded by running away with their remaining four children, not an easy task (Rawick 1973:69). Some mothers were able to persuade their owners to keep their children, and used a variety of means to try to negotiate the best circumstances for them, with varying degrees of success.

How prevalent the separation of young children from their families was is open to debate. Some studies have estimated that no more than 1 percent of children under the age of eight were sold from their parents, but others estimate the number at 5 percent to 7 percent (Schwartz 2000:89). From the ex-slave narratives, many who remembered being separated by sale from parents were between 9 to 12 years of age when it happened. During the 1850s, several southern states, including Alabama, made it illegal to sell children under the age of five away from their mother in response to growing anti-slavery sentiments in the North. For children who recalled losing parents, it is clear from their adult memories that one could never be old enough to endure the loss with anything but pain.

The experiences of black women who attempted to raise families despite physically and mentally demanding labor were in contrast to the ideology of motherhood that was popular in white middle-class circles. Ladies magazines, proscriptive literature, and novels of the time romanticized women's role in the domestic sphere, proclaiming that women were the sacred protectors of the home and its inhabitants. The home existed as a spiritual refuge from the stresses and secularism of the economic sphere, where men worked. While white middle-class women used their position as guardians of morality to push for political and social reforms, with abolition being a particularly relevant example, they remained incapable of understanding the reality experienced by working-class or enslaved women.

In her discussion of black womanhood during slavery, Angela Davis (1983) emphasizes that white models of womanhood, derived from the ideology of the cult of domesticity, could never describe or account for the experiences of black women. "The cleavage between the home and the public economy, brought on by industrial capitalism, established female inferiority more firmly than ever before. 'Woman' became synonymous in the prevailing propaganda with 'mother' and 'housewife,' and both 'mother' and 'housewife' bore the fatal mark of inferiority. But among Black female slaves, this vocabulary was nowhere to be found" (12). Davis is particularly outraged by Harriet Beecher Stowe's representation in *Uncle Tom's Cabin* of the slave woman Eliza as "white motherhood incarnate"(27). In Davis's reading, Eliza's climactic crossing of the Ohio River is attributed to

"God impart[ing] superhuman abilities to gentle Christian mothers," when in fact "these women [slave mothers], unlike Eliza, were driven to defend their children by their passionate abhorrence of slavery. The source of their strength was not some mystical power attached to motherhood, but rather their concrete experiences as slaves" (29).

While the ideologies of white middle-class motherhood would have been outside the experiences of enslaved women, they were certainly exposed to these realities through interactions with white families. This would be particularly true of women who worked in domestic service. The contrast between the control and liberties white women had with their children versus their own experiences must have been stark. Like a thousand other elusive rights and privileges reserved for those with white skin, the privileges of motherhood were denied to African-American women. While white middle-class women's rights advocates saw the domestic sphere as a prison constructed to disenfranchise women, for African-American women, the domestic sphere represented an impossible—and not necessarily evil—fate. White middle-class women and their children remained secluded from demands of labor, and free of sexual tyranny. For women who had grown and raised children under enslavement, models of white motherhood and mothering certainly would have left an impression that may have influenced constructions of African-American mothering after enslavement.

African-American Ideologies of Mothering

The ex-slave narratives gathered by the WPA Federal Writer's Project in the late 1930s provide an important window into the experiences of families and individuals during enslavement. The narratives have many flaws and shortcomings, which have been discussed fully by others (e.g., Blassingame 1979; Foster 1997; Schwartz 2000). Interviewers were often white and blinded by their own biases, presenting the narratives in a demeaning tone. Racial dynamics between interviewee and interviewer led to cautious responses from many former slaves. By the 1930s, many of the survivors of enslavement had been children at the time of Emancipation. Their memories were not always clear, and often focus on playtime and the happiness of childhood. In a few interviews, informants released pent-up anger in eloquent tides that shocked their interviewers. These narratives are particularly revealing.

Despite their flaws, the narratives provide a fascinating look into the memories of some of slavery's youngest survivors. These individuals were among the first generations of former slaves to marry and raise children as freed people. They were part of the generation that created their own ideologies of family life and mothering for their communities. The narratives provide insight into the collective memories that shaped and colored their own approaches to family and children. Through these narratives, we can see that "mother" as an icon became every bit as romanticized among African Americans as it was in the white community.

Memories of separation and loss are a predominant theme in the narratives. As would be expected, the loss or removal from parents and siblings constituted important landmarks in a life history. While it would be impossible to provide an exhaustive account of these sufferings in such limited space, it is worth considering several examples. Charles Aarons recalled being taken from his family in Virginia to be sold at a Mobile slave mart at the age of 10 years. He never saw or heard of his parents or siblings again (quoted in Rawick 1979a:1). Laura Clark had a similar story; born in North Carolina, she was sold to a trader and brought to Alabama with 10 other children. "Warn't none of dem ten shillun no kin to me, and he never bought my mammy, so I had to leave her behind" (quoted in Rawick 1979a:72). Clark's story is particularly revealing, for it is the experience of a young child told after a lifetime of reflection, and perhaps haunting regret:

> I recollect Mammy said to Old Julie, "Take keer my baby childe (dat was me) and iffen I never sees her no mo' raise her for God." Den she fell off de waggin where us was all settin and roll over on de groun' jes' acryin'. But us was eatin' candy what dey done give us to keep us quiet; and I didn't have sense 'nuff for to know what ailer Mammy, but I knows now, and I never seed her no mo' in dis life. When I heered from her atter S'render she done dead and buried. (quoted in Rawick 1979a:72)

Delia Garlic, who was sold away from her mother as a young woman, apparently after avoiding the advances of an employer, was haunted by her last memory of her mother. "I has thought many times through all dese years how mammy looked dat night" (quoted in Rawick 1979a:130).

Informants recalled not only their own separations from loved ones, but accounts of their parents' losses as well. Ann Bishop recalled her mother telling of being taken from South Carolina by a speculator who separated her from her own mother and father, whom she "never did see no more in dis life" (Rawick 1979a:35). Lizzie Baker, in her eighties at the time of her interview, shared her mother's lifelong search for her siblings.

> Dey sold my sister Lucy and my brother Fred in slavery time, an' I have never seen either of 'em in my life. Mother would cry when she was telling me about it. She never seen 'em anymore. I jes couldn't bear to hear her tell it widout crying . . . we tried to get some news of brother and sister. Mother kept 'quiring about em as long as she lived and I have hoped dat I could hear from em. Dey are dead long agos I reckons, and I guess dare ain't no use ever expectin' to see 'em. (Quoted in Rawick 1974a:69)

Still other children carried with them memories of watching others separated from loved ones. Perhaps no image was more enduring than that of slave sales or slave traders. Sally Brown recounted memories of these events, "Oh! It wuz pitiful to see chillun took from their mothers' breast, mothers sold, husbands sold from wives. One 'oman he [the speculator] wuz to buy had a baby, and of course the baby come befo' he bought her and he wouldn't buy the baby; said that he jest wouldn't" (quoted in Rawick 1979b:96). Mary Childs remembered seeing a group of young boys, "just like horses in a pasture, whom the speculators were feeding up and keeping for auction" (quoted in Rawick 1979b:198).

In some narratives, children of former slaves remember their parents' determination to claim them from white owners with the coming of freedom. Viney Baker remembered going to sleep with his mother on a straw mattress when he was a child. When he awoke, he found his mother was gone. He soon learned that a slave speculator had come and bought her during the night. She had been taken away without saying goodbye to her son. Unlike so many others, however, Baker was to see his mother again. After the surrender, he was still being held by his former owner, when Baker's mother returned. "I reckon I wuz twelve year old when my mammy come ter de house an axes Mis Allen ter let me go spend de week en with her. Mis Allen can't say no, case Mammy might go ter de carpet baggers, so she lets me go for the weekend. Mammy laughs Sunday when I says something about going back" (quoted in Rawick 1974a:71).

Jeff Davis was separated from his parents when they were sold to two different plantations. He was left to be raised by an aunt. His mother was able to return to the plantation years later by accompanying her recently widowed owner home. Davis recalled his confusion at being told by the woman he thought was his mother that his mother was visiting. He dismissed the notion until, "when de wagon got to de house, my mammy got out an' broke and run to me an' th'owed her arms 'roun' my neck an' hug an' kiss me, I never even put my arms 'roun' her or nothin' of de sort. I jes' stood dar lookin' at her. She said, 'Son ain't you glad to see your mammy?' I looked at her an' walked off." He later realized, upon greater thought, that he did remember her, and went to ask her forgiveness for being so rude. While Davis's mother was able to reunite with her son, his father was lost to the family forever (quoted in Rawick 1974c:117–19).

Also shocking and embedded deep in the memories of former enslaved people was the trauma of seeing parents whipped or abused. Oliver Bell stated that his earliest memory was of seeing his mother whipped (Rawick 1979a:27). Henry Cheaten remembered wanting to kill a black overseer who beat his mother (Rawick 1979a:66). George Washington Browning broke down in tears during his WPA interview, explaining his outburst by saying, "Whenever I think of my mother plowing in the field I have to cry" (quoted in Rawick 1979b:111). In one dramatic interview, Cornelia Andrews denied having been whipped during enslavement. Her daughter, who had been educated at Cornell, angrily stormed into the room and forced her mother to open her shirt, revealing crisscrossed heavy scars from a cowhide whip. Andrews then bitterly acknowledged that she had been publicly whipped for being slow and breaking dishes (Rawick 1974a:28). In this instance, we clearly see the outrage expressed by a daughter on her mother's behalf. Even 70 years after the end of enslavement, Andrews was ashamed of the punishment inflicted on her, and her daughter refused to allow her to blame herself.

Formerly enslaved people remembered the sense of helplessness that overcame them as they witnessed the abuse of parents and loved ones (Schwartz 2000). The last children of enslavement remembered the workloads their mothers endured with both anger and pride. Lila Nichols recalled, "We wucked all de week, my mammy plowin' wid a two-horse plow all de year when she warn't cleanin' new ground or diggin' ditches; an' she got two days off when her chilluns wuz borned" (quoted in Rawick 1974b:149). Janie Scott said of her mother that she "was strong and could roll and cut logs like a man, and was much of a woman" (quoted in Rawick 1973:338).

Sexual abuse, which must have been one of the worst violations for a child to be privy to, were referred to in narratives as well, and stories of triumph against this adversity were recalled across generations. Writing for the *Voice of the Negro*, Adda Hunton (1904:281) observed, "There is hardly a daughter of a slave mother who has not heard of the sublime and heroic soul of some maternal ancestor that went home to the God that gave it rather than live a life of enforced infamy." Martha Allen's mother was the object of their owner's son's attention. "De young Marster sorta wanted my mammy, but she tells him no, so he chucks a lightwood knot an' hits her on de haid wid it. Dese white mens what had babies by nigger wimmens wuz called 'carpet gitters,' my father's father wuz one of them" (quoted in Rawick 1974b:14). Still others expressed their disgust with the men who would rape black women and then treat their own flesh and blood as property.

Memories of mothers were romanticized as well, obviously colored by ideals of domesticity and the protection of womanhood. Nathan Beauchamp had a poetic recollection of his Indian mother, who died shortly after freedom, "I remembers de way de sun sparkle on her teeth when she smile" (quoted in Rawick 1979a:26). The Rev. W. B. Allen warmly remembered awaking to the 3 A.M. bell that called the enslaved people awake for work. "I was so young then that I didn't have to get up with the first bell, but I usually waked up and can remember that my old black mother always sang as she prepared breakfast in the big, open fireplace. . . . Then, after everybody had gone to work, I'd get up and go to the hearth and find my breakfast—where my mother had left it for me" (Rawick 1979b:9–10). "Mother" was a recollection of beauty and nurturing.

It is clear from a review of the ex-slave narratives that "mother" held many strong associations for African Americans. Unlike the cult of true motherhood, in which white women were romanticized primarily as the moral keepers of the house and nurturers of children, "mother" held a number of different, yet equally romanticized connotations for African Americans. "Mother" was the embodiment of love and protection lost, a longing, and a reminder of helplessness and tragedy. "Mother" was a face for the unspeakable outrages and suffering of slavery. Yet, "mother" was kinship, determination, and strength in adversity. The mothers of enslavement were symbols of families lost and ruptured, and a desire to recover lost loved ones. "Mother" was deserving of protection and love and respect. Finally, "mother" became a symbol of righteous anger—the person who would fight to reclaim what slavery had put asunder.

For African-American mothers following enslavement, to mother "appropriately" could never be separated from what white racism dictated their motherhood to be; what motherhood had been during enslavement; and notions of what a freed mother could be according to the African-American community. These discourses were further entangled in broader social discourses surrounding competing constructions of American motherhood that characterized the mid-nineteenth to twentieth centuries.

As daughters, wives, and mothers, the Perryman women would find themselves enmeshed in a web of competing and conflicting mothering ideologies and controlling images of black womanhood. Caroline Perryman and perhaps her sister Sally would have remembered some of their mother's experiences as an enslaved woman, as well as their own lives as enslaved children. Given the death of several young mothers within the family, mothering within the Perryman family would mean raising children of other family members. Lucrecia Perryman mothered during enslavement, and after. For her, the birth of each child after freedom would have been an opportunity to re-create her mothering and to engage in mothering in ways not previously available to her. Because she had experienced communal mothering and parenting during slavery, her later vocation of midwifery, which entailed motherwork for her community, was a natural extension of the values and experiences she had as an enslaved women. This vocation engaged her in additional ideological debates, including when and if to become a mother, as well as placing her in a position to shape constructions of African-American mothering practice and appearance in her community.

Narrative Interlude II
Marsoline Collins

18 Jefferson Street, Turnerville, Mississippi
Interview Date: May 17, 1937
Interviewed by: Hazel Neumann

Marsoline Collins was born in 1855. She is the first cousin of Georgia Thompson, who directed me to her. Mrs. Collins lives in a house that was built just after the war. The trees surrounding the house are tall and strong, and although old, the house has been well maintained, with a bright coat of whitewash on the outside. The front room serves as Mrs. Collins's parlor and is well lit, and the air is fresh. It is a very pleasant space.

She has few memories of slave times but was very congenial and liked having a visitor. Like many women of her race, it would be difficult to determine her age by looking at her. She has few wrinkles, finely kept hair, and dignified but simple dress. I couldn't get her to talk much about slavery or the plantation where she was raised. She mainly wanted to talk about happy childhood memories. It seems that most of her immediate family members have died, and her living children live up North. She talked to me over a cup of tea.

"I was born on Hilltop Plantation—right over there by Great Oak. I lived in Jackson till a few years back. Came back here to be closer to extended family after my husband died. It's too expensive to live in the city, and all that Jim Crow getting worse and worse. That's right, Georgia and I are cousins. Our mothers were sisters. Her mama went to live on Great Oak after she married Georgia's daddy. Marriages abroad—that's what we called them—were common back then, my mama used to say. Oh yes, I remember a little bit about life back then. There were five of us then, me, my sister and brother, and my parents. I didn't know my grandparents. My mama and papa would work in the fields. I was just itty-bitty, so I didn't have to do much. All the little ones went to the kitchen during the day. We were watched by an old slave woman. She was so old and wrinkled; she looked like a raisin, all shrunk up. Sometimes we were scared of her, on account of her having blue gums and blue eyes, but she had a pretty smile. She must have had 30 children to watch, including babies. The mothers would come in from the fields to nurse a couple of times a day. It used to kill them to leave their babies, and the overseer would come by to make sure they went back to the field. As I got bigger, I would help watch the littler ones. I only saw my mama and papa for a few hours at night, but my mama would try to make us a hot supper, and we would help with chores before going to bed.

"When the war came, Mr. James, the man that owned our plantation, took my papa with him to the battle as a man servant. He knew that papa wasn't going to run away from him because he wanted to get back home to us—that's why he took him. Mr. James got shot in one of those battles, maybe Chickamunga? Anyways, they cut off his leg and sent him home. My papa took care of him. After freedom, Mr. James helped my papa get a good job as a waiter up in Jackson. It was a good living, so my mama was able to stay home with us children.

"My, were things different! She had three more babies, two more boys and a girl. We lived in Jackson in a little rented house. Mama was so proud of that house. It had real glass windows and floors that you couldn't see the ground through. She made that house real pretty. We had curtains, and a pretty shiny tea set that used to sit on the table in our front room. I remember it so well, it had little pink flowers and green leaves. I don't think we ever used it, it was too pretty to use. Papa used to joke about how she was putting on airs, having all those nice things. She would just smile. When we were slaves, we children never had shoes, and we only had two sets of clothing in any year—one for summer and one for winter. We used to wear those clothes until they hung off us in strips. Mama was a good seamstress, and would fix them as best she could, but the fabric was so poor, there was only so much you could do. A lot of little children went naked in slave times. After that, my mama would make all of the children beautiful and well-made clothing, with shiny buttons for the boys and lovely lace for the girl's dresses. And shoes! I hated having shoes at first. We used to go barefoot all year before. My toes ached, and my ankles blistered and sweated when we first got shoes. Then my feet softened up so much, I couldn't go barefoot anymore, so that was that. Yes, we all looked so fine when we went to church on Sunday. That was a big church we went to, a big A.M.E. Church. I have a friend who lives on the other side of Turnerville who I first met there as a child. It was a strong community, yes, ma'am.

"My parents put all their children in school after slavery. The Freedmen's Bureau set up schools, and off we all went. I was pretty old to be starting school. I learned my letters, and I can read all right. My younger siblings were real good at it though. I remember mama making me sit by the oil lamp, scratching my letters over and over again on an old slate. Oh, the sound those slates would make, scratch, scratch, scratch, like a tree branch on a roof. The other big change I remember is medicines. In the slave days, when you got sick, mama or papa would go in the woods and get some leaves. They would make a tea for you to drink, or soak them and put them on your head. Some of the teas were awful. But what was really awful was the castor oil momma used to get after freedom came. Oh, she would go to the store and get these big green bottles with this brown sticky oil in it. She would dose us with that regular. It was supposed to keep you healthy. Only reason I ever brushed my teeth in those days was to get the taste out of my mouth. Those were good times, though. I didn't see much of my mama during slave times, but I could see she was much happier after. I would tell my little brothers and sisters about slave times, and how things used to be. They would say I was crazy or lying—they just couldn't imagine. I know that times were hard for a lot of folks after slavery ended, but we did all right. Yes, we did all right. Now, honey, I'm happy to talk more about those old days, but I'm talked out for now. Why don't you come back another day?"

May 17, 1937

Dear Sweet-Pete,

Well, of course you know I miss you, and based on your letters, you seem to miss me somewhat as well, or at least some of the comforts of marriage I represent (that is not to say I do not miss those comforts as well!). It has been good to be away, though, from a writing perspective. I do not believe I have ever had such an extended time to observe, ponder, and record as I do now. If I am to someday write for an audience larger than that of our friends, it is important that I continue this project as long as I can.

Just a short letter tonight, I think. I bored you with too many mundane busy-work details of my days in my last letter. I am settling in better to my task now. I have had a series of interviews since I last wrote a few days ago, with none of the discomfort of the first. Part of the success, however, may be that most of the people I have interviewed were very young children at the time of slavery. They really remember very little of what may have been experienced, and those memories they do have are like those of most children—selectively merry.

Still, it has been a bit of a relief to avoid stories of broken families and lives. In my current condition, I find that I am more prone to sentimentality, and likely to cry at the least provocation. I fear you would have laughed at me earlier today. One woman I interviewed spoke of a teapot her mother used to have, and it sounded so much like that of my granny's that I experienced a strong wave of nostalgia and had to feign a sneeze so I could wipe my eyes. This particular woman was a joy to interview. She spoke so lovingly of her family and experiences as a child, that it made me hope that one day our own child will have such memories.

The paper runs short, so I shall end this.
Your loving wife,
Hazel

4

Mothering and Domesticity in Freedom: Ideology and Practice

For newly freed African-American women, to possess authority over the bodies of their children and to be responsible for their rearing was a new and empowering experience. This was true within individual households, but also at the level of national discourse, where redefining public perception of black mothers became an important focus of black political movements. In this chapter, I will review national discourses as they related to African-American women and mothering. I will then turn to the household of the Perrymans and explore how they may have articulated with these discourses through everyday practice and their material lives, first as a two-parent household, and later as the widowed Lucrecia became sole head of the household.

The freedoms and civil rights promised by Emancipation were short-lived. As post-Reconstruction southern states systematically disenfranchised black men, stripping them of only recently earned voting rights, it became of increasing importance for the black community at large to engage in the struggle for women's suffrage (Giddings 1984). The cult of true womanhood, while exiling white women to the household, also provided them with a new entrée into social justice discourses. As the culturally designated moral center of white middle-class households, white women declared it was their right to assert themselves in political matters that jeopardized the sanctity of the domestic realm (Meyerowitz 1994a:7).

For black women to claim the same moral imperative required that black womanhood be rehabilitated in the minds of the white populace. Hundreds of years of degradation and ingrained stereotypes had entrenched racist, sexist stereotypes of black women. It was necessary for black political leadership to defend black womanhood and to demonstrate that the criteria of true womanhood applied to them as well (Giddings 1984:87–88). Increasing the difficulty of this task, white suffrage movements had become increasingly racist following the enactment of the fifteenth Amendment, which ensured the right of black men to vote. The unsteady coalition between abolitionists and suffragists that had fueled the movement to end slavery now became fractured, with elite white women turning against newly enfranchised African-American men. White suffrage leaders such as Cady Stanton voiced the opinion publicly that it was an outrage that ignorant black men should receive the vote before white educated women (A. Davis 1983). As black men were stripped of the vote, it was increasingly imperative that black women not be lost in the fight for women's vote (A. Davis 1983). Mothering was both a personal and politicized undertaking.

Black feminists (e.g., Collins 2000; A. Davis 1983; Giddings 1984; Roberts 1997) have emphasized that black women, given the circumstances and aftermath of enslavement, have always been more engaged in feminist agendas than white women. The realms of motherhood and domesticity for African-American women were not private spheres, as they were for white women, but instead a part of very public practice. Ruth Feldstein (1994) has powerfully illustrated this point in her textual analyses of Mamie Till Bradley's contrasting portrayal in black and white newspapers after the brutal lynching of her 14-year-old son, Emmett Till, in 1955 Mississippi. Till, according to his murderers, had brought his death upon himself by whistling at Carolyn Bryant, a young white mother of two small children. Bryant's husband was one of the murderers. Feldstein convincingly demonstrates that the trial of Till's murderers became a referendum on motherhood itself, with the issue of who and what constituted a "good" and "natural" mother being central to public discourse and the court trial itself. Pitted on one side was the supposedly threatened sanctity of white motherhood and virtue, represented by Carolyn Bryant; on the other side was the grieving black mother, Mamie Till Bradley. Feldstein situates Mamie Till Bradley in these discourses as a knowingly engaged actor who consciously contested stereotypes of black motherhood through her actions and public persona, first at her son's public funeral, and later, during the course of the trial and its aftermath. Mamie Till Bradley, like so many other black women before her, realized that black womanhood and motherhood, as constructed by the white populace, would continue to be used to oppress African Americans in the United States. Faced with the greatest horror many mothers can imagine, Mamie Till Bradley fought a public battle for her son's right to justice, and for her own right to be a righteously angry and grieving mother.

Motherhood was the business of the entire black community, not just individual households. For freed black women, then, motherhood and its associated domestic sphere were things to be done correctly—not just for the sake of children, but also for the good of the race. This sentiment can be seen in the writings and speeches throughout the history of African-American politics, expressed by leaders such as Maria Stewart, Sojourner Truth, and Frederick Douglass.

Maria Stewart, who is recognized by scholars (e.g., Collins 2000; Giddings 1984; Richardson 1987) as the earliest of the black feminist leaders, called as early as 1830 for African-American mothers to shape racial uplift. In an 1832 address to the Boston Afric-American Female Intelligence Society, Stewart exclaimed, "O woman, woman! Upon you I call; for upon your exertions almost entirely depends whether the rising generation shall be anything more than we have or not. O woman, woman! Your example is powerful, your influence great; it extends over your husbands and your children, and throughout the circle of your acquaintance" (quoted in Richardson 1987:55). To those who would question women's involvement in the quest for racial equality, Stewart answered in this way in 1834:

> What if I am a woman; is not the God of ancient times the God of these modern days? Did he not raise up Deborah, to be a mother, and a judge in Israel? Did not queen Esther save the lives of the Jews? And Mary Magdalene first declare the resurrection of Christ from the dead?... St. Paul declared that it was a shame for a woman to speak in public, yet our great High Priest and Advocate did not condemn the woman for a more notorious offence than this; neither will he condemn this worthless worm.... Did St. Paul but know of our wrongs and deprivations, I presume he would make no objections to our pleading in public for our rights. (quoted in Richardson 1987:68)

Although Stewart's political addresses dated to the 1830s, in 1879 her collected works were published and again made available, this time to an audience that included formerly enslaved women (Richardson 1987).

Anna Julia Cooper also drew attention to the role black mothers had to play, In *A Voice from the South,* a collection of her public essays published in 1892, she wrote: "Woman, Mother—your responsibility is one that might make angels tremble and fear to take hold! To trifle with it, to ignore or misuse it, is to treat lightly the most sacred and solemn trust ever confided by God to human kind. The training of children is a task on which an infinity of weal or woe depends" (22). Cooper, like other black women of her time, recognized the unique challenges in asserting their womanhood that faced women of her race. In the following anecdote, she provides a telling example of how readily black women's roles in their families were ignored, as well as illustrating tensions in feminist movements that claimed to be inclusive of black women and white southern women.

> Of Wimodaughsis (which, being interpreted for the uninitiated, is a woman's culture club whose name is made up of the first few letters of the four words wives, mothers, daughters, and sisters) Miss Shaw is president, and a lady from the Blue Grass State *was* secretary. Pandora's box is opened in the ideal harmony of this modern Eden without an Adam when a colored lady, a teacher in one of our schools, applies for admission to its privileges and opportunities. The Kentucky secretary... is filled with grief and horror that any persons of Negro extraction should aspire to learn type-writing or languages or to enjoy any other advantages offered in the sacred halls of Wimodaughsis. Indeed, she had not calculated that there were any wives, mothers, daughters, and sisters, except white ones. (80–81)

Cooper's story reminds us that even within the feminist movements of the late nineteenth and early twentieth centuries, black women were pushed to the periphery or left to their own devices. The struggle to assert and reaffirm a black woman's natural right to mother, and to be acknowledged as a good mother, was fought solely from the black community.

Angela Davis (1983) notes that African-American feminism has always been more articulated with issues related to working mothers than has white feminism, with black women more frequently juggling those roles. Ida B. Wells, best known for bringing international attention to lynching in the American South, publicly juggled a family life and high-profile activist career after her marriage, as well as serving as editor for the *Conservator,* the first black paper in the city of Chicago. Following the 1896 birth of her first son, Wells-Barnett took the child with her on national tour so that she could continue to breast-feed him (McMurry 1998:241–242). Though Wells-Barnett did not see a contradiction in her priorities in desiring to continue her activism and have a family, she found that white feminists such as Susan B. Anthony viewed her as somehow abandoning the quest for women's rights. Wells-Barnett observed in 1898 that Anthony "would bite out my married name in addressing me" (quoted in McMurry 1998:243). For African-American women, motherhood and activism were not contradictory or mutually exclusive. For women who had been stripped of their mothering rights during enslavement, mothering *was* activism.

High infant mortality rates among African-American communities increased the resolve of the political establishment to direct its focus on educating African-American women about mothering. The *Crisis,* the official organ of the NAACP, regularly published comparative infant mortality statistics for the black and white populations. Ultimately, W. E. B. Du Bois (1932) supported birth control as a means of decreasing infant mortality—parents would be better able to provide for fewer children, ensuring that more children survived to adulthood. Proper mothering, was, of course, part of this equation. Improvements in mothering were necessary for improvements in the race, and accordingly, advice on child rearing was among the information to be found in the *Crisis.* In 1911, Mrs. John E. Milholland contributed to a column called "Talks about Women." The column on hygiene was directed toward "the homemakers and to those mothers who above all else want to make a success of their own particular work in life. To these women, who only too often have their hands as well as hearts full of the cares of their little folk, a word regarding that privilege is sometimes helpful. . . . Above all, it should be the mother, not the teacher or some little interested stranger who looks after the child's development" (29).

While the educated elite of African-American society extolled the virtues of motherhood and black domesticity, more significant is the way these values were reflected in the actions of recently freed people. As Gutman (1976) and others (e.g., J. Jones 1985; Giddings 1984; Kolchin 1972) have documented, African-American couples rushed to marry at the end of the Civil War. Long-married couples were able to reaffirm—legally—marriages of already long duration. Couples separated through sale or forced to marry others against their choosing were able to marry. Freedmen's Bureau records include numerous marriages, sometimes involving as many as 26 couples at a time (Kolchin 1972:60).

Once married, couples worked out the labor dynamics within the family. In many cases, the decision seems to have been made that the wife would stay at home, limiting her labors to the domestic sphere. In his study of African-Americans in Alabama during the period of Reconstruction, Kolchin (1972) found that in some rural districts of Alabama in 1870, as many as 80 percent to 95 percent of the African-American women had "at home" listed in the census as their occupation. These numbers were smaller in urban areas; for example, in Ward 2 of Mobile, only 31.8 percent of the women were described as "at home" (68). One white Mobilian complained in 1866, "The negro women were told that women should not work, and they announced that they never intended to go to the field or do other work again, but live like white ladies" (quoted in Fleming 1911:445).

As scholars have noted elsewhere, this trend can be seen in several different lights. From a masculinist perspective, the retreat of women from labor external to the household can be seen as the reassertion of black men's authority over women (Giddings 1984) through the appropriation of the patriarchal household model. Just as easily, this trend can be seen as African-American women choosing not to work following slavery, preferring to focus their attentions on their immediate circle of family (Giddings 1984:62; J. Jones 1985).

African-American women had good reason to avoid working out of the home. Even for educated women, domestic service positions were the most likely source of work in the South. In the North, particularly during World War I, and afterward, black working women were able to gain employment in manufacturing and metalworking, and some were able to find employment as clerks, stenographers, and bookkeepers (Giddings 1984:142–143). Work conditions for African-American women remained poor, in either case, with lower salaries and substandard work spaces being the norm. Domestics were expected to work long hours for little (and sometimes no) compensation, finding themselves working away from their own children to raise someone else's. The sexual, physical, and verbal abuse that characterized working as domestics during enslavement were still standard parts of the work experience. "Many Negro maids say their greatest fear is being in the house alone when the white man comes in" (T. Harris 1982:84).

Laundress positions offered some advantage over working for a single house. A laundress could work for several families at a time, but because she would most typically do her work at her home, she needed to interact with them only when picking up or dropping off clothing. Laundry could be done collectively, shared among women, and could involve help from their children. Given this, it is probably not surprising that in 1870, neighbors Lucrecia Perryman and Emira Hansberry, wives of African-American landholders, when in the workforce, entered as laundresses. This employment allowed them to contribute to their family's income without needing to be absent from the protective sphere of their homes.

Domesticity and Class

For white women, the categories of "good mother," "domestic sphere," and "middle class" could not be separated, for to be one, it was necessary to be all. One could not be a good mother if one was not of the middle class, and one could not be middle class unless one could demonstrate proper control of the etiquette and prescriptions related to the construction of the domestic sphere (Ryan 1981; Wall 1994). The performance of good mothering was also a performance of a class identity—and a racial identity—although for white society, this was an unspoken assumption. As we detail the materials recovered from the Perryman site and how they relate to the performance of class identity among white families, we must continual challenge ourselves to question what meanings these practices have in an African-American household. As Paula Giddings (1984) has observed, "much of what has been interpreted as mere imitation of white values among middle class Black women was a race-conscious mission"(99).

For middle-class white women, domesticity had become a complicated code of behavior and materiality, encoded in ever changing rules of etiquette. The elaboration of etiquette, particularly in the realm of food service and entertaining, is documented in the abundance of prescriptive literature of the middle to late nineteenth century, and in the proliferation of seemingly endless variations in cutlery and tablewares that accompanied them. The ability to converse in recent fashions, and to demonstrate knowledge of arcane service rituals provided a means of social jockeying among white middle-class society (S. R. Williams 1987).

Diane DiZerga Wall (1994), using period etiquette books, has illustrated how place settings became increasingly elaborate during the Victorian period as etiquette became the means through which middle- and upper-class women reified their families' socioeconomic positions. One way that competitive etiquette is demonstrated archaeologically is through teawares. Wall (1991, 1996) and others have noticed the tendency for teawares associated with the white middle class to be more expensive than the rest of the ceramics, including those associated with dining, which were often plain or minimally decorated ironstones or whitewares. Wall (1991), in an oft-quoted paper, suggested that this difference represented the split between the private, almost sacred nature of family dining in the cult of true womanhood, versus the public display of a family's wealth and status as conveyed through tea parties.

Until the second half of the nineteenth century, the dichotomy between private and public practice was reinforced in the architecture of middle-class housing as well, with entertaining in the parlor, and family dining in the kitchen or living room. Following the Civil War, dining rooms became the focus of architectural change. Clifford Clark (1987) found that although 1850s architectural plan books revealed separate dining rooms to be absent from most houses, by 1867 plan books used descriptions of dining rooms to evoke a sense of family unity. "A good dining room, according to the plan books, should reinforce the spiritual unity of the family" (149).

A well-furnished dining room was considered by the 1880s to be an essential component of any middle-class dwelling. Accompanying this shift came a change in the way the dining room was perceived. Once seen as the sacred refuge of the family from the public sphere, middle-class families increasingly engaged in dinner parties, welcoming non-family members into the dining room. Accompanying this transformation were altered attitudes about design and furnishings. Household decoration became a medium for self-improvement and artistic development—in essence, a canvas for creatively displaying the personalities and values of the family who inhabited it. China cabinets and other pieces of furniture that would display the personal belongings of the family became the norm in dining rooms, as did elaborate shelving systems, wallpaper, wall hangings, planters, and lighting, which would combine to best highlight the linens, ceramics, and silverwares being used there. Clark (1987) writes: "Even poor immigrants, much to the disgust of social reformers in Boston who urged them to adopt the slow-cooking Aladdin oven and eat stews, rejected the reformers' vision; instead they continued to demonstrate their conviction that one of the marks of success in America was eating a roast of beef or a steak" (172).

Social jockeying and the reinforcement of difference through materials was not confined to the white middle classes. Research in Annapolis has provided us with insight into the lives of members of the African-American upper class. John and Maria Maynard were among the African-American families studied archaeologically in Annapolis. Maynard had been born free and, after purchasing the freedom of his family members, established himself as a landholder. The Maynard family was clearly part of the African-American elite in Annapolis. In 1849, the appraised value of his possessions was $549, making the family wealthier than 53 percent of the African-American population. The land owned by the family after building their house was valued at $1,000 in 1860 (Mullins 1999:2). At the time of his death in 1876, Maynard's probate inventory lists $105.50 worth of goods, including Victorian furnishings and decorative goods (Warner 1998:204). Newspaper items that demonstrate the family's connections to other elite African-American families and institutions in Annapolis provides further evidence of the family's status. The materials used by both Warner and Mullins in their analyses were deposited between 1889 and 1907, after the death of John Maynard (and possibly Maria), and before the marriage of their daughter, Maria Louisa. According to Mullins (1999), the family's fortunes fell after Maria's marriage in 1908 (13).

In Warner's (1998) opinion, one of the ways that the Maynard and Burgess families reified their position in the middle class was through participation in tea socials held among these families, as evidenced through the greater abundance of teawares associated with the family when compared to other African-American sites in Annapolis. While the Maynards were engaged in the typical white middle-class pursuit of the social tea, they did not do so in ways that were simply emulative of white practice. Mullins (1999) observes that in contrast to the white Victorian convention of using matched ceramic sets, the Maynards used ceramics with a wide range of decorative motifs and styles—perhaps as a conscious rejection of the white practice, since the Maynards-Burgesses could well afford matched sets.

How, then, would the Perrymans be perceived within the African-American community? We have not been able to find evidence related to their religious or social lives that might provide insight into their community networks. That Lucrecia was able to support herself as a midwife after Marshall's death suggests a certain amount of recognition within her community, as well as a certain level of respect and trust granted her. Economically, the Perrymans occupied a precarious space. Though the family had been able to purchase tracts of land and a cemetery plot, their economic fortunes were dependent upon the continued labors of Marshall Perryman.

I have not found any evidence as to what the Perryman household income was. To locate the family economically, it is worth considering, based on comparison with documented pay averages, what their salary may have been. Marshall held an unskilled labor position as a porter. In 1860, the average pay for laborers was $1.01 a day (E. W. Martin 1942:409); adjusting for inflation, this would be approximately $1.57 in 1870 (Derks 1994:2). This income may have been supplemented in part by wages earned in tips. This base salary, however, would be similar to the $1.50 a day earned by farm laborers in New York in 1870 (Derks 1994:12). The wage rates set by the Freedmen's Bureau can also be used as a guide. From 1866 through no later than 1874, the Freedmen's Bureau recommended that men between the ages of 18 and 40 be paid a minimum of $25 a month (Fleming 1911:422). These wages would be a bit less than a dollar a day assuming a minimum of a 26-day work month. By 1884, the value of the dollar had dropped, and a salary of $1.25 a day was typical for laborers (Derks 1994:14). Based upon labor practices of the time, Frank and Marshall probably worked 6 days a week, for an average workweek of 60–66 hours.[*] With Marshall's and Frank Perryman's salaries combined, the Perryman household income may have been as much as $980 annually in 1870 or as much as $780 a year in 1884, at the time of Marshall's death. These of course are only the roughest of estimates based on national averages—the wages paid in the South

[*] Unfortunately, it is impossible to know how much Lucrecia may have been contributing to the household economy, since there is no clear way to estimate how much time she spent on this enterprise or for how long. Unlike other laundresses who appear in the city directory, this is not the case for Lucrecia.

have been traditionally lower. It may be that working for Vail provided other advantages, such as discounted or free groceries, a possibility we will discuss from the archaeological perspective.

Let us quickly contextualize the Perrymans' income, at least as suggested by his occupation. In his study of alcohol consumption in the 1880s, Rorabaugh (1987), based on his reading of the census, suggests that what constituted the middle class of the United States at that time included lawyers and ministers, merchants and storekeepers, at the high end, and master craftsmen such as carpenters, blacksmiths, middle managers in factories and stores, and lesser clerks, at the low end. He found the middle class to make $500–$2,000 a year. A family of four required an annual income of $400–$600 a year to survive, and the average unskilled laborer made in the vicinity of $250 a year (25). This would be a much smaller salary than estimated for the Perryman men. Marshall and Frank Perryman, by 1880, were supporting 12 people on their salaries and covering the expenses of two houses. That Marshall was able to continue to purchase land and pay his property taxes during the 1878–1885 economic depression that encompassed Mobile as the cotton industry declined (Summersell 1949:45) suggests that the Perrymans fared better than others in the city. At the same time, it is difficult to believe that the Perrymans' existence could have been described as luxurious.

Land-ownership did provide the family with stability in residence and pro-tection from landlords—advantages not enjoyed by most African Americans in Mobile. The family was also able to accumulate some material evidence of wealth. At the time of Marshall's death, the 1885 Mobile tax record contains the only appraisal of the family's property, with the value of "furniture, plate, pianos, watches, jewelry" listed as $84, and the land at $200. That Marshall's belongings were appraised separately from the land at all suggests that the family owned some valuable possessions. Often, for smaller estates, the value of land and other property are collapsed into a single value. Unfortunately, no probate list exists for the estate. Among the finer items recovered from the site were porcelains and a gold-plated watch fob. The archaeological materials commu-nicate not only information about accumulated wealth at the site, but also, it is from these items that we have the greatest hope for understanding how the Perrymans may have viewed their own socioeconomic status. These materials also provide insight into how domesticity was constructed through ceramics during and after Marshall's life.

Although not often discussed in the archaeological literature, literacy, edu-cation, and fair skin were defining aspects of the most elite African-American families in the South. Connections to white families provided some people of mixed race opportunities not available to other African Americans (Gatewood 2000). Communities of free people of color were to be found in most antebellum southern cities, and communities of elite African Americans established them-selves in northern cities such as Boston and Philadelphia. In the former French colonies of the Gulf Coast, caste-color systems were well established and clearly linked to color gradation. Mobile had an established wealthy free colored population dating back to French rule. These families often held substantial wealth, beyond that held by many white families (Nordmann 1990).

For the elite African-American communities, higher education was often expected. By 1900 African-American women were earning degrees not only from traditionally black colleges, but from institutions such as Oberlin, the University of Chicago, Cornell, Radcliff, and Wellesley (Giddings 1984:76). The 1912 Negro Year Book, published by the Tuskegee Institute, reported that since the decade of 1820–1829, 3,856 African Americans had received college degrees, with the vast majority of these (3,477) being earned since 1880 (Work 1912:102). Census records indicate that neither Marshall nor Lucrecia could read—given the norms of enslavement, this is not surprising. Court documents involving Marshall Perryman indicate that he "made his mark" rather than signed paperwork, supporting the findings in the census. But the Perrymans obviously valued education, and with the exception of Caroline, all of their children were recorded as having attended school, and all were literate. Among Lucrecia and Marshall's great-grandchildren were college graduates, but not before.

In her study of the black middle class of Birmingham, Feldman (1999) identifies home-ownership as one of the distinguishing features that provided entrée into the black middle class (40). She reports that in 1890, Alabama African Americans owned 6,889 homes statewide (46). In Birmingham in 1910, the rate of home-ownership was 4.4 percent among African Americans. Occupationally, the families she studied in Smithfield, a suburb of Birmingham, included doctors, lawyers, dentists, and business owners.

Christopher Scribner (2001) has described Mobile's population of black elite as being very small, numbering fewer than 70 people, or less than 1 percent of the city's African-American population. Included among this number were African-American businessmen like A. N. Johnson, an undertaker and newspaper publisher, who was connected to the National Negro Business League. Among his other enterprises, Johnson owned the People's Drug Store, located on Dauphin Street, one of three African-American owned drugstores in the community (165). C. M. Witherspoon owned Gulf City Drug Store, and Dr. J. Scott owned Southside Drugstore (Ewert 2001:150). The black business district of Mobile in the early twentieth century consisted of 33 businesses located on and around Davis Avenue, and included grocery stores, funeral homes, restaurants, drugstores, and hardware stores, and a Mutual Aid Society (Scribner 2001:166).

While economically insecure given their employment, the Perrymans' status as homeowners placed them in a privileged position relative to many other African Americans of that time. As such, they certainly could be perceived as having achieved lower-middle-class status—or at least a status that seemed to be beyond "laborer." But what of other trappings of middle-class ideology? It is worth considering briefly how the Perrymans would come to be exposed to notions of the cult of true womanhood and its associated material culture. Archaeologists often rely on the prescriptive literature available at the time and do not always consider the other ways through which ideas and practices are transmitted. Prescriptive literature and advice columns would be accessible to the family through their children, in the form of housekeeping books, and in black newspapers.

Churches were often involved in movements related to racial uplift, and would be another avenue for exposure to white middle-class ideologies. Most important would have been experiential learning. Contact with white families, as enslaved people or as employees, would forcefully illustrate white privilege and the ways that privilege and difference were communicated through social practice and material culture. As domestics, during enslavement and freedom, African Americans would have seen the domestic sphere on display. Not only would domestics witness this realm, but they also would be responsible for knowing the ins and outs of etiquette as it pertained to their work. For African-American women, the protection that white women and children enjoyed within the domestic realm would have been particularly noteworthy. We know that Perryman was likely to have entered white houses as part of her work as a laundress.

In historical archaeological analyses of domesticity, dining room etiquette, as reflected by the ever-ubiquitous ceramics, is often the focus. Certainly, the ceramics recovered from the Perryman household belie how the family responded or ignored fashion and stylist trends that characterized American society at the time. While archaeologists tend to be very excited by a discovery of ceramics, it is important to place them into perspective. While the purchase of ceramics did require some investment of funds, and although these were items used on a daily basis, they represent just a small portion of the material culture that furnished and shaped the practice of everyday life in any household. That caveat aside, I too will now indulge in the historical archaeological passion for hypothesizing what and how much the Perrymans chose to communicate about themselves through their tablewares.

Let us have a brief word about the context and materials of the two archaeological deposits associated with the Perrymans. In the case of the earlier 1885 deposit (Feature 3), we can be reasonably assured that most of the materials found there were items that would have been familiar to Marshall Perryman, since they were broken and deposited roughly around the time of his death. As such, these would have been items acquired during the Perrymans' lives together, when Lucrecia was situated in the role of full-time wife and mother. Only nine ceramic vessels were recovered from this deposit, of which four are tablewares, one is decorative, two for beverage storage, and two for cooking. The decorative piece is a blue dry-bodied stoneware canister, clearly intended to evoke Josiah Wedgwood's Jasper ware. This is a fine piece of ceramic, comparatively speaking, and would have communicated a certain level of luxury.

Figure 4.1 Rebecca at the Well Teapot

The tablewares consist entirely of teawares: two "Rebecca at the Well" teapots, a plain whiteware teacup, and a plain ironstone saucer. The saucer is marked with a Johnson Brothers of England mark that was used beginning in 1883 (Godden 1964:354–55), suggesting that it was acquired shortly before Marshall's death. The plain ironstone ceramics are typical of those recovered from white middle-class family sites, and are generally interpreted as being popular because they emphasized the sacred simplicity of family life (Wall 1994).

The Rebecca at the Well teapots deserve our further attention as well. These are a familiar sight to historical archaeologists, for they appear with great regularity at nineteenth- and early-twentieth-century sites. The ceramics are of a type known as Rockingham, which are yellow-bodied ceramics generally bearing a mottled brown glaze. The decoration on the teapots is molded. Many different versions of the Rebecca teapots were manufactured, but these two contain identical version of the motif and appear to have been made by the same manufacturer. The teapots, one of which holds two pints and the other five pints, depict a woman bending over a well, drawing water (Figure 4.1).

The design originated on an English stoneware pitcher labeled "Arabic" and was copied on Rockingham teapots by Edwin and William Bennett of Baltimore, who dubbed the design "Rebekeh at the Well" and embossed it as such on the teapot (Claney 1996:117). Our teapots do not include the embossed label, suggesting that at the time of their manufacture, the image was well established and required no further introduction. The woman represents Rebecca of the Old Testament, who had been identified as the woman chosen to be the wife of Isaac based upon her offer to draw enough water from the well to satiate his camels. The story fit well with the nineteenth-century American popular view of woman as the spiritual and physical protector of the household. As such, the scene depicted on a teapot, the ceramic embodiment of the woman's family role, became popular in American households. The teapot was even paneled in the style of the popular "gothic" tablewares used to communicate the sanctity of the home (Claney 1996:122). The Bennetts' introduction of the teapot coincided with the Odd Fellows establishment of the "Degree of Rebekah" to confer on members and their wives, in what Claney observes was a shrewd marketing decision. The Odd Fellows was one of the old-line secret societies that had an African-American order. Peter Ogden founded the Order of Odd Fellows for African Americans in the United States by becoming a member of the Grand United Order of Odd Fellows in England, securing a charter and setting up the first lodge March 1, 1843 (Work 1912:138).

Rebecca at the Well teapots remained popular through the 1930s, but by the early twentieth century, given the high profile of the women's movement, their meaning had shifted from being a glorification of the domestic sphere to one of nostalgia (Claney 1996:124). At the time when these teapots were discarded at the Perryman site, Rebecca imagery was still a potent symbol to American women defining themselves and their roles within their families (Claney 1996:127).

While the materials recovered from Feature 3 constitute a decidedly small sample, it is not the only source of information available regarding potential ceramic use during Marshall's life. Ceramics and other goods acquired by the couple would have continued to be used (and broken) following Marshall's death, thus being deposited much later. The ideal way to identify such materials would be to have examples of ceramics or ceramics marks that were not manu-factured after 1885. The artifacts were not so cooperative, however, and yielded no ceramics of that chronological description. The well did, however, contain a number of ceramics whose production overlapped with Marshall's lifetime (Table 4.1). Of course, there is always the possibility that older, secondhand ceramics entered the assemblage after Marshall's death.

One hallmark of Victorian respectability at the table was the use of matched tableware vessels. Ceramics were alternately sold in sets, which contained desig-nated numbers of place settings and service vessels, or a individual piece could be bought from open stock. In the 1897 Sears catalog, a dozen plain, 8-inch dinner plates could be purchased for 95 cents, or a 100-piece dinner set of a slightly better ceramic could be purchased for $7.95 (Israel 1997:678). For other patterns, tea sets of 44 or 56 pieces, or dinner sets of 55, 100, 112, or 124 could be purchased. Open stock sales allowed one to build a set slowly, or to replace broken pieces at different times. Advertising copy in the catalog provides some insight into what were perceived to be the current biases of fashion. For in-stance, the 100-piece W. H. Wetherby and Son set of ceramics were advertised as "suitable to decorate the tables of the wealthy" and guaranteed to be "genuine English semi-porcelain ware, not first or second grade American, but the gen-uine English" (Israel 1997:678). Decorated Haviland porcelain was proclaimed

Table 4.1 Pre-1885 Ceramic Vessels Recovered from the Well

Manufacturer	Date of Mark	Mean Date	Description of Vessel(s)	Number of Vessels Recovered
E. & C. Challinor	1862–1891	1876.5	White ironstone flatware	1
George Jones	1864–1907	1885.5	plain whiteware plate	1
Goodwin Brothers	1876–1893	1884.5	molded whiteware kitchen bowl	1
John Edwards	1880–1900	1890.0	plain whiteware soup plate	1
Cook and Hancock	1881–1903	1892.0	brown transfer-printed oval serving dish	1
T. Maddock and Sons	1882–1902	1892	plain ironstone tureen blued ironstone dish	2
Wallace and Chetwynd	1882–1901	1891.5	embossed luncheon plate	1
Johnson Bros.	1883–1916	1899.5	plain whiteware soup plate plain ironstone dinner plate blued ironstone flatware blued ironstone saucer	4

to be "the finest French China" and "thin and transparent, the shape entirely new; every piece embossed heavily and traced with gold" (Israel 1997:680).

The composition of the ceramics recovered from the well suggests that the Perrymans invested both in sets of tablewares as well as accumulating pieces one by one. A surprisingly large number of ceramics—a minimum of 82 vessels—was recovered from the well.

Among the tablewares, teawares and plates are the most common forms (Table 4.2). Within vessel forms, a variety of sizes is represented. Soup plates ranged from 20 to 26 cm in diameter, plates from 18 to 26 cm. Saucers as small as 12 cm in diameter and as large as 18 cm were found. Teacups and bowls showed the least variation, with three of the four measurable tableware bowls measuring 16 cm across, and eight of the nine teacups measuring 8 cm in diameter.

The assemblage does not exhibit much in the way of surface decoration. Twenty-six of the whiteware tableware vessels are plain, and 12 others are decorated with banding or embossing. Surface decoration suggests that the Perryman

Table 4.2 Distribution of Ceramics by Vessel Type

Form	Number Recovered (Minimum number of vessels)
Bowls	4
Plate and Soup plates	30
Teawares	38
Service vessels	15
Beverage Storage	32
Food Storage	3
Bathwares	4
Food preparation	18
Other Forms	22
Total Number of Ceramic Vessels Recovered	**166**

households had several different matched sets or partial sets of ceramics (Table 4.3). The predominant set of ceramics consisted of plain white tablewares, made of both ironstone and improved white earthenwares (Figures 4.2 and 4.3).

The decorative regularity of the set belies the diversity of the assemblage. At least 10 different manufacturers of these wares are represented archaeologically. Johnson Brothers accounts for at least two vessels, and CC Thompson Pottery Company is represented by at least two plates. Unfortunately, a number of unmarked or incomplete plates were also recovered from the site. Four of the unmarked plain teacups and four of the unmarked saucers match one another. This circumstance leads me to believe that at some point the Perrymans acquired a large set of plain whitewares, manufactured by one producer. Since a wide variety of manufacturing dates are represented in the assemblage, I take this as evidence that the plain tableware set was added to by the family through time. Whether this set was started while Marshall was alive is open to speculation. While plain ceramics were the cheapest tablewares available, the uniform white sets were symbolically laden, seen within the cult of true motherhood to represent the purity and sanctity of the household.

The family also owned a small number of ironstone vessels that exhibited a grayish blue glaze, giving them a very different appearance from the other bright white vessels. Two Johnson Brothers saucers, a John Maddock oval serving dish, and an unmarked oval serving dish were found with this coloring. In the case of these ceramics, one of the Johnson Brothers' saucers was recovered from the early deposit, and the second from the well. These bluish gray ironstone ceramics faded from popularity by the early 1900s, so the smaller number of these ceramics may reflect the increased difficulty of attaining them or a lack of interest in the style. Given that one of these vessels was recovered from the earlier deposit, these ceramics may have been procured while Marshall was living. This

Table 4.3 Possible Matched Ceramic Sets Recovered

Description of Set	Vessels Represented	Manufacturer	Date of Manufacture	Number of Each Found
Plain (ironstone or whiteware)	whiteware soup plate	Johnson Brothers	1883–1916	1
	whiteware soup plate	John Edwards	1880–1900	1
	whiteware soup plate			1
	whiteware plate	CC Thompson Pottery Co.	1890–1910	2
	whiteware plate			6
	ironstone plate	T. Maddock and Sons	1882–1902	1
	ironstone plate	Johnson Brothers	1883–1916	1
	ironstone plate	J & G. Meakin	1897+	1
	ironstone plate			2
	whiteware teacup			4
	whiteware teacup	"Germany" with lion mark		1
	whiteware saucer			5
	whiteware serving bowl			1
	whiteware serving bowl	Brockman Pottery Co.	1888–1912	1
	whiteware serving bowl	McNichol, Burton and Co.	1885–1892	1
	whiteware oval dish			1
	whiteware oval platter			1
	ironstone tureen	John Maddock and Sons Royal Semi Porcelain	1896+	1
Ironstone with blue-gray glaze	ironstone saucer	Johnson Brothers	1883–1916	2
	ironstone oval dish	Maddock & Co., Burslem, England		1
	ironstone oval dish			1
Embossed	whiteware soup plate	Sebring Porcelain		2
	whiteware plate	presumably the same		1
Plain porcelain	soup plate			1
	plate			1
	teacups			4
	saucers			2
	teapot lid			1
	tureen base			1
	tureen lid			1

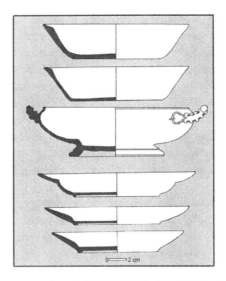

Figure 4.2 Examples of plain ceramics recovered from the well

style of ceramics would have been popular, though of decreasing popularity, throughout the period of the Perrymans' marriage. Johnson Brothers is a well-known ironstone manufacturer, and the fact that they are English, rather than American-made ceramics may have enhanced their desirability to the family.

Three plates with matching embossed scroll decorations may represent a third set of ceramics used by the families. Two soup plates and one plate marked "The Sebring Porcelain," have matching embossed decorations. Produced between 1887 and about 1900 (Lehner 1988:470), these ceramics were procured after Marshall's death. A final potential matched set of ceramics was composed of plain white porcelain. The vessels are unmarked (Table 4.3), but this group includes 11 vessels of matching color, paste, vessel shape, and thickness. Tablewares, teawares and service vessels are represented, providing the best evidence from the site that the family had purchased one complete dining service, but the lack

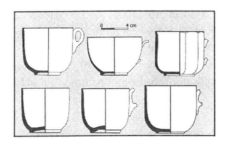

Figure 4.3 Examples of teawares recovered from the Perryman well

of marks has made it impossible to date their manufacture. Porcelain was, of course, among the most expensive and desirable of the ceramic types available at the end of the nineteenth century (Henry 1987). The presence of service vessels also attests to the display value of these pieces. Safely housed in a glass-fronted sideboard or china cabinet, these pieces would have be spoken the family's ability to acquire items of wealth.

The ceramics discussed above account for 49 of the 88 vessels recovered from the well. The remaining vessels include unmatched molded and embossed ceramics annular decorated wares, as well as a small number of transfer-printed and decalcomania decorated vessels. The greatest variety in decoration is seen in the teawares from the well. Teawares were the most brightly decorated, including embossed, hand-painted, overglazed transfer-printed, gilt, and decalcomania-decorated vessels. Among the teawares, the porcelain wares stand out as the most diverse. Three of the porcelain teaware vessels demonstrate the influence of Japanese aesthetic traditions so popular in American households at the turn of the twentieth century. One overglazed transfer-printed Japanese teacup was recovered from the site. In addition, two teacups with molded bamboo handles were recovered. Although not of Japanese origin, the bamboo styled handles were clearly influenced by the *Japonisme* craze that began in the late nineteenth century. Even though the teacups used by the Perrymans are of varying decoration, they are mostly similar in size, suggesting, perhaps, an attempt to create a sense of unity for the collection.

Overall, the ceramic table assemblage suggests the presence of the dichotomy in decoration reported for white middle-class homes. Items intended for family meals, be they manufactured from porcelain, ironstone, or whiteware, emphasize whiteness and a simplicity of design that suggests a visual unity to the assemblage, even though the individual pieces were created by a number of different manufacturers in at least three countries. Dates from the ceramics suggests that even after Marshall's death, family members continued their attempts to present a well-matched table. Whether the sets identified archaeologically were used by Lucrecia and her children, by Carolyn and her first or second husband, or even represent some of the ceramics of the Cunningham family, it is striking that the identified sets of ceramics suggest that the users were conforming to similar aesthetic and stylistic principles. The Perrymans' ceramic assemblages suggest that the Perrymans turned to popular cultural representations of the family and household life to help shape their own homes. To read the ceramic assemblage merely as an indicator of class aspirations would be to ignore the more fundamental aspirations she held—to raise and nurture her own children.

Food at the Table

As I shall examine more closely in a following chapter, the faunal and macrofloral remains left by the Perrymans have since been mainly consumed by the processes of nature. I can offer only that beef, chicken, pork, oysters, and fish were consumed at the site, but any attempt to suggest relative preference for any meat over another would be meaningless. What little we can glean of the family's diet must be drawn primarily from the remains of commercially produced and packaged foods. Marshall and Frank Perryman's employment with a grocer may have provided access to foodstuffs not ordinarily to be expected, based on their income. This advantage, if it indeed ever existed, would have ceased with the end of Frank Perryman's employment with Vail. A substantial number of artifacts, at least 88 vessels recovered from both deposits, once contained food (Table 4.4). Of the containers for which contents could be reasonably identified, based on either form and/or embossing, condiments were the most common. Oils, extracts, catsup, Worcestershire sauce, horseradish, pickles, pepper sauce, and mustard were among the most abundant. Among the condiments were products that had been imported from England, such as preserves, pickles, and sauces. These imports are not surprising, for Mobile had long ties with England, resulting from its cotton exports (Amos 1985).

Food preparation through the 1880s was still simple in its execution and presentation. The creation of small, dainty, picturesque foods that tested the creative talents of cooks became increasingly popular toward the end of the nineteenth century as improvements in stoves allowed for greater control over cooking (Kasson 1987; Cowan 1983). We are able to gain some insights into how the different condiments may have been used based on period cookbooks. Jellies and preserves were often served as accompaniments to roast bird, lamb, pork, and game meals (H. Campbell 1881), catsup and Worcestershire sauce were used to flavor gravies, or in the case of catsup, as a pickle to accompany beef.

Mobile sits on the Mobile River, which feeds directly into the Gulf of Mexico, long renowned for its oysters, shrimp, and gulf fish. It is hard not to imagine that some of the other foodstuffs are related to enjoying this regional bounty. We know that at least one fish and 29 oysters made it into the Perryman well. Cookbooks (e.g., H. Campbell 1881) confirm that olive oil was one recommended frying medium for fish.* Mustard could be used to thicken "fish gravy" or as a dredge in frying. Catsup, Worcestershire sauce, pepper sauce, and horseradish combine into a sauce popular for raw oysters and other seafood.

Glasswares and Alcohol Consumption

No table setting was complete without an elegant set of glittering pressed glass vessels to accompany it. With increases in industrial productivity, pressed glass vessels became both ubiquitous and inexpensive by the 1870s (Leach 1993). The Sears catalog is filled with pages of sets of tumblers, berry bowls, goblets, pitchers, covered butter dishes, and such Victorian oddities as celery glasses

---

* It is more likely, however, that olive oil (or sweet oil) was being used for its medicinal qualities.

Table 4.4 Food Storage Vessels

Form	Product Brand (if discernable)	Minimum Number Found in 1885 Pit	Minimum Number Found in 1911 Well
Oil/vinegar bottle			4
Vinegar bottle			1
Oil bottle			5
Preserves	Durkee	1	
Preserves	Campbell Preserves Camden		2
Preserves		4	4
Mustard barrel	Charles Gulden	1	2
Mustard barrel			2
Catsup bottle	Curtice Bros. Food Product		1
Catsup			3
Horseradish jar	H. J. Heinz Co. No. 37		1
Horseradish jar			2
Worcestershire sauce bottle	Parker Brothers	1	
Worcestershire sauce bottle		1	4
Pepper sauce bottle		1	3
Extract bottle	Sauer's Extracts		10
Extract bottle			4
Pickle jar	H. J. Heinz Co.		1
Pickle jar			2
Commercial jars			12
Milk jug			2
Fruit sealer	Fish and person, "... de Mark"		1
Fruit sealer	Mason Pat Nov 30		1
Fruit sealer cap	Patd Sept. 20th 1898		1
Fruit sealer	Patd Feb ...		1
Fruit sealer			10
Lid liner	Boyd's Genuine Porcelain Lined		1
Potted meat jar			1

and spoon holders. Like ceramics, pressed glass could be purchased in large sets or piece by piece. Faced with the possibility that consumption of these objects would fail to meet production, glass companies reissued their older (and other factories') patterns under new names, which they hoped would inspire buyers to collect more pieces than they would otherwise. The United States Glass Company in 1907 issued a series of patterns struck from molds first used in the 1870s under various state names. Other companies issued commemorative

Table 4.5 Glassware by Vessel, Shape, and Pattern

Type of Vessel	Number of Vessels Found	Number of Different Patterns Represented
Berry bowls	4	2
Covered bowl	1	1
Celery vase	1	1
Cordial or egg cup	1	1
Goblet	8	4
Tumbler (not including commercial tumblers)	9	4
Butter dish	1	1
Spoon holder	1	1
Cordial	1	1
Covered sugar box	1	1
Pitcher	1	1
Oval dish	1	1
Decanter	1	1
Salt cellar	1	1
Eccentric dish (probably shaped as a stove)	1	1
Chicken dish	1	1

pieces showing religious or political events. A large contemporary collectors' literature exists for pressed glass (e.g., Jenks and Luna 1990; Miles and Miller 1986), so many of the patterns produced have been identified to manufacturer and date. Collectors use pattern names when they are available through company documents; otherwise, they create pattern names based on design attributes. Because glass manufacturers reused molds, dating any particular piece can be difficult, and, some glass companies continue to strike new pieces from original molds of patterns popular with collectors. At least two of the identified patterns appear to have been produced only during the 1870s and 1880s, and could have been in the Perryman family's possession prior to Marshall's death.

Fifty-four pressed glass vessels were recovered from the Perryman site. Of these, 19 of the tumblers are typical of the type produced to hold commercial goods, such as processed cheeses, peanut butter, jelly, and tobacco (particularly snuff). Just as today, these tumblers were reused as drinking vessels after their initial function was served. If we remove these from consideration, we find that a range of vessels and patterns are represented among the pressed glass (Table 4.5).

Within the assemblage, there is no evidence that the family had a matching set of any particular glass pattern. Likewise, the family does not seem biased toward a particular theme or manufacturer (Figure 4.4). The only duplication of

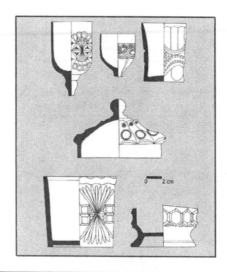

Figure 4.4 Examples of the Perrymans' pressed glasswares

pattern occurs among vessels of the same type, for instance, three goblets from the site were of the same pattern, and similarly, five matching tumblers were recovered, as were three matching bowls. This pattern suggests that the family purchased matching sets of particular vessels, but not a complete matching table set. I was intrigued to note that some of the less used forms, such as butter dishes, celery vases, pitchers and spoon holders, were represented by single examples (Table 4.5), suggesting that the family maintained a complete set of pressed glass, but that the set did not match. Family members would consume beverages from vessels that matched those others at the table were using, and eat from matching bowls. Vessels such as the butter, celery, sugar box, pitcher, and spoon holder were communally used, and not necessarily at the same time. In other words, although the pressed glass assemblage on the surface appears to be quite disparate in its composition, it did meet some criteria of the Victorian ideal, for the corporate nature of the family would be reinforced by their use of place settings that matched one another.

Also of relevance to us is what may have been served in those matching tumblers and goblets. One of the issues that divided the working and middle classes was alcoholic beverage consumption. Consumption of whiskey and other hard liquors had decreased among native-born Protestants as a result of increasingly evangelical religious teachings during the nineteenth century. In contrast, growing immigrant populations, like the Germans, Irish, and Italians, brought with them culturally rooted drinking practices. Most notably, with more climate-suited brewing techniques, the Germans were able to increase the popularity of beer until it became a more popular beverage than whiskey (Rorabaugh 1987:27–29). Rorabaugh reports that per capita consumption of beer more than doubled between 1870 and 1885, causing considerable concern among the middle class. Middle-class women drew upon their role as keepers of domestic purity (and as part of their attempts to gain suffrage) and entered into the temperance struggle, leading sit-ins at saloons during the 1870s. It is also Rorabaugh's contention that "in 1885, when the middle classes sat down to Sunday dinner, they did not drink alcoholic beverages. To have drunk whiskey would have been low and vulgar; to have drunk beer would have been to associate with immigrant working-class culture. . . . The middle classes were forced, in the name of propriety, either to give up alcohol or to drink sparingly—and guiltily" (42). Wine was sometimes drunk, but remained expensive for most consumers. Instead, suggests Rorabaugh, milk, water, coffee, and recently introduced flavored mineral waters were served in houses of the middle class. Abstinence from alcohol consumption was not limited to the white middle class. An 1841 observer of Philadelphia's black upper class described them as practicing abstinence and sobriety and exhibiting a concern for moral conduct (Gatewood 2000:11).

Now archaeologists can attest to the point that simply claiming publicly not to be engaging in a behavior does not preclude that behavior being visible in one's trash. I was involved in the excavation of a Prohibition-period house site occupied by a Santa Monica police officer that contained more glass whiskey hip-flasks than I have ever seen on a single site. Therefore, any discussion of alcohol consumption should proceed with one eyebrow firmly raised in skepticism. In a study of middle-class versus working-class tobacco and alcohol consumption, Recknor and Brighton (1999) found that out of seven middle-class households studied, only two seemed to conform to mainstream temperance rhetoric in their assemblages. In considering alcohol consumption in the Perryman household, I will not address the 25 stoneware jugs believed to have once contained whiskey that were recovered from the site. I suspect that these represent Lucrecia's medical practice, not recreational consumption. Those containers aside, alcoholic beverage consumption seems to have been a regular feature of life in the Perryman home (Tables 4.6 and 4.7), both during and after Marshall's lifetime.

The small 1885 trash pit contained one stout bottle and six hard liquor bottles. While it could be argued that the presence of these bottles might just as easily be a result of reuse as consumption, this argument is more difficult to

Table 4.6 Alcoholic Beverages Recovered from Early Feature

Type of Alcohol	Number of Glass Containers	Number of Ceramic Containers
Beer		1
Hard liquor	6	

Table 4.7 Alcoholic Beverages Recovered from Well

Type of Alcohol	Number of Glass Containers	Number of Ceramic Containers
Beer	32	1
Hard liquor	43	5*
Wine	6	
Bitters/liqueur	3	

*These vessels alternately could have contained mineral water.

make for the later well feature. In the well feature, hard liquor, especially in the form of flask-sized whiskey bottles, was the most abundant alcoholic beverage represented. Joseph A. Magnus's Cincinnati whiskey was the most frequently occurring, with five examples found. As I will discuss further, whiskey had a number of medicinal and household uses beyond merely drinking, and any interpretation of whiskey consumption should acknowledge this circumstance. Thirty-three beer bottles, including seven Budweiser examples, were also found, as were a smaller number of wine and liqueur bottles. Given that the number of adults living in the households was limited at any given time, it seems safe to suggest that members of the Perryman household do not seem to have eliminated the consumption of alcohol from their household. Indeed, they even drank of that lower-class beverage, beer. We also see the consumption of wine within the household, providing evidence of more expensive alcohol tastes.

Though the Perrymans would not receive special recognition from any temperance societies, they also consumed a beverage more acceptable to middle-class Protestant households: mineral water. Eight soda bottles were recovered from Feature 3, including an example embossed with "Conrad's Soda" and two Saxlehner's Bitterquelle Hunyadi Janos bottles. Hunyadi Janos mineral water was named after a Hungarian national hero whose defense of Belgrade from the Turks in 1456 led to 70 years of Hungarian independence. The product claimed to be a safe and gentle aperient that aided habitual constipation and treated inflammation, congestion, and gouty disorders (Schulz et al. 1980:142).

Fifty-four mineral and soda water bottles were recovered from the well. Most of the bottles are the short-neck type with bead or blob finishes, a number of which had been used with Hutchinson stoppers. Most of the containers held locally produced sodas. E. Carre, D. Palliser's Sons, Steins Spring Bottling Works, Spring Hill, Choctaw Soda Works, and Phoenix Bottling Works are among the regional brands present (Table 4.8; Figure 4.5).

Mineral or soda waters, while increasingly consumed as beverages by the middle class, were also considered part of a health-conscious diet. Beginning in the 1870s, mineral waters were popularly consumed for their powers to cure

Table 4.8 Mineral Bottles Recovered from the 1911 Well

Embossing	Minimum Number Found
Choctow Soda Works	2
Coca-Cola	2
D. Palliser's	5
Phoenix Bottling Works	8
E. Carre Company, Mobile, ALA	14
Spring Hill ALA Bottle Works	1
Stein's Spring Bottling Works	7
unidentified soda bottles	15

a variety of ills, including "constipation, piles, asthmas, bronchitis, diseases of the skin, dyspepsia, diabetes, kidney and urinary tract infections, paralysis, and nervous prostration" (Armstrong and Armstrong 1991:89). Mineral waters were a principal target of the Pure Food and Drug Act of 1906, which attempted to crack down on patent medicines and other products that used unproven health claims in their advertising. E. Carre, D. Palliser's, and Phoenix Bottling Works all are listed under "Mineral Waters" in Mobile city directories. Also listed was G. Van Antwerp and Son, a local pharmacist whose drugstore bottles were found in abundance at the site, underscoring the medicinal uses of these beverages. We will return to this line of exploration in the next chapter.

Decoration of the Home

If the home was to be the canvas on which a middle-class family creatively expressed its values, what can we learn from the Perrymans? Clark (1987) writes: "By the 1880s, the ideal of the artistic middle-class house had become extremely popular. These houses were designed to be read like a book whose symbolic meanings would be almost self-evident to contemporaries"(158). Perhaps, then,

Figure 4.5 Mineral water bottles recovered from Perryman site

the Perrymans invested some of themselves into the decorative items that graced their home. Who, though, would have been their contemporaries? During Marshall's lifetime, and perhaps beyond, their neighbors, the Hansberrys, or other similarly situated families, may have joined the Perrymans in their home socially. Certainly, the documentary record hints that the wives may have worked together. These families would have met together as generational peers, as a couple with children of similar ages, and as fellow African-American landholders. Accordingly, the hopes, aspirations and experiences expressed through the domestic materials of their households would have been recognizable to one another. After Marshall's death, Lucrecia's midwifery practice would draw other visitors, potential mothers and perhaps their families, to the Perryman home. These contemporaries would have entered the Perryman home from a different subject position, that of one requesting advice and services from a trusted community member. Lucrecia's home would be searched by these visitors for evidence of her accomplishments and abilities as related to her practice, and her belongings would be read accordingly.

The Perrymans' house would not have appeared remarkable from the outside. Appraisers for the city of Mobile certainly did not expect it to be, for they did not even add to the assessed value of the property to account for the houses' values, and there is no evidence of improvement to the structures in the tax record. The wooden frame structures shown on the 1878 Mobile map measured no more than 25 feet square, representing a 625-square-foot living area for each house. While the Hansberry family lived in a similar-sized house, white neighbor Jonathon Seed appears to have had a house at least three times as large. Yet, to put things in perspective, the Perrymans' house would have been approximately three times larger than the average slave cabin.

Let us briefly imagine what we might encounter upon entering the Perrymans' modest home. Based on the number of oil lamps recovered, visitors would have found a brightly lit interior. The lamps found are of the tabletop variety; at least one featured a decorative globe, and another had faceted glass fobs on the reservoir. Presumably the simple elegance of the porcelain tablewares would have been highlighted in a china cabinet or on shelves. If the Japanese and Japanese-inspired teawares were visible, the visitor would have no doubt that the Perrymans were aware of the recent popularity of Asian motifs in household décor. Small, yellow molded and wheel-turned clay flowerpots may have held ivies or other decorative plants in or outside of the house. Victorians were partial to using plants to bring naturalistic themes inside of their homes, and the raising of plants was seen as a wholesome pastime for young women (Beecher and Stowe 1870). Plants were typically situated on shelves, around windows, and on mantels.

Perhaps it was interspersed with these domesticated elements of nature that we would find placed a number of white parian figurines. A Victorian sense of balance would require that the matching parian cherub vases be situated close

Figure 4.6 Cherub vases from the Perryman well

together, so that the visitor might observe them in one view. The cherubs are so evocative: one sits perched on a tree stump, gently strumming a lute, while its companion playfully holds a hand to ear, poised to catch every note (Figure 4.6). Although they are rendered in white, their soft round cheeks, full pouty lips, and gently curly hair could grace children from any number of racial backgrounds. Their nicely formed limbs and full bellies exemplify vigor and good health. Would a formerly enslaved woman see these figures and think of children taken, or consider her newfound ability to raise children as she saw fit—would she see the opportunity to raise children whose innocence could be somewhat protected from the realities beyond the domestic sphere? Upon seeing these figures, would a nervous pregnant woman see a materialization of her hopes for a successful pregnancy, and the result, a beautiful and healthy child?

After gazing at the charming vases, perhaps one's attention would be drawn to the other figurine, this one of a huntsman, carrying a bird in one hand, his rifle slung over his shoulder. Although the head is missing from the one found in the well, examples like it seen in antique stores often feature a childlike head on an adult body. Are we seeing an endorsement of rural life? Or perhaps we are meant to observe an appreciation for an existence in which hunting is done with childlike pleasure, rather than as a desperate supplement to a meagerly provisioned diet? Or maybe our huntsman is communicating a sense of ties to the land? Ah, have you noticed the colonial figure perched hence? I think he may be from the top of a teapot or similar ceramic, I cannot quite see from here. Are the Perrymans telling us that they too are patriots, even though Marshall Perryman, who has paid his poll tax every year, has never been allowed to register to vote? Finally, I cannot help but point out the milk-glass dish shaped as a chicken sitting on its nest. I presume that we are allowed to gaze upon it with a gentle smile, for it is both charming and humorous. It is a much more manageable fowl than those found wandering in the neighborhood, and perhaps

Figure 4.7   Matchbox lid, depicting Semele and Zeus

beckons us to remember that we remain rooted in the mundane activities of everyday life.

Also visible, perhaps, would have been the family's porcelain spittoon, conveniently situated near a chair for easy use while reclining. Of course, tobacco consumption is looked down upon by certain members of society. Certainly such a fine piece would not be hidden away. Another fine piece of tobacco paraphernalia might have been visible for inspection, a redware matchbox lid that bore a highly ornate embossed design of a woman feeding an eagle from a plate, a motif reminiscent of mythological themes (Figure 4.7). The most obvious source of the image is the story of Semele and Zeus. Zeus seduced Semele in the form of an eagle and impregnated her. Hera appeared to Semele as her sister to convince her that she must trick Zeus into appearing to her in his true form. Semele makes the request of Zeus after forcing him to grant her an unspecified wish, but as a mortal she cannot handle the sight of the god in his glory; she is burned alive. Zeus rescues the unborn child from her ashes and places it in his thigh, hiding it from the jealous Hera. The child is Dionysus, who later rescues the shade of his mother from the underworld, and she becomes a goddess.

The story became the subject of an opera by Handel, first performed in 1744. The association of Semele with fire, both at the time of her seduction and at the time of her death, certainly explains the association of the imagery with a matchbox—serving almost as a play on the idea of igniting passions. Given the connection to Dionysus, the image certainly has associations with mothering and midwifery. The pregnant and dying Semele has her child delivered and gestated by Zeus. The myth also can be seen as illustrating the bond between mother and child, for it is Dionysus who realizes Semele's dreams of becoming a goddess. Though Handel's opera was written in the 1700s, the imagery of Semele and Zeus/Jupiter was still popular in late-nineteenth-century art; as such, the meaning of the image would have been accessible in a variety of media. The subtext of the piece, that a woman can achieve greatness through her children, would certainly resonate with those embracing the cult of true womanhood.

What furniture graced the home, we can only imagine. The number of display-worthy items suggests, however, that some amount of surface area was necessary to accommodate these things. Tabletops, cabinets, mantels, railings, and window moldings were all possible venues for display.

Children's Play

One of the responsibilities of the women in the cult of true womanhood was to nurture the individual potential of each child in a way that recognized his or her unique needs and talents. At the same time, mothers were expected to shape children into disciplined members of society, capable of self-regulation and control. To a degree, these character skills were learned through the example of the mother. In Lydia Child's 1831 *The Mother's Book*, we can see an already established emphasis on how the mother presented herself to her child. Child instructs: "The uniform gentleness, to which I have before alluded, and the calm state of the mother's own feelings, have much to do with the affections of the child" (1989:6). Representing the self-sacrifice that came to be associated with what Hays (1996) has termed "intensive mothering"(x), Child reminds women, "The care of children requires a great many sacrifices, and a great deal of self-denial; but the woman, who is not willing to sacrifice a good deal in such a cause, does not deserve to be a mother" (1989:15–16).

Play was one of the means through which children developed their characters and the skills necessary to being a successful member of society. According to Child, "something ought to be mixed with these plays to give the child habits of thought. Toys amuse him for the time; but he grows weary of them, and when he does not hear, or see them, they do not furnish anything for him to think about. But should you, while tossing a ball, stop and say, 'This ball is round; this little tea-table is square' . . . it would give him something to think about" (1989:11).

Although this work considers mothering, the activities of children are muted in the archaeological record of the Perrymans. No toys were recovered from the earlier deposit. Given the small size of the deposit, this is not especially surpris-ing. Materials thrown in the well were intentionally deposited there. Often, toys most revealing about children's activities are those lost or discarded by children themselves. Our materials from the Perrymans' house sites were recovered from subsurface features, not the scatter of odds and ends that could be expected throughout the yard area, and would be most likely to record activities that took place there, including child care and play. Further, objects that masquerade behind one function could have easily been incorporated into children's activities. The buttons recovered from the site could have been strung together as necklaces, used as counters in games, or served as eyes for cloth dolls. The sole tobacco pipe recovered from the site, which showed few signs of having been smoked, could have been used to blow soap bubbles while laundry was being washed in the yard. While we can imagine a hundred ways that mundane objects could be used by children, jumbled together in a back-filled well only the mass-produced toys speak to us of children's play and mother's supervision.

The presence of dolls is perhaps not surprising given the number of girls known to have been born into the Perryman family. The most impressive of the dolls recovered was a bisque "Floradora," manufactured by Armand Marsielle of Köppelsdorf, Germany, between 1890 and 1939. Floradora was a girl doll with a bisque shoulder head, long curly brown wig with a side part, and a red satin bow. Our specimen has blue glass eyes and rosy cheeks, and her smile reveals four upper teeth. She would have measured 21 and one-fourth inches in height (Lavitt 1983:205). The doll could have been the plaything of any number of Perryman children or grandchildren. She would have been expensive to acquire, and an impressive possession to behold, perhaps limiting the handling she received. Upon her demise, her head was dumped in the well with the rest of the trash.

One of the other dolls is a Frozen Charlotte, a small single-piece doll commonly available in the late nineteenth and early twentieth centuries. Broken limbs are all that remain of two other dolls presumably owned by the family. Two toy tea set vessels, a saucer and a teapot, were found. Children were constant occupants of the Perryman land, first as Lucrecia and Marshall built their family, then as their grandchildren and great-grandchildren were born. Any toys owned by the household would have had constant users, so only those items broken beyond use were found. The one possible exception is a lone blue clay marble found in the well. It is perfectly intact, and although small, still attractive. I wonder if it was tossed away with other trash accidentally, or perhaps sent on its way by a mischievous owner. I suspect it would have made a satisfying "plop" as it hit the water. Marbles have long been popular and inexpensive toys, subject to many children's imaginings. They could also be used insidiously as teaching devices. Child (1989:15), for instance, cited marbles as a means of introducing arithmetic to children, for they could be encouraged to count the objects.

It is easy to dismiss toys as a peripheral category of artifacts, yet toys have much to tell us about dominant ideologies and the ways they manifest themselves in the worlds of children. Toys are laden with multiple meanings regarding gender, work, class, and race. For instance, at Oakley Plantation, I found that the planter family gave the children of their African-American domestics many of the children's toys. Playing at tea, therefore, had the insidious overtone of preparing the Freeman children for a life of servitude (Wilkie 2000a:149–151).

In contrast, much of Lucrecia Perryman's family consisted of semi-skilled workers who had avoided domestic service positions. Lucrecia's grandchildren who did become involved in service positions as laundresses were able to take their work out of white homes. In this setting, the presence of toy tea sets is probably more reflective of the family's aspirations for class mobility and the sanctity of the role of motherhood. Nonetheless, in their baby dolls the children saw a reinforcement of whiteness as the ideal of beauty. As we shall discuss further on, however, these ideals do not seem to have been reinforced on the canvas of the black bodies within the households.

Activists recognized the possible psychological impacts of black children playing with white dolls, and by 1911, the National Negro Doll Company of Nashville, Tennessee, was advertising in the *Crisis*. "Your child would be happy," the ad proclaims, "if it had a Negro doll such as are sent out by the National Negro Doll Company. . . . Every race is trying to teach their children an object lesson by giving them toys that will lead to higher intellectual heights. The Negro doll is calculated to help in the Christian development of our race" (*Crisis* 1911:174). The dolls ranged from 50 cents to $8.50, which made them easily accessible to only the more affluent African-American families.

The expense of these dolls is indicative of a trend about which W. E. B. Du Bois voiced his concerns in a 1922 issue of the *Crisis*:

> Grown ups think of little children as "cunning," "pretty," "cute" and amusing. The new mother dresses them up like living dolls, in ribbons, frills and furbelows, and with many a "Don't get dirty" "keep out of the mud," "Be careful," "Naughty, naughty" she proceeds to impress it upon the one-year-old that the chief end of man is to be an impossible prig. Our jails are full of children who were once unbelievably cunning. Thus with overdressing and "showing off," our children are spoiled. This is particularly the case with groups like American Negroes of the better class who are striving to improve their conditions and push their children up and up. (Du Bois 1922:247)

At the heart of Du Bois's editorial seems to be concern that the African-American middle class is being seduced by material privilege associated with their position, and being distracted from the quest for racial improvement. I think that this editorial is important in that it highlights African-American activists' articulation with the cult of domesticity being as much about the reconstitution of the view of black mothering as it was about anything else.

Beauty Ideals and Bodily Presentation

Personal discipline and bodily sacrifice marked Victorian culture, and were hallmarks of the white middle class. Control of the body is perhaps most pronounced in Victorian dining etiquette. According to John Kasson (1987), Victorian dining

Table 4.9 Personal Hygiene–Related Artifacts from 1911 Well

Type	Brand	Minimum Number of Vessels Recovered
Cologne bottle	Lazell's Perfumes, New York	3
Cologne bottle	Ed Pinaud, perfumers, Paris	1
Cologne bottle	Colgate Perfumers, New York	1
Cologne bottle		2
Toilet water	Colgate and Company, New York	1
Toilet water	Ponds	1
Toilet water		1
Deodorant	Mum Mfg Co. Phila, Pa.	3
Ointment		4
Skin cream	French Gloss	1
Hair cream	Seven Sutherland Sisters Hair Grower	1

was an event in which "diners sought to cloak their bodily needs and invest the occasion with dignity by distancing themselves from organic processes. Symbolic demonstrations of bodily control testified to their commitment to social order and constraint"(135). Personal presentation required that similar control be exercised over biology, and hygiene was an arena in which Victorian ideals held strong sway. Sixteen glass containers recovered from the Perryman well once held colognes, cold creams, and deodorant (Table 4.9). Lazell's Perfumes, of New York, was the most popular identified brand, represented by three bottles. The deodorant "MUM," which promised to remove odor from perspiration, was also represented by three examples. I will discuss these items again relative to their possible role in midwifery practice, but they deserve further consideration here as well. Given the number of these products advertised in black periodicals of the time, noticeably missing from the assemblages are products related to the bleaching of skin or hair straightening.

Perhaps no artifacts recovered from African-American sites demonstrate the complexities of ethnogenesis and ethnoracial assignation better than those related to hair straightening and skin bleaching (Mullins 1999; B. Williams 1992). These objects represent the pressure imposed on African Americans (for a variety of reasons) to alter their very physical being in order to better navigate the social-political and economic landscapes in which they lived. Products such as Hinds Honey and Almond Cream, Nadinola Cream, Bleaching Black and White Cream, a variety of lye-based hair products, and hot combs have been recovered from African-American urban historical sites (Gums 1998:69–71; Mullins 1999; Wheaton and Reed 1990), though not from the Perrymans' well.

Skin lighteners and hair straighteners have long polarized the African-American community. One of the foci of the hair controversy was Madame C. J.

Walker, founder of an empire of hair care, which included hair growers, restorers, the hot comb, and a chain of beauty parlors. Walker asserted that her intent had been to improve scalp health among African-American women so that they could experience the growth of longer, thicker hair (Giddings 1984:188–189). While Walker's intent may have been to provide opportunities for black women to achieve greater beauty, some of the black community questioned the motives of women who used straighteners and bleachers.

In a 1904 essay in the *Voice of the Negro*, Nannie H. Burroughs condemned hair straightening and skin bleaching among African-American women. "Many Negroes have colorphobia as badly as the white folk have Negrophobia. You say this is not true. Then, what does this wholesale bleaching of faces and straightening of hair indicate? From our view it simply means that the women who practice it wish they had white skin and straight hair"(277). Men, argues Burroughs, are partly to blame for this circumstance, for "the white man who crosses the line and leaves an heir is doing a favor for some black man who would marry the most debased woman, whose only stock in trade is her color, in preference to the most royal queen in ebony" (277). Women, she advises, should spend more time improving themselves rather than worrying about their appearance. "Putting in modern improvements may enhance the value of a house, but putting on modern improvements by straightening hair and bleaching faces will not enhance the value of any real woman" (278).

Yet, magazines and newspapers that targeted African-American consumers were filled with advertisements for these products. *Half-Century Magazine*, devoted to developing the domestic spirit of African-American women, noted that it would not accept advertisements from "Clairvoyants, Fortune-Tellers, Saloons, Intoxicating Liquors, Get-Rich-Quick Oil Mills or Mining Stocks, Buffet Flats, or Pictures ridiculing Colored People," but it did include advertisements for skin bleachers and hair straighteners. In the same issue of *The Voice of the Negro* that published Burrough's essay, advertisements for Hair Grower can be found.

Whether arising from what bell hooks (1992, 1994) has referred to as a failure of African Americans to see themselves outside of the lens of white racism and to resist allowing their minds to be colonized by white values, or simply a recognition that lighter skin and straighter hair provided certain advantages, a demand for these products existed. The prevalence of eugenic thinking in American society reinforced among the white community the notion that lighter skinned African Americans were biologically and intellectually superior to darker skinned persons. Writing in *Half-Century Magazine* in 1918, M. A. Majors comments, "We grant that a people long regarded by reason of a light skin to be better than those of a dark skin, are better by reason only of a difference in superior environment, which also helps to urge the individual or race so blessed to entertain nobler attributes, and to lessen the tendency toward hopelessness and misery" (16).

Incentives for using these products varied (and the reader is directed to I. Banks 2000 for a fuller discussion of hair treatments), including a desire to give the appearance of accommodating to white beauty values, or to appropriate white beauty characteristics as a means of resistance. Some women interviewed by Ingrid Banks (2000) saw these products as allowing the consumer greater freedom to adopt a variety of fashionable hairstyles, not as any endorsement or rejection of African-American beauty.

Despite having white dolls, the women of the Perryman family apparently did not feel compelled to alter their skin or hair. In part because of the employment in which they worked—whether as laundresses, midwives, or mothers—they were able to avoid the kinds of service positions that would have placed them in extended contact with white employers. Domestic workers often felt pressured, as many professional African-American women today do, to straighten their hair while in the white-dominated workplace (I. Banks 2000). It could be suggested, delicately, that the Perrymans may not have needed these products, for there is some documentary evidence to suggest that at least part of the family was considered from time to time to appear mulatto. Yet, I would counter that it is this very reason why we might expect to find bleaching products at the site—if already fair, a person could expect even greater results from the products. Similarly, based on information available about the men and women the Perryman children married, there is no evidence that they attempted to marry only within a particular color caste. With the number of women living at the site, if regular use of bleaching products was occurring I would expect there to be some archaeological evidence of it.

As it is, there is only one product that may be related to racialized perceptions of beauty: Seven Sutherland Sister's Hair Grower. African-American hair was often portrayed in the media as unable to grow as long as European hair (Giddings 1984), so it is possible that this product could have been used in this way. The product's advertising pictures the long flowing tresses of the Sutherland Sisters. Unlike products such as Thomas' Magic Hair Grower, or East India Hair Grower, which specifically targeted African-American consumers, this product was not promoted in this way. Hair growers were as commonly used by men as women, and for treating baldness and thinning, not just hair length. Unlike products specifically sold as straighteners or bleachers, this product's implications are rather ambiguous and fail to provide much insight.

Domesticity and Motherhood in the House of Perryman

We have now toured the Perryman house, examined the family's medicine cabinet, observed their children's toys, interrogated their china, and stolen a glance in their pantry—but what have we learned? Or, at least, what do we think we have learned? It would be easy to interpret the seeming conformance to white middle-class etiquette in dining and beverage service and household decor to an appropriation on the part of the Perrymans of that social class's trappings, to assert their right to be recognized as equal citizens. Or perhaps we could interpret these practices as evidence of materialistic ambitions to accumulate wealth following the deprivations of enslavement. Indeed, these are valid interpretations, and have been suggested by other archaeologists for other sites. My purpose in presenting dialogs that shaped African-American activism, however, was to suggest another, perhaps more subtle possibility for the nature of these practices, that of the reconstruction of the image of black womanhood and motherhood.

If we consider the evidence spread before us, the archaeology suggests that the Perryman family adopted some practices of the middle class, but ignored others. In some cases the omissions are little things, for instance, using mismatched glasswares for communal vessels rather than a completely matching set. What the middle class communicated through its use of matched sets was multifaceted: the matched sets conveyed a sense of wealth—in a world of rapidly changing fashions, families were able to purchase entire sets of china that met the requirements of the most recent trend. The uniformity of the sets conveyed order and discipline and, in the context of family dining, the corporate nature of the family. In each of their sets of china, no matter the cost of one set relative to another, they consistently selected plain-bodied, white or off-white ceramics. Within white middle-class circles, these plain wares communicated the sanctity of the hearth, home, and family. While the greatest evidence of colorful design on ceramics was found in the Perryman teawares, even in this category of vessel, white vessels predominated. Although middle-class households were increasingly turning to *à la Russe* service, which entailed plates being brought pre-prepared to the table (Kasson 1987:135), the number of service vessels, such as tureens and serving bowls, recovered from the Perryman site suggest that the Perrymans still shared their meals "family style." Tablewares are not the only arena in which the Perrymans adopted predominant symbols of the cult of true womanhood. The Rebecca at the Well teapots be speak the family's engagement with another powerful symbol of domesticity.

In what little evidence we have regarding the culinary practices of the family, there is little to suggest that they were involved in the consumption of exotic food products. If anything, there is some evidence that the family ate regionally available foods, including fish and oysters, which had developed negative associations among some African-American middle-class families (Mullins 1999). Abstinence from the consumption of alcohol, a choice common among white middle-class families and some black elite, does not seem to be the Perrymans' choice. Similarly, the family did not leave any evidence to suggest they engaged in altering their bodies to look more phenotypically white, thus ignoring another convention of the white middle class, which emphasized the necessity of pearly white skin for its women (Peiss 1998).

It may be tempting to suggest that the décor of the house attests to middle-class ambitions and sensibilities, yet here again, the focus of decorative objects seems to be as much directed toward communicating values of domesticity and motherhood as on anything else. Even the decision to decorate could be seen as a mothering decision. For instance, in 1906, Fannie Barrier Williams wrote, "I sometime feel a heartache for many of our young people because they have so few inspirations that lift them up above the vulgar things of life. Their tastes are formed out of surroundings and experiences that do not make for morality and high living" (213). The creation of a nicely decorated home that featured pieces of art, or mundane objects decorated with classical scenes, would have served to construct an enriching and nurturing environment for one's family.

In looking at the materials recovered, first from the 1885 deposit, and then from the 1911 well, we can see continuities in the family's performance of domesticity and womanhood. During Marshall's lifetime, Lucrecia and Caroline Bowers were living a role that many African-American women of their time, and they themselves during enslavement, would have envied—that of full-time mother. The materials that surrounded the Perrymans in everyday acts of life seem to reify that opportunity in ways familiar to similarly situated white women. After Marshall's death, the mothering role was transformed for both of these women. For Lucrecia, the loss of both of her male providers required her to enter the workforce to support her young children and grandchildren. Caroline's family was also supported by her brother and stepfather, and eventually, she and her own husband split. The untimely death of her sister introduced new children to the households. With her mother working outside the home for the first time in more than a decade, Caroline was probably responsible for much of the care of her youngest siblings and nephews, in addition to her own son. While the nature of changes in their lives differed for the two women, the outcome was the same. Each of them found their role expanding from mothering for their children to motherwork for their broader community.

Narrative Interlude III

Christine Freeman

260 Washington Street, Turnerville, Mississippi
Interview Date: May 19, 1937
Interviewed by: Hazel Neumann

"Come in, Come in! I heard there was a lady going around asking about the old days! I'll help you best I can. But you better sit down, it's hot outside!" Mrs. Freeman enthusiastically waves me into her parlor. Her house is located in one of the poorer Negro sections of Turnerville, down the street from one of the local churches. Her yard is neatly swept, and flowers decorate her porch. Her house is of the shotgun style, with three rooms in a line, front to back. She has me sit in a well-used but comfortable chair in the front room and brings me a cup of tea. It is hard to guess how old she is, for she is very spry. If her estimate of being at least 25 years old when freedom came is correct, she is 97 years old. I start off as I start all my interviews, and ask her where she was born.

"I was born in Louisiana, south of here on a plantation called Bayou Landing. We never saw the owner, he lived somewhere else. Just an overseer ran our place. It was a large cotton plantation off the Mississippi River. We could watch the steamboats come up and down the river, going to or from New Orleans." She closed her eyes, as if she were seeing the past in her mind. "Those plantations had been growing cotton so long that the soil was giving up, the war just hurried them on their way. It was after the war that my husband and I moved north to Jackson, where he had a sister. We made a lot of friends there, but city life required too much of your time be someone else's, so we decided to sharecrop outside Turnerville after a few years. Now my church helps pay my expenses and makes sure I get plenty to eat. One of my daughters lives here in town and helps me too. The others are spread out all over. I worked in the fields as a young woman. When the fields are full of cotton, it looks just like snow. It would be pretty unless you know you have to pick it."

She paused, presenting me her fingertips to examine.

"Do you know I have no feeling left in my finger tips after all those years of picking cotton? The plants have sharp barbs that tear up your fingers, but you can't stop because they give you a quota to make. Women always were expected to pick more than men on account of our small hands."

I asked her if she had been married as a slave. She lit up at this question,

"Oh, honey, I was a lucky girl. There was a handsome young man who was sold to our place when I had just become grown. He was called Jamaica Joe, 'cause he had been born in the islands. He had the smoothest skin, and the darkest eyes and hair. He was strong, one of the best field workers, and always helped the slower and weaker workers. One day, I had to go to the field with a fever. It had come on me quickly, and I didn't have time to take a tea to break it. It was picking time, and the overseer was feeling particularly fierce. He told us whoever picked the least cotton would take 25 lashes. I worked and worked, but my eyes couldn't see right, and I felt so poorly I could hardly stand. I barely filled my sack that day, and I was dragged out of the line to take my lashes. Joe stepped forward and said he would take my 25 lashes and 10 more if the overseer would let him take my place. He did. We nursed each other and decided to get married. We lived together 50 years before he died."

She stood up and carried a framed photograph that had been sitting on the table next to her. "Here's my Jamaica Joe." The picture showed a 40-something man, of fine features and well-dressed. Mrs. Freeman gently laid her hand on my shoulder, "I hate to pry, but it seems to me that you are adding to your family." I must have blushed, for she laughed and said, "Honey, there's a ring on your hand, no shame in that." She returned to her seat.

"Joe and I had nine children, five in slave times and four after. I am happy to say that five are still living. It is an awful thing to bury a husband, but worse to bury a child. I intend to leave this earth soon enough that they are around to bury me and tend my grave."

I haven't yet talked to any informants about what it was like to give birth during slavery, so I asked,

"Who attended you when you had a baby in slave times?"

"On our place there was an old African woman who caught all the babies. She delivered the first three of my babies. Her daughter took over after her death, and delivered the rest—even the ones after freedom. There weren't any doctors that helped with births in those days. I can't imagine having a man there for something like that. Are you using a doctor or a granny?" I told her that I would be going to the hospital for my baby's birth. She seemed skeptical.

"Why do you need a hospital? You're not sick, just having a baby." To divert the conversation away from me, I asked her what would happen during a midwife birth.

"Well, the first time is always the scariest, because you don't know what is coming. All of your friends and family who have babies get you pretty worked up and worried with all their stories. Living close together in the quarters, you could hear the hollering when someone was giving birth. Some women really like to holler so everyone knows what they're doing, other women keep it to themselves. Some say if you yell too much during birth you'll have a colicky baby. Once the pains are coming on regular, the midwife comes. I was pretty worried with my first one. I didn't have kin on the plantation except for Joe, and the midwife did not want him in the room. She rubbed on me with tallow so I wouldn't tear, and walked me around to keep the contractions moving, but I was so upset and scared that she was afraid they would stop coming. The old midwife left me in the cabin, crying and fussing, and went to get a hat from Joe. When she came back, she set this big old sweaty field hat of his on my head and said, "That will make you feel better."

Well, Joe was a big man, and his hat kept falling over my eyes as I walked around. Suddenly, it came to me in my mind's eye how I must have looked. Here's this naked woman, wearing out the floorboards, walking in circles, with a smelly hat drooping over her nose. I started to giggle, then I started to laugh—big belly laughs that made the contractions seem to get stronger. It was a few minutes before I could stop, but when I did, I felt much better and ready to have that baby. I later found out that the midwife had slipped an old ax under my mattress while I was distracted. I don't know which really worked, the ax or the hat, but after that I had new strength. I had that baby squatting over the floor, and after a good dose of castor oil, pushed out the afterbirth with no trouble. I was able to stay with my baby for the first week without going out to the fields. You can't imagine how good that feels to a poor body that's been slaving in the fields and then has a baby. I had no problems with my other children; I knew what to expect. I always kept a hat of Joe's with me, just so I didn't lose my sense of humor."

May 20, 1937

Dear Peter,

   Now that your spring term is nearly over, you are probably more aware of my absence. I look forward to you visiting me at the end of the month. I wonder what you will think of Turnerville and our riotous cultural scene. I have become comfortable with the quiet rhythms of daily life in this place, although I have been here for just a short time. How quickly one falls into routines.

   My interviews now have a purpose. I met with a wonderful woman yesterday; although she has lived most of a century, her mind was sharp, and she spoke in poetry. She noticed my "condition," which means others will shortly as well. I do not see my field supervisor with great regularity, so perhaps my secret will remain mine a while longer. It was my "condition," however, that encouraged this woman to talk about her own experiences of marriage and childbirth. I think you would have been fascinated as well to hear her stories of African birth attendants and folk practices. I realized, listening to her, that most of my understanding of slave mothers' experiences comes from Harriet Beecher Stowe and other abolitionist-motivated authors. Perhaps in some small way I can help this part of slavery be recorded. After all, is not part of the goal of this Writer's Project to record the ex-slaves' versions of the past? I also feel like delving further into the folk beliefs could be something I can draw upon as a writer.

   I am grateful, dear, that you helped secure me this position, and cannot wait to discuss the experience with you in person.

Your loving wife,
Hazel

5

Midwifery as Mother's Work

African-American midwives could be described as the symbolic mothers of their communities. Several researchers have equated their positions and influence within their communities as equivalent to that enjoyed by minister (S. Smith 1995). The prestige they held was not arbitrary, for midwives literally held the community's future in their hands. Pregnancy and childbirth were often viewed in the nineteenth century as a frightening but inevitable and natural condition of women's lives. The woman who had never lost a friend or relative in childbirth was rare (Leavitt 1986). Women approached births with concern and, sometimes, fatalism (Faust 1996). While other women friends and relatives might be present and provide support during a birth, it was ultimately the midwife who directed and facilitated labor and delivery. Birth had been a woman's business, experienced by women, and overseen by women, so while modern pundits might view statistics showing that African-American lay midwives had overseen 50 percent of all births in the United States during 1910 as alarming (Ladd-Taylor 1988:255), a woman about to deliver would have been comforted to know that her midwife had safely supervised a multitude of deliveries or that she had overseen possibly even her mother's births.

When Lucrecia Perryman became a midwife following Marshall's death, if her experiences were like those of other women, it was not a decision made of her head, but of her heart and faith. Women were called to midwife, called to catch babies and comfort mothers. It was not a field, despite accusations to the contrary by the white medical community, which offered much financial security. Midwives served families least able to pay, taking payment in whatever form was available, if they were paid at all. Often, as was the case for Alabama midwives Onnie Logan and Katherine Smith, women called to midwifery were the daughters or granddaughters of midwives. Logan's grandmother had midwifed during enslavement, and her mother midwifed when Logan was a child. Smith's grandmother had also been a midwife, and in their autobiographies, both women proudly recounted the successes their ancestors had achieved through their skill and faith in God.

Midwifery is a powerful example of what Patricia Hill Collins (1994) has termed "motherwork." "Work for the day to come is motherwork, whether it is on behalf of one's own biological children, or for the children of one's own racial ethnic community, or to preserve the earth for those children who are yet unborn" (48). Molly Ladd-Taylor (1988) has described midwifery as "an extension of maternal responsibility, passed through generations" (255). Midwifery was the motherwork of creating mothers.

For African-American women living in the rural South after Emancipation through at least the 1950s, if you were having a baby, the likelihood was that you would be seeing a midwife. Although the popular press and sentiment had come to favor hospital births, the reality was that hospitals were few and far between, expensive, and, in many cases, off-limits to the black community (Ladd-Taylor 1988; Dougherty 1982; Susie 1988). Onnie Logan (1989) recalled, "I don't remember a single doctor deliverin a black baby at home. Not in my whole life. Cause if they sent for him the baby woulda been there and probably some of em walkin before he got there" (59). African-American midwives, or "grannies," as they were often called in the black community, provided pregnant women of both black and white races with experienced, patient-oriented, inexpensive home births. African-American midwives learned their medical knowledge through apprenticeships with older active midwives. A woman was not recognized as a midwife until she had witnessed, assisted, and, finally, supervised the birth of numerous babies. In contrast, many medical students during the late nineteenth and early twentieth centuries graduated as obstetricians without having witnessed (let alone supervised) a single birth (Susie 1988:1).

In addition to their medical expertise, midwives were bearers of cultural and communal standards. Midwives linked generations of families, often delivering the children of children they had delivered. By virtue of delivering a woman's child, the midwife became a recognized member of the family; children were raised recognizing the woman who had supervised their birth, often referring to them with an honorific title like auntie (Dougherty 1982; M. Campbell 1946). Women who became midwives often did so as a spiritual calling from God. For all these reasons, midwives were considered pillars of their communities, in addition to the esteem in which they were held for their medical specialization (Clement, Grunden, and Petarson 1999; Coe 1995).

Midwives, through their apprenticeships to older women, created a cross-generational chain of magical and medical continuity. Typically, a woman was called to midwifery after she had raised her own children and was beyond childbearing years herself (Coe 1995; Susie 1988). It was not unusual for a woman to begin her career in midwifery in her forties or fifties, and women in their eighties were reputed to be actively working as midwives. Given their long careers, midwives also linked generations of families, often delivering the children of children they had delivered (Susie 1988; M. Campbell 1946), thereby providing cultural and structural continuities within the African-American community. Midwives passed important cultural knowledge from one generation of women to another.

Midwives did not merely "catch babies," but trained women to be mothers. In the postpartum period, midwives would spend extensive amounts of time with the new mother, sometimes actually living with her, teaching her how to feed, clean, and care for the baby (Susie 1988). Magical and medical rituals protected the infant from disease and malevolent spirits (M. Campbell 1946). In teaching the basics of motherhood, midwives actively modified the traditions of one generation to suit the new realities of the next, combining cultural conservatism and innovation in their practices (M. Campbell 1946; Susie 1988). It was the ability of midwives to meet the changing needs of new generations that encouraged continuities in cultural practices and beliefs.

Midwives' medical practices were situated within African-American traditions of diagnosis and treatment. Health was perceived as balance maintained—balance in the blood that ran through a person's veins, balance in the person's spiritual and personal life. High blood, or blood that was too hot, or blood that was low, or running cold, or blood that was dirty or infected, would cause disorders of the nerves, head, stomach, lungs, or kidneys. Bad blood between people could also lead to illness as well, in the form of spiritually inflicted harm. Spiritually inflicted harm could take natural forms, such as nervousness, fatigue, weight loss, or sexual dysfunction; or more dramatic forms, such as infestations of animals, as evidenced by rashes, welts, swellings or lumps, or in the most disturbing form, creatures visibly moving under the skin in the main body cavity or the arms and legs (H. Mathews 1992a; Hyatt 1973). Like other African-American healers, midwives mediated between the physical and metaphysical concerns of their clients, employing a combination of motherwit, medicinal herbs, and sympathetic magic. To those outside of the ethnomedical system, this combined approach to healing was characterized as superstitious and backward, charges that ultimately helped the medical profession to outlaw lay midwifery. To the clientele of midwives, be they black or white, the midwive's practices conformed to the reality of the world they experienced, and to ignore the health of the spirit would have been a disservice. Spiritual oppositions were an intrinsic part of life—arising from family tensions, marital disputes or community discord. These were social relations necessary for survival among the impoverished populations that accounted for much of the midwife's clients, who turned to family and community members for access to food, goods, mutual support, and comfort as a matter of everyday practice.

The greatest spiritual antagonism that existed was that between man and woman. In Harry Middleton Hyatt's (1973, 1974) comprehensive series of interviews with conjurers during the early twentieth century, conflicts between the sexes were the most commonly described problem they were called upon to solve. Attempts to keep a mate, leave a mate, and ensure a mate's fidelity were described at great length.

In conjuring, men and women were spiritually distinct, and could render control over one another (in favorable and unfavorable ways) through the manipulation of personal belongings or bodily fluids, with seminal fluid and menstrual blood being the most powerful. In essence, those in most intimate contact were the best situated to harm one another. Hyatt, in his study of conjurers, found literally hundreds of spells and rituals related to the control of one's spouse or lover. For instance, a woman's menstrual blood, mixed in her lover's food or drink, once ingested, would leave him impotent with any other woman (1973:2501). Similarly, burying a woman's exuvia in a teacup near her doorstep would render her unable to leave her mate (1974:3012). While charms and rituals could be highly idiosyncratic, based on the personal style of the conjurer involved, an underlying "grammar," so to speak, of substances and materials seem to be linked in reproductive magic (Wilkie 2000b).

Cow feet and hooves, the color blue, Vaseline, perfume, sulfur, hats, coins, and bottles were (and sometimes still are) employed in many instances involving issues of sexuality or reproduction. A woman wishing to attract a man can do so by dousing his hatband with perfume (Hyatt 1973:2663), whereas a man can make a woman fall in love with him by wearing her hair in his hat. The importance of the hat could be derived from several of its attributes. Its location on the wearer's head means that the hat band will absorb sweat, a very personal fluid. The hat also sits on the head. Individuals gifted as conjurers are said to be double-sighted, with the second pair of invisible eyes situated over the visible ones, in the forehead. As such, the head is a powerful part of the body.

The color blue, most typically discussed in archaeological literature for its protective powers (Stine et al. 1996), is often associated in conjuring literature with the pursuit or repelling of love. Blue stone, blue candles, and blue bottles are often used in spells intended to draw, repel, reignite, or extinguish love. Blue is strongly associated with the *orisha* Yemalia, often represented as the Virgin Mary, who is the Yoruba diety of motherhood, love, and water (R. Thompson 1983).

Vaseline, a popular brand of petroleum jelly, was a common component of magical cures for impotency and venereal disease. Tea brewed from cows' hooves and sulfur could be used to take away or restore a man's ability. Often, these different ingredients could be found in combinations; Hyatt (1973), for instance, recorded a cure for venereal diseases that called for "sulfur, Vaseline, castor oil, and blue stone to be boiled together in a salve" (2026). It is important to note that cures such as these combine a holistic approach to medicine, and many treatments presented by conjurers as treatments for spiritually caused illnesses contained ingredients that treated physical as well as psychological symptoms.

Angela Davis (1998) has explored the musical tradition of the blues as a site where women could engage in discourses revolving around their newfound individualism, particularly as related to their ability following Emancipation to control, celebrate, and explore their own sexuality. While Davis has demonstrated that blues is one record of how these new freedoms engendered tensions between the sexes among the working classes, I would suggest that an exploration of spiritual tensions between the sexes, as mediated by conjurers, is another such site and deserves to be the focus of further scholarship.

While conjurers often dealt with men and women engaged in discord, midwives more typically engaged in acts that reinforced the complementary nature of men and women, and used that complementariness to bring strength to women undergoing the transformative and dangerous event of birth. The complementary nature of men and women was even discussed by members of the African-American middle class, as a means of justifying the embrace of the public private sphere dichotomy by African-American families. The following musings of Anna Julia Cooper (1892) on differences between the genders could be ascribed to the spiritual realms as well:

> All I claim is that there is a feminine as well as masculine side to "truth" that these are related not as inferior and superior, not as better and worse, not as weaker and stronger, but as complements—complements in one necessary and symmetric whole . . . that both need to be worked into the training of children, in order that our boys may supplement their virility by tenderness and sensibility, and our girls may round out their gentleness by strength and self-reliance. (60)

Midwives recognized the importance of the convergence of male and female spiritual powers at the time of birth, and sought through a variety of practices to draw on these complementary powers. Following birth, midwives engaged with the spiritual world on the behalf of the infant, trying to ensure its protection from malevolent forces. As we shall see, material objects like hats, blue glass bottles, castor oil, and Vaseline, used by conjurers for mediating gender tensions, were also employed by midwives. Examples of these very items are present at the Perryman site. Because midwifery was a vocation more than a profession, many of its practitioners were devout, religious women of great faith. Many believed that God guided their hands through difficult deliveries (e.g., Dougherty 1978; Susie 1988; M. Campbell 1946; Logan 1989) and that delivering babies was in His service. As such, the use of a nurturing spiritual power for the benefit of mothers and children would have also been possible only through His will.

Sources Available about African-American Midwives

Though midwives were important individuals within the African-American community, little unbiased historical information is available about them and their practices. The American Medical Association (AMA) targeted midwifery for extermination during the early twentieth century, spreading misinformation about the supposed inabilities and malpractices of traditional midwives. By the 1920s, most midwives had to be licensed by the state in which they practiced and were strictly controlled in how they practiced. Many midwives retired in disgust, and the apprenticeship system, which had perpetuated the training of midwives since the period of enslavement, disappeared (Mathews 1992a).

Oral histories collected from midwives largely post-date the period of licensing, when women were afraid to discuss traditional practices or felt that they had to decry the old ways to protect their licenses (Coe 1995; M. Campbell 1946; Mathews 1992a). Perhaps one of the more valuable studies is Beatrice

Mongeau's (1985) dissertation research into North Carolina midwives. Although her dissertation was not completed until 1979 (and became available on microfilm in 1985), her field research was conducted in the 1960s. Her research demonstrates that midwives were actively contesting many aspects of regulatory control and documents pre-regulation practices. In her study of memories of Virginia midwifery, Gertrude Fraser (1998) found, "by keeping the history of midwives and the experiences of homebirths on the periphery of public memory, residents protected it from scrutiny while guarding their ambivalence about what had become stigmatized traditions and experiences" (7). There is adequate evidence available to suggest that even after regulation, midwives sought to maintain as many traditional practices as they were able (Ladd-Taylor 1988; Dougherty 1978, 1982; Mongeau 1985). Today, traditional African-American midwifery continues only in isolated areas of the rural South (Fontenot 1994).

A limited number of oral history interviews are available describing the experiences of midwives who worked in the American South, including two narratives of Alabama midwives. Onnie Lee Logan, who worked as a midwife in Mobile County, Alabama, from 1947 to 1984, told her story to Katherine Clark, and the book was published in 1989. Later midwifery experiences in Alabama were recorded in the life experiences of Margaret Charles Smith, whose story was published in 1996. Smith had worked as a midwife in the town of Eutaw, and throughout Greene County, Alabama, from 1949 until 1981. All of these women were working during the period after regulation was in effect. Their stories do, however, provide some insight into the kinds of practices that were common before regulation. Likewise, ex-slave narratives and other ethnographic sources provide some references to women's birthing experiences. It is from these sources and the archaeological materials that we will now consider the rhythms and events that marked the career of an African-American midwife.

The Call to Midwifery

Within African-American communities, healers of greater age often commanded more power and respect, as accumulated experience translated into greater knowledge. Hyatt's interviews (as well as the ex-slave narratives) contain various references to healers of more than 100 years of age. Some healers certainly played upon this circumstance by exaggerating their age. It is worth noting that Lucrecia Perryman was listed as increasingly older beyond her years in the U.S. censuses gathered while she was a midwife.

Though these strategies may have enhanced one's prestige in the community one served, it would ultimately be used to justify the elimination of midwives. In white society, with the increasing emphasis on scientism and modernity, the new and the most recent were privileged over the tried and true. Many of the calls to outlaw African-American midwifery in the 1920s quoted a fictional midwife who claimed "she was too old to cook or clean, but could still catch babies" (Susie 1988).

Midwives before regulation learned their trade through apprenticeship to an older, established midwife. An apprentice would accompany her mentor, assist with births, and direct births under the midwife's supervision. Once her mentor determined her to be accomplished enough, she declared her apprenticeship to be over, freeing her to begin her own practice or, as was commonly done, assume the practice of the older woman (Dougherty 1978). Given their long careers, midwives also linked generations of families, often delivering the children of children they had delivered (Susie 1988; M. Campbell 1946), thereby providing cultural and structural continuities within the African-American community. Midwives passed important cultural knowledge from one generation of women to another. Expectant mothers often relied upon the same midwife birth after birth, and found comfort in the continuity (S. Smith 1995). Even though Lucrecia Perryman is not listed as a midwife until the 1889 Mobile city directory, she would have been practicing as an apprentice before this time.

A strong spiritual element marked the decision of women to enter midwifery and helped older midwives select apprentices. Women were drawn to midwifery because of a calling. Many attested that doing God's work of delivering babies was so important that they would do it for free. In many cases, they did, as their often cash-poor clients could not afford to pay for their services. One woman remembered her calling for Molly Dougherty (1978) "I was plowing in the field, plowing cotton, when a voice within told me he wanted me to be a midwife, to take care of mothers and babies" (151). This woman then experienced a dreamlike vision in which she learned how to develop calves and was shown by a small child how to prepare the umbilical cord. I was struck, in reading this description, both by the inclusion of the cows symbolizing the work of midwifery and by the similarity of this account to accounts by people who have experienced being born again as Christians. Dougherty reported that similar kinds of visions and knowing came to women selecting apprentices. Once called, women saw themselves as having no choice but to respond. "After I got the call, I couldn't stay home; if I knowed a woman was in labor, I was gone. I just had to be there, just had to help" (quoted in Dougherty 1978:153).

Often, being related to a midwife predisposed a woman for calling. Marie Campbell (1946), who wrote about the experiences of granny midwives in Georgia, met a woman descended from a line of midwives. "One old midwife claims a tradition of midwifery being practiced by women in her family 'all the way straight back' to their tribe in Africa where some midwife ancestor of hers was captured and sold into slavery. She brought the practice of her profession with her to America, handing it down to some close female relative, usually a daughter, in each succeeding generation" (6). Enough midwives seem to have derived authority from connections to Africa to suggest that both the time depth of the midwife's line of succession as well as her cultural authenticity were important elements of a midwife's repution.

A Note on Treatments

Accounts of pre-regulation midwifery suggest that midwives, as part of their practices, created and employed a number of traditional remedies, ranging from herbal- and animal-product teas to tonics and bitters. Onnie Logan (1989) said of her mother's midwifery practice: "In those days the doctors didn't tell em what to do. They used the old home remedies, mostly come from the Indian remedies. The midwife then would always carry her herbs that she was goin to make teas out of to give them somethin warm to drink. They made teas outa this and teas outa that and drank it all down through the times" (53). That Lucrecia Perryman produced medicines, including alcohol-based herbal remedies and possibly "food medicine," can be inferred from three types of archaeological evidence—the abundance of bulk liquor containers, the presence of knapped glass scrapers, and the faunal assemblage from the site.

Whiskey is commonly named by African-American informants and mentioned in oral histories as an important ingredient in "home remedies" (Wilkie 1996). The use of alcohol as a solvent for medicinal ingredients is common to many commercial pharmaceutical and home remedy traditions throughout the United States. In addition to the chemical properties of alcohol that make it an appropriate medicinal base, African-American informants have described at length the use of whiskey or "spirits" in a wide range of magical cures, including the creation and feeding of charms, and as elements of potions (Wilkie 1996).

Among the ceramic vessels from the site are 25 one-gallon or larger stoneware "whiskey jugs" and 25 stoneware gin bottles. A minimum of 51 liquor bottles and flasks were also recovered. All of the stoneware jugs conform in shape and style to those used in the area at the turn of the twentieth century to sell and store whiskey, and none exhibit the distinctive spout that often identifies molasses jugs. While it is impossible to know whether these items were acquired full of alcohol or if they were obtained empty and filled with another liquid, the curation of so many of these vessels suggests that Perryman stored large quantities of liquids. The limited oral historical and ethnographic materials available on pre-regulation midwifery do discuss the importance of homemade pharmaceuticals to a midwife's tool kit. In addition, midwives have been tied not just to the use of alcohol in these remedies, but also to the production of "moonshine." I encountered a woman who remembered that a midwife who practiced during the early twentieth century in North Carolina (and from whom she was descended) maintained her own still for making medicines. During Prohibition, she was able to continue her midwifery practice by providing local authorities with free "hooch." The large number of whiskey jugs curated by Perryman may be indicative of medicinal production and storage at the site. Given the number of flasks recovered in addition to the jugs, I suspect that the jug whiskey (probably of a lower quality) was used in the medicinal practice, whereas the flasks were used for family consumption.

Among the bottles found at the site are 10 "Sauer's Extracts" bottles. Extracts, such as essence of peppermint, lemon, ginger, and vanilla, were sold both for cooking and as ingredients in medicinal remedies (Schroeder 1971:790). The presence of these bottles further suggests that Perryman was producing medicines. Peppermint, in particular, was an important ingredient in many traditional African-American magical and medical cures, and a main ingredient in the commercially manufactured "Dr. Tichenor's Antiseptic" recovered from the site. Peppermint washed on the front steps is believed to draw good luck to a house; used on the hands, it brings love and friendship; and, when added to medicinal teas, relieves a wide range of stomach disorders (Wilkie 1996b). It is, unfortunately, impossible to know which extracts were contained within the Sauer's bottles.

The probable production of home remedies by Perryman is also supported by the large number of knapped glass scrapers recovered from the well; at least 12 of these tools were found. Though oral history connects these tools to men's working of wooden agricultural implements, I have found these tools in predominantly female households whose members were not involved in agricultural pursuits (Wilkie 2000a). In addition, the greatest abundance of these tools have been recovered from sites that provide little evidence of use of commercially produced medicines, sites where the archaeology suggests that traditional medicinal production took place. Therefore, it is possible that these tools (among other known and possible uses) may be related to the processing of ingredients for medicinal teas. The scrapers would be convenient for peeling or grating roots or stems of plants. Until microwear analysis is conducted on these tools, however, their functions will remain uncertain.

There is also evidence that Perryman may have been making food medicines at the site. Faunal remains were recovered only from the well feature of the site, and the saturated conditions of that context were poorly suited to the preservation of faunal remains. Faunal materials recovered from the site were badly decayed, and in many instances bones were preserved only as a stain in the soil. Those archaeological remains that we were able to retrieve are almost exclusively from large mammals, with teeth being the most common elements recovered. Given such poor preservation, the faunal assemblage from the well is probably not representative of the range of dietary habits of the Perryman family. Some trends visible in the evidence are worth noting, however.

Animal bone was identified, when possible, by element or portion of element and species. Comparative zooarchaeological specimens, housed in the archaeological facility of the Department of Geography and Anthropology at Louisiana State University, were used for species and element identification. When evident, butchering marks and cut marks were noted. There was no attempt made to determine the minimum number of individuals (MNI) present since the

Table 5.1 Zooarchaeological Remains from the Site

Species	Element	NISP*	MNE**
Bos taurus (cow)	cranial fragments	7	1
	mandible fragments	14	2
	teeth	24	10
	vertebra	7	2
	radius (sawn)	2	1
	distal tibia (sawn)	3	2
	rib fragments	3	1
	calcaneum	4	4
	scapho-lunar	1	1
	naviculo cuboid	2	2
	astragulus	3	3
	metatarsal	1	1
Sus scrofa (pig)	mandible fragments	3	1
	scapula	1	1
	humerus	1	1
	phalange	1	1
Gallus gallus	femur	1	1
Unid. large fish	vertebra	4	4

*NISP = number of individual specimens present.

**MNE = minimum number of elements present. This measure was used since the assemblage was so fragmentary, and because on many historical sites butchered parts, not entire animals are represented.

Perrymans would have purchased butchered cuts of meat rather than purchasing whole animals, making MNI counts irrelevant. Instead, minimum number of element counts per species were employed (Table 5.1).

A total of 278 bone fragments was recovered from the site. Of these bones, 194 fragments are probably from large mammals, but are too broken to be attributable to species or element. The unidentified bones include 100 burned fragments. Whether this burning occurred during food preparation or during depositional activities is not known.

Only 86 of the bone fragments were identifiable. Beef (*Bos taurus*) or cow constituted the largest number of identifiable bones, followed by pork (*Sus scrofa*). Some fish, bird and horse/mule bones were recovered. Noticeably absent is any chicken (*Gallus gallus*) or other barnyard fowl. Yard fowl require little supervision, little feed, and provide a reliable supply of eggs and meat. Given that Lucretia Perryman occupied a substantial piece of land, it seems likely that she would have kept some chickens and other fowl in the yard. The absence of evidence for these species may be a result of the poor preservation of faunal remains at the site.

The cuts of beef recovered from the site are at first glance suggestive of a poor diet. Beef cuts at the site were drawn, almost exclusively, from the head and lower limbs, parts with little meat. The presence of cranial elements, teeth, and fragments of mandible suggest that the Perrymans may have been boiling down cows' heads, similar to the way that pig heads are boiled to make hogs' head cheese. The vertebrae, ribs, distal femur, ulna and tibia would have carried more meat, but only the vertebral cuts could be considered decent quality cuts of meat. The cow scapho-lunars, naviculo cuboids, astraguli, phalanges, and calcanea are found at the lowest extreme of the animals' legs, and provide little in the way of meat. The presence of these foot elements could be related to Perryman's midwifery activities. One invalid's food that utilizes a cow's lower limbs is calf's foot jelly, which was made by boiling extremities to reduce the cartilage and other attached tissues to edible form.

Before the development of commercial gelatin, any molded dessert or salad relied upon the jelling properties drawn from calves' feet. In addition, calf's foot jelly was considered an "invalid's food" (Beeton 1907:1371). The gelatin was prepared by gently boiling calves' feet in water, skimming the surface when necessary, and draining the particles. The process was time consuming, but had the advantage of being prepared from cheaper cuts of meat. Related food medicines were "Beef Iron Wine," which was produced commercially (Schroeder 1970: 26), and promised to build muscle and give strength, and "beef tea," which was a brothlike preparation. Helen Campbell (1881) described the production of beef tea for convalescents as follows: "one pound of lean beef prepared as above [cut into little pieces and put into a wide-mouthed bottle]. Add a pint of cold water,—rain-water is best,—and soak for an hour. Cover closely, and boil for ten minutes; or put in the oven, and let it remain an hour. Pour off the juice, season with half a teaspoonful of salt, and use. A little celery salt makes a change" (253). As late as 1916, even pediatricians were advocating beef juice and beef tea as excellent sources of protein for infants (Grulee 1916:137–138). Lucretia may have prepared calf's foot jelly for her own consumption, as she was over 70 years of age by time the well was filled, or she may have made the jelly as a nutritional food for clients recovering from, or perhaps anticipating, childbirth. It is worth noting that these beef-derived medicines developed from the mid-nineteenth century research of Justus Von Liebig. Liebig sold a beef tea for invalids (Bagnall 1999). The use of these medicines, among others, firmly situated Lucrecia in contemporary scientific mothering discourses.

The potential use of cow products is particularly interesting in this context given the associations of cows and reproduction already noted. Cow hoof teas are known to be used to treat another female-specific complaint, menstrual cramps (Wilkie 2000b). It would appear that this animal may also be associated with other aspects of reproduction.

Interviews with midwives who worked after the period of regulation showed different reactions and relationships between midwives and older cures. Some remained convinced of the medicines' uses and continued to produce them. One of Dougherty's (1978) informants said, "Well, I know the nurses call it a superstition but I know it works" (160). In discussing their own relationship to traditional treatments after the period of regulation, Alabama midwives Logan and Smith expressed a combination of disdain and distance from the remedies, much as described by Gertrude Fraser in her study of Virginian midwifery (1998). Logan (1989) stated:

> I didn't use as much of those old remedies. I didn't use it cause really along about my time they was plenty of medicine that you could go buy. Vicks salve for fever and for colds but I always have said its made outa the same stuff that lil weed is. See all a that start comin in that you could go to the to the drugsto' or you could go to the sto' and buy it during my time. So I didn't have to deal with those home cures but I've heard of it so mech so until I know they used it in those days. I'm glad I wasn't here to have to in those times. I knew Better. Everything had improved since those times. With all of that science I didn't have to come in contact with so much of that other stuff. But you know it took me a long time. Women in those days they just beginnin to get away from it. Especially our black girls. They want to continue to do like what mother said and grandmother said. It hadn't been too long they've gotten away from all that. I can see why. I don't blame em. That's what their old grandparents brought em up on. (64–65)

In Logan's statement we see both a distancing from and a justification for the use of traditional medicine. Her attitudes are similar to those expressed by women involved in Litt's (2000) study of scientific mothering on African-American women, a subject I will explore more in a later chapter. She also illustrates the creativity of midwifery, the way that new products were used in similar ways to replace older remedies. Lucrecia Perryman's midwifery practice provides evidence of this process. As a midwife trained during the period of regulation, Logan would have learned that she could not publicly support the use of such medicines herself (at the risk of losing her license), yet at the same time, she would have found herself wanting to fill the requests of her patients. Her comments also demonstrate that birth was a multigenerational event involving women of many ages.

Margaret Charles Smith expressed similar sentiments in her consideration of traditional teas. She expressed frustration with the fact that her midwifery training, which dictated that she use no traditional remedies, was at odds with the wishes of her patients, who requested the old products. When she obliged and provided traditional remedies, other patients heard of the medicines and requested them as well. With the notoriety that came with powerful healing came the increased chance that regulatory agents would hear that she was violating the terms of her license. Smith stated: "I had to stop fooling with teas and things in labor because my name was getting out. 'Miss Margaret, how come you are not using some of that stuff you used on Emma of Lucille. She was telling me about what good stuff you had. Why don't you give me some? Fix some for me so I can get through with this baby" (Smith and Holmes 1996:99). Smith admitted that she had been practicing as a midwife for some time before she stopped dispensing traditional medicines. Midwives found themselves caught between two sets of expectations: those of the regulatory agencies, and those of their patients. They mediated between these competing demands as best they could, but because they were stripped of the power to work according to what their own experiences had taught them, they served neither group as effectively as they would have liked.

Prenatal Care and Preparations

Ideally, from a midwife's perspective, a woman would visit a midwife when she first suspected she was pregnant, and the midwife would estimate a delivery date and recommend ways for the woman to care for herself during pregnancy. Midwives complained, however women frequently did not approach them until it was time to give birth (M. Campbell 1946). Onnie Logan (1989) recognized that lack of good nutrition, little to no prenatal care, and harsh work conditions led to increased complications and mortality rates for African-American women, and disputed the notion that difficult deliveries were the fault of the midwife's. The midwife would check on her patient throughout the pregnancy, especially as the due date neared, would supervise the birth, and attend to the mother and child following the birth. They might teach a mother how to care for an infant in advance of a birth or help them sew clothing for the baby. One midwife recalled that the child would be visited daily until the cord fell off (Ladd-Taylor 1988).

Medical intervention began during the prenatal period. A number of teas and treatments were employed to make pregnant women more comfortable and to ensure a healthy pregnancy. Sourwood root and wild cherry bark tea were used to relieve body aches typically suffered by pregnant women (M. Campbell 1946:35). Black haw root tea was used to prevent miscarriage (M. Campbell 1946; Coe 1995; Logan 1989). The beef teas and jellies already discussed would have been nourishing to women plagued with morning sickness or particularly demanding pregnancies.

In addition to evidence of nutritional foods being prepared at the Perryman site, several commercially produced food medicines were recovered, including Johann Hoff's Malt Extract, and Leibig Malt Extract. While I will discuss these products again, nourishing pregnant mothers could have been one use.

Labor and Pain Management

The midwife would be sent for once contractions began. Midwives often recalled being sent for at all times of the day or night (M. Campbell 1946). During the early stages of labor, midwives engaged in what later public health officials would refer to as "fussing" (Mongeau 1985:84). "Fussing" involved beautifying a woman's body in preparation for the transformative event of birth. A woman's hair was braided and pomaded, her calves and legs oiled, her arms and groin were talcum-powdered, and her person was sprinkled with sweet water, or perfume. Mongeau (1985:84) describes "fussing items," such as Vaseline, cocoa butter,

Figure 5.1 Artifacts potentially related to "fussing" period of labor

rose water, talcum, toilet waters, pomades, face creams and sweet soaps as some of the items banned from midwives' bags following regulation. The toilet waters, perfumes, and creams I discussed in the previous chapter (Figure 5.1) could have been used in Perryman's midwifery practice as easily as by her family. "Fussing" has physiological as well as ritual functions. The rubbing, combing, and massaging would relax and comfort the mother and provide a distraction during the first stage of labor, which can go on for hours. Ritually, the body is made beautiful in anticipation of greeting the new child. Strong, positive smells can counteract any ill will or malevolent spirits that may linger in an area.

During childbirth, women were encouraged to find comfortable positions in which to labor. They were encouraged to walk around, and were usually massaged by the midwife. Baths and compresses of herbal teas were used to simultaneously relax laboring mothers and stimulate contractions. Midwives saw their participation in the actual birth process as non-intrusive, using no medical appliances and, generally, not violating the birth canal beyond the mouth of the vagina. Oils and massage were used to facilitate delivery itself. For instance, a Florida midwife described using hot water to expand the birth canal, and oils to soften the perineum (Susie 1988:185). Likewise, midwives used massage to correct problem presentations of the baby, for instance, turning a breech-positioned infant to a normal head-first delivery (Dougherty 1982).

A number of herbal teas were used to strengthen or cause contractions. Bamboo briar root was used to encourage contractions as well to expel the placenta (Smith and Holmes 1996:39). Dirt dauber tea, sometimes seasoned with pepper, was used to induce vomiting to cleanse the system and encourage contractions (Smith and Holmes 1996:47). Dogwood berries consumed during childbirth would ease the pain of contractions and facilitate birth (M. Campbell 1946:35). In Louisiana, a tea brewed from egg shells was said to ease the pain of contractions (Clayton 1990). Onnie Logan (1989) described sassafras tea, and hen feathers tea that her mother used during labor and childbirth for her patients. Regarding delivery, she said: "I'll tell you what they used to do even when they got in labor. It was big hand on givin em a big dose of castor oil. That would work their bowels off real good and bring the contractions close together. My grandmother did that. They would always use that homemade grease. They didn't have Vaseline but they had animal fat that had been cooked all the water out of" (53). Vaseline petroleum jelly was one of the more abundant products represented at the well: ten empty jars were recovered. Oral history suggests this product had many uses in midwifery, one of which being to coat the birth canal.

Cathartics were used both during labor and soon after. Some oral histories make mention of cathartics given to mothers immediately after birth to "clean the mother out and to heal her up inside" (Coe 1995:18). Castor oil was an ingredient commonly attributed by public nurses as a pre-regulation period medicine used by midwives (Doughtery 1982). A bottle of "Burnett's Cod Liver Oil" and four Castoria bottles were found among the Perrymans' refuse and could have been used to aid labor and delivery.

You might remember that a number of mineral water bottles were also recovered from the site. The prevalence of mineral water bottles in the well may reflect in part Lucretia Perryman's midwifery activities. Paul Mullins has recently argued that African-American consumption of mineral waters reflects in part a syncretism with traditional African-American beliefs regarding the curative powers of May water (the first rain waters to fall in the month of May). The curative powers attributed to mineral waters in the popular media would have been compatible with traditional beliefs, while also providing a medium for consumption that was compatible with the fashion of middle-class America (Mullins 1999). This kind of dual-focused consumerism, combining traditional needs with new means of material expression that also communicated to non–African Americans, is present in much of African-American ethnomedical practice (Wilkie 2000a). The use of commercially available May water may represent an adjustment to life in an urban, racially mixed consumer environment in which the appearance of conformity with European values and practices was necessary. Mineral waters also advertised themselves to have a cathartic effect, may have provided a gentler means to keep laboring mothers hydrated, promote the cleansing of the bowels before delivery, and perhaps speed contractions.

Midwives employed metaphysical pain relief as well, drawing upon sympathetic magic to lessen labor difficulties. Perhaps the most commonly cited example was the placement of a knife or ax under the mattress of a laboring woman to "cut the pain" (Dougherty 1982; M. Campbell 1946; Fraser 1998).

Two pocket knives were found in the well. Pocket knives, of course, are useful, multifunctional artifacts, but they could have had ritual uses, too. Both knives and axes bear power-laden meanings in African Diaspora contexts, as well, and within Santeria and Voodoo are strongly associated with the Yoruba male *Orisha Eshu-Elegba* and *Ogun* (R. Thompson 1983). The syncretized religion of Voodoo was well established throughout colonial French Louisiana, particularly New Orleans. The use of knives and axes in the context of labor and delivery may also have associations with male power, similar to that embodied in deities such as Ogun. The use of knives under mattresses is also apparently still common today in Egypt—suggesting another African or possibly Muslim origin to the practice. While the pocket knives recovered from the Perryman site were likely used in a variety of contexts and for a variety of functions, the possibility that they were used in Perryman's midwifery practice should not be discounted.

Drawing upon male power in the birth room was done in another way. Fathers, although not typically allowed to attend births, were asked to provide one of their hats for the woman to wear. One of Marie Campbell's (1946) informants was asked whether she thought the practice worked. The midwife provided an anecdote about a young unmarried woman who was giving birth to her first child. Her lover had been scared by her pregnancy and was ignoring her in favor of a woman his mother wanted him to pursue. During labor, the midwife saw the girl was having a difficult time, and left for the father's house. She insisted that the man's mother provide a hat for the girl, exclaiming, "Bad enough for a woman to bear her pains for a man that she's snoring in the face of every night but to bear them for a man that's running after a school teacher his momma picked out . . . " (113–114). After being denied, she grabbed the man's hat from a rack and marched back to the birth room. The girl safely delivered a baby boy. The story did not end there. The man came to retrieve his hat later and saw the baby. He repeatedly visited and soon asked the young mother to marry him. The midwife explained that the couple were happily expecting their second child and that their circumstances proved the midwifery practice could have powerful effects.

Campbell clearly took the story as a clever play on the hat practice having an unintended consequence leading to a happy conclusion. However, I cannot help but wonder if that midwife was employing magic to bind—intending to bring the young family together from the outset. After all, she could just as easily have placed an ax or pocket knife under the bed to ease the labor pains. Instead, she chose a hat, commonly used in spells to attract and bind, to bring the father's presence into the birth room.

Onnie Logan's (1989) autobiography also illustrates that midwives were involved in maintaining the health of their patients' relationships to their partners and recognized that sexuality was an important part of that relationship. "Mens are ready for their wives as soon as the baby come out. And I can see the point. They're ready for em. And to my idea, I declare they ought to give themselves a week. I tell em further than that cause I know they ain't gonna go as far as I say"

(121–122). Logan's comments also suggest that there may have been some proscriptions on sexual intercourse during at least some portion of the pregnancy.

Another midwife, Rosalind Stephenson, helped relationships in another way—she banned fathers from the delivery room. "I just be 'shamed that they be in there. 'Cause, see—have you seen a baby born? This way I be thinkin' the boy gonna be teasin' her. I don't be wantin' 'em to see nothin' to tease their girlfriends or their wives. We never know these men . . . make their wives hurt'em. 'Cause if [they] have a little fallin' out, he may tease that girl or his wife. And that's why I don't like 'em or want 'em in there" (quoted in M. Campbell 1946:217). This midwife ensured that whatever disruptive influences men might bring to the birthing experience were headed off, and in such a way protected mothers from needing to perform in a certain way while laboring and delivering.

Delivery often took place in a squatting or kneeling position, using gravity to aid the woman bearing down, often on the floor. Onnie Logan remembered boiling old quilts for mothers to give birth on—after regulation, public health officials deemed this practice unsanitary, preferring woman to give birth on pads of newspaper (Doughtery 1982). Before regulation, Logan also remembered midwives carrying laundry bags to hold their equipment, and sometimes tearing these apart for women to birth on. The photograph of Lucrecia Perryman from the William E. Wilson photographic collection (Figure 5.2) shows her holding such a bag. Floor births were a practice that midwives were particularly against altering following regulation (Litt 2000), and was in direct opposition to the attitude of the professionalized medical industry that a delivering woman should be passively positioned horizontally on a bed (Leavitt 1986; Litoff 1978).

Postpartum Care

Upon birth, the infant was cleaned and rubbed with Vaseline or tallow to protect the newborn's skin and keep it warm (Coe 1995). Amniotic fluid was said to be "hot" in character and to prevent the baby from breathing, so babies were quickly removed from the birth site (Dougherty 1978:155). As a prevention for sore eyes (gonococcal blindness), a mother's breast milk might be squeezed into the infant's eyes (Dougherty 1982:262). In some instances, midwives required mother and baby to live for the first days after delivery in a darkened room to protect the baby's eyes (Susie 1988; M. Campbell 1946). Special attention was given to the umbilical cord and placenta. The cord was cut and left to dry and fall off naturally (typically between day 7 and 10). The placenta was carefully burned and buried. In some cases, a tree was planted over the placenta—the growth of the tree being connected to the thriving of the child; in other cases, the location of the placenta was not revealed (M. Campbell 1946; Fraser 1998; Susie 1988).

Many midwives saw expelling the afterbirth as a more dangerous proposition than the actual delivery of the child. A number of practices for removing afterbirth were recounted. Some midwives required their patients to drink water or buttermilk to hasten the afterbirth (Dougherty 1978). Returning again

Figure 5.2 Photograph of Lucrecia Perryman, circa 1900. Courtesy of the Historic Mobile Preservation Society.

Table 5.2 Midwifery-Related Artifacts

Product/Artifact Type	Potential Use	Number Recovered
Toiletries	grooming the mother, "Fussing"	19
Food medicines (malt extracts)	supplement diet of mother, during pregnancy or postpartem, supplement infant's diet	7
Infant foods	to serve as a supplement or replacement for breast milk	2
Vaseline	coat newborn, lubricant for delivery, treat after pains	10
Cathartics: Castoria, cod liver oil, sweet oil	to clean out mother for delivery, speed contractions, delivery, after birth	10
Blue glass bottles	to blow in to deliver afterbirth	61
Vaginal syringe pipe	douche following delivery of afterbirth; to treat fallen ovaries	1
Pocket knives	to cut labor pains	2
Stoneware whiskey jugs	as a solvent for medicinal tonics	25
Pharmacy products and extracts	raw ingredients for medicinal tonics	47

to the role of the color blue in spiritual practices, within midwifery, blowing in a blue glass bottle was believed to cause the release of a retained placenta (M. Campbell 1946:35). Sixty-one blue colored bottles were recovered from the site, and certainly could have been reused in this way. Particularly intriguing from this perspective are the six blue ten-sided Phoenix mineral water bottles. The shape of the bottles combines the paneled look of the gothic—associated with mothering and womanhood in ceramic assemblages—with the blue color of Yemalia. It is tempting to wonder whether this particular mineral water bottle, with its shape and color conveying the importance of domesticity from two different cultural discourses, played a role within Lucrecia's midwifery practice, either for the use of the contents or as a breathing device.

Additional medical products may have been included in the site assemblage for their uses in midwifery (Table 5.2). In addition to the medicine bottles, several

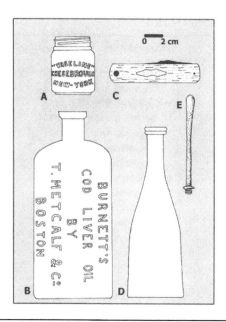

Figure 5.3 Artifacts likely to be related to Perryman's midwifery practice

additional non-traditional artifacts seem to be related to medical care: a white metal vaginal pipe (Figure 5.3), a rubber hot-water bag, and rubber tubing for a douche kit. Onnie Logan remembered using douches to treat "fallen ovaries" or "after pains" following birth. The patient was first douched with vinegar, then wrapped around the middle with an elastic band, her abdomen rubbed with lard or Vaseline, and a medicine-soaked ball of cloth was inserted vaginally and left overnight (Logan 1989).

Ritual could also mark the mother and new baby's incorporation into the community. Dougherty (1978:161) recounts a fascinating practice in Florida, in which on the first day out of bed, the mother carried the baby outdoors, walked around the house counterclockwise, and stopped at each of four corners, which were said to symbolize the four directions of the wind. This practice calls vividly to mind the Bakongo cosmogram (Figure 5.4), which represents the cycle of birth and death. The Bakongo cosmogram takes many forms in the Diaspora, and though we archaeologists are sometimes guilty of wanting to see representations of this icon everywhere, this example is particularly evocative and suggests a strong continuity in African midwifery traditions.

A child was named typically nine days after birth, during which time the parents had an opportunity to watch the child and evaluate personality and physical traits that might suggest a name (Mongeau 1985; Fontenot 1994). After this period, a midwife was usually done with her duties. But until then,

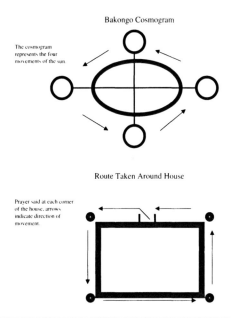

Bakongo Cosmogram

The cosmogram represents the four movements of the sun.

Route Taken Around House

Prayer said at each corner of the house, arrows indicate direction of movement.

Figure 5.4 Bakongo Cosmogram as related to birthing ritual of introduction

between the birth and the naming, midwives aided the new mothers in ways other than medical, often helping to cook and clean the house, and making sure other family members were tended to so that the new mother could rest.

Midwifery as a Living

As religious women who felt they were called to their vocation, African-American midwives often proclaimed that they would help a woman in her misery even if she could not afford to pay. Often, if received at all, pay was low. While a physician might receive no less than $50 for a delivery in the early 1900s, a midwife would charge no more than $5 to $10. Often, the midwife's clients were cash-poor, and would pay the midwife in produce, products, or promises. Lucky midwives received animals or fresh produce. One midwife described her best pay to have been the gift of a speckled hen pup that turned out to be a great bird dog that was in demand as a hunter and breeder. She estimated she netted as much as $600 from that particular birth (M. Campbell 1946:45). Most midwives were not so lucky, receiving moldy produce or worthless gifts. Another midwife recalled receiving a large china platter that was decorated with a rabbit on it. "A nice dish, but it fairly turned my stomach to eat off a platter that had a rabbit on it big as life and with some fur on" (M. Campbell 1946:46).

In contrast to the observations of Beatrice Mongeau (1985), midwives did not live a wealthy existence; in rural areas they also worked on farms for their

Table 5.3 Glass Canning Jars Recovered from the Site

Type of Sealer	Number Found
Aqua embossed, "7 61 Nov 4 6"	1
Aqua, unmarked	2
Aqua, embossed "Trademark" with picture of a man carrying a fish	1
Clear, unembossed	2
Lt. Blue, "Pat'd Feb"	1
Lt. Blue, unembossed	1
Lt. green, "Mason Pat'd Nov. 30"	1
Lt. Green. "Pat'd. Sept. 20th 1898"	1
Lt. Green, unembossed	2

livelihood, and in cities they worked often as domestics or laundresses. Despite accusations that they were unclean, midwives appear to have done much sterilizing of blankets, quilts, and sheets before and after deliveries. Working as a laundress would provide control over cleaning items related to midwifery practice. In addition, laundresses were able to work their own schedule, picking up laundry and returning it upon completion. Midwives could not anticipate when they might be called away on a birth, so working as a laundress would have provided an alternate source of income that was related to their work but provided the scheduling flexibility necessary to midwife. It is interesting to note that Lucrecia's only other occupation was that of laundress.

It is tempting to wonder if any of the objects recovered from the site represent payments for midwifery services. Any of the animal resources recovered from the well could have been received as payments. Likewise, 14 fruit sealers, or canning jars, of 13 different varieties were recovered from the site (Table 5.3). Sealers were often sold in sets, so more overlap between types might be expected if their deposition resulted primarily from the family's home canning practices. The diversity of the assemblage might suggest that these were goods received from other families as payment for services. The mix of ceramic types, particularly teacups, from the site may also reflect tokens of thanks. How much Lucrecia's midwifery practice contributed to the economy of the household is unknown. She certainly did not earn enough to pay property taxes. The incentive to midwife was not pay, but a different and greater reward.

Midwifery as Motherwork

Lucretia's calling to midwifery as a widow seems to have also arisen out of her concerns for motherhood. As a midwife, she was able to support herself transmitting the knowledge of her first and truest profession, motherhood. As we have seen, midwives did for more than oversee births. As a midwife, Lucretia would have been teaching pregnant women how to care for themselves during pregnancy, what to expect during the ordeal of childbirth, and, afterward, how to care for their newborns. After experiencing 11 pregnancies, raising numerous children, and enduring the deaths of six of her children and at least one grandchild, Lucretia was also especially able to respond empathically to women who experienced the loss of pregnancies or babies. As part of the training that Lucretia provided (if her medicinal assemblage is any gauge to measure by), she taught women to use those commercially produced medicines embraced by "good" white, middle-class mothers. Black children would have been raised on the same medicines advertised to assure white mothers of healthy, pink-cheeked cherubs. The racial ambiguity of the cherub figurines displayed in the Perryman household stated to observers that beautiful, healthy children were also within the reach and the right of black women.

Evidence of medical practice recovered from the site is intriguing on several levels. First, there is some evidence to suggest that Lucretia Perryman, like other midwives of her time, was involved in the production of medicinal remedies, presumably for use by her patients either before or during labor and delivery, or for the care of their infants after birth. If the 25 stoneware jugs are taken as evidence of this industry, it would appear that Lucretia Perryman invested a great deal of time and effort into this endeavor. Faunal remains from the site suggest that one specific medicinal product made at the site was calf's foot jelly. At the same time that Lucretia Perryman was involved in the production of traditional remedies, she was also using (and perhaps distributing or recommending) commercially produced equivalents of these medicines. The food medicines and Vaseline are examples of such equivalents.

The evidence of medicine production and commercial medicine use were drawn from a single contemporaneous deposit, thereby suggesting that commercial products were not merely used increasingly through time as substitutes for traditional remedies, but used at the same time in Lucretia's practice. In addition, Perryman seems to have incorporated non-traditional medical paraphernalia like the vaginal douche into her midwifery practice. The archaeological evidence, therefore, suggests that Perryman combined ethnomedical conservatism and innovation in her practice.

Such a combined approach to her medicine would serve Perryman well. The birth experience was one shared by the women of a household. Women of multiple family generations would attend to a laboring woman (M. Campbell 1946; Logan 1989; Susie 1988). The midwife, given her age and stature, was a tie to older generations of women in attendance. Through medicinal and magical conservatism she reinforced the values of this older generation. In addition, such conservatism would offer the older women a sense of comfort; the childbirth experiences of the younger generation remained familiar to them, neither threatening nor upsetting. At the same time, through innovation (by the introduction of functionally equivalent commercially produced medicines or new techniques and devices) the midwife acknowledged generational change, while providing a way for the younger generation to link meaningfully to older generations.

Such a mixed strategy allowed for internally controlled culture change. New mothers would experience birth, child raising, and child care in ways familiar to the older generations of their families, yet in a way that better reflected their expectations of the world. Grandmothers, mothers, daughters, and granddaughters, through shared experiences and understandings of reproduction, birth, and child care, would also, in essence, share an understanding of what it was to be an African-American woman. In such a way, the midwife represented a generational mediator for her community. Despite the racism and oppression that in part shaped the experiences of the African-American community, it is clear through the actions of midwives that members of the African-American community actively sought to construct and maintain a sense of shared heritage and cultural identity among their clientele. In the limited number of traditional midwifery practices preserved in the ethnographic record, we can see continuities in traditions that originated in or were influenced by African cultural practice.

While midwifery's practices provided generational continuity among African-American women, spiritual practices also provided a means for gender mediation. Midwives were emphatic that men not be involved in the actual birth experience (e.g., Susie 1988). Yet metaphysical tensions between the sexes characterized the practices of other magical mediators in the African-American community. Through the incorporation of rituals that used artifacts that symbolically represented male power or that physically belonged to the child's father, midwives were able to use male spiritual power within the female experience of birth as a healing, rather than divisive, influence. In such a way, midwives were gender mediators who recognized the spiritual implications of the differences between men and women while celebrating these differences.

Birth, though of relatively short duration, is an event within a woman's life that alters her perspectives and place within her community in countless and irrevocable ways. Relationships with mother, father, husband, and friends change in immediate and drastic ways. The birth of a child links a woman in new ways to the generations that preceded her, and those generations yet to come. The midwife played a pivotal role in this transformation, providing a means of creating support networks among generations of women while also striving to mediate the tensions between men and women that arise from the addition of a child. It is only through continued consideration of the construction and maintenance of gender ideologies and roles that we can build multidimensional interpretations of African-American life that acknowledge the interpersonal dynamics that shaped family experiences.

Narrative Interlude IV

Olive Johnson

1411 Sandhill Road, Turnerville, Mississippi
Interview Date: June 15, 1937
Interviewed by: Hazel Neumann

On the advice of Mrs. Freeman, I approached the local A.M.E. Church about locating other former slaves in the town. The minister kindly provided a list of his older congregation members and let me know what foodstuffs or medicines I should take to each place. Miss Johnson is one of the oldest congregants. I was warned that she may not be up for an interview because she is ill with some sort of chronic lung problem. I was asked to bring her some medicines, fresh fruits, and vegetables, and deliver a pot of stew made for her by another church family.

When I arrived at Miss Johnson's cabin, I was greeted by a young man who said he was Miss Johnson's grandson. He was happy to receive my sack of goods, and told me that, although his grandmother was not well, it was worth attempting an interview. The house smelled like a sickroom, with a scent of decay underlying the masking scents of mint cleanser. I was not sure that in my condition it was a good place to visit. Miss Johnson was able to talk to me a bit. She is a fragile-looking woman, but her mind is remarkably sharp. She was born in 1847 and lived on a plantation in Alabama's cotton belt. She couldn't remember if the plantation had a name. The plantation had an absentee owner and like others I've heard about, had an overseer run the day-to-day affairs. While most of the people I've interviewed were field workers, Miss Johnson worked as a seamstress for the plantation slaves and for the overseer. She wove fabric and sewed the slaves' clothing. On occasion, she was asked to sew clothing and bedding for the overseer. Shortly after our interview began, Miss Johnson had a coughing fit and had to end our visit. I do not know if it was because she was feeling poorly, but I felt that I had a harder time speaking with her than some of the other people; she kept her answers brief and never smiled or provided any kind of visual or verbal encouragement. Her grandson indicated that I could interview her again in a few days, if I liked.

June 18, 1937
Second Interview, Olive Johnson

I returned to Miss Johnson bearing more food and carrying a resolve to do a better job of communicating in this attempt. In looking over my earlier interview notes, I found that most women I have talked to enjoyed discussing aspects of their family life. Once Miss Johnson is propped up comfortably in her chair and holding a cup of tea, I asked,

"Miss Johnson, did you have any family on the plantation?"

"No. I was sold away from my kin as a child. Never saw or heard from any of them again."

"Oh, I'm sorry." I decided to try again. "I've met your grandson, so I assume you have children. Were they born before or after slavery?"

Miss Johnson looked at me expressionlessly for a moment, set down her teacup and remarked,

"*You* have children on *your* mind. Why would you think I'd want to have children in slave time? To see them sold? To see them worked in the field? I never had any children. My grandson is by my dead husband's boy."

I was silent, taken aback by the woman's blunt irritation with me. I tried to think of a way to salvage the interview, and instead said, "I'm very sorry to have upset you, Miss Johnson, perhaps I should go now."

I had risen to my feet, when she responded,

"Sit down. You brought me food, I'll pay you with a story." Her tone was even, but I could see in her face that this was an order, not an invitation, so I sat. I was worried but also excited. Not since my first embarrassing attempt at an interview with Georgia Thompson had I encountered any anger. In the 20 narratives I had done since, people had recalled positive memories. I waited in anticipation. Miss Johnson turned away from me to face the doorway of the cabin, or perhaps she was addressing someone unseen to me, a phantom or other haunt. She spoke in a dead, even tone.

"Long ago, there was a young girl who had to work hard every day of her life, without a break, without a family, without anyone to love. Everyone she had ever loved was taken away from her, so she decided to keep to herself. Her days blurred together, rising before dawn, crawling onto her corn shuck mattress long after dark, and spending the time in between hunched over a loom or a sewing a miserable garment out of miserable cloth for miserable people. Food was scarce, but work was plenty. She survived by keeping herself locked up tight inside herself, away from anybody might try to hurt her. She wasn't a pretty girl, but she also wasn't a shame to see, men looked at her. Her boss looked at her. Her boss was a cruel man. His skin was white and red, but his heart was blacker than the blackest field slave. He liked to control his workers with hate and pain. He would beat workers for moving too slow, for looking too happy, or for looking too unhappy. If he hated you, that was one thing.

"A body can heal from the lash, and he wouldn't risk killing a slave. He'd lose his job. Oh no, it was another matter though, if you were a woman and he liked you, and he liked most of the slave women at one time or another. He gave a woman this look, it was an awful look, like he wanted to chew on a person's soul. That look would terrify a woman because she would know what was coming.

"This bossman, he decided he liked the look of the girl, and one night, he came to her cabin. He beat her, and he took her. Night after night, he did this until he decided she was too beat up and too used to look at anymore. When it was over, she found out it wasn't over. He'd left her with a baby inside. The shame was too much. She couldn't have that baby—not that devil's baby, not inside, not where she had tried to keep herself safe. She tried roots, she tried herbs, she tried magic, but that baby was stuck in there tight. Finally, she took a sharp stick and drove it up into herself, and the baby finally came out.

"She nearly bled to death, and they had to call the doctor. The bossman knew why, the doctor made sure to tell him that. Bossman knew who the father was, even if the doctor didn't. At least that made her happy, that he knew his ugly white baby wasn't good enough to grow in her body. After that, it was him who couldn't bear to be looked at by the girl. He convinced the owner to sell her. She thought she had won. She never was able to have babies after that, even after she married a good man. Maybe that bossman won after all."

She turned to me for the first time since beginning her story and said, "Thank you for delivering the food and medicine. I think you should write down that story of slave times for people to hear. I think I've told you all the stories I know."

June 18th

Dear Peter,

It is late, but I absolutely needed to write to you. I have had an incredible experience today, and it has filled me with doubt as to what I am trying to accomplish here. I interviewed a woman today who clearly endured the worst horrors that slavery could offer, and I cannot find words that can do anything but undermine the impact of her story. She was raped by an overseer and left barren from an abortion. She seems to have been so devastated by the experience that her pain has rendered her beyond pain. Why did she choose to tell me this story? Did my pregnancy provoke her pain? Did she feel it was time for the story to be heard? I had spoken to this woman earlier and had not guessed the story that she kept in her heart. Now I cannot help but wonder, how many interviews have I recorded that were censored versions of the past? How many times have I been told what an informant thought a woman of my color and class wanted to hear? Am I engaged in a farce? Can we ever hope to reconstruct the experiences of these people, and if we were successful, could we bear the knowledge? I am filled with grief, for this woman, but also for the unknown others, all the unknown others. I so wish you were here with me tonight.

Love,
Hazel

6

To Mother or Not to Mother

Motherhood is not an inevitable condition of adult women's lives; rather, it is a role that some women choose to avoid, delay, or stagger according to their own needs and desires. The ability of women to control their own bodies, however, has been at the center of political and religious debates throughout the modern period (e.g., Fried 1990; Riddle 1997; Mohr 1984). Beginning in the nineteenth century, the professionalization of physicians accompanied drastic changes in the naturalized perceptions of women's bodies, particularly as related to sexuality, pregnancy, and birth. The perverse control over African-American women's bodies exercised by slaveholders represents the most extreme manifestation of a broader societal trend to sever women's ability to control their reproductive lives and physical person.

Midwifery cannot be seen as separated from other aspects of reproductive health. Midwives treated women for a number of fertility-related conditions, providing services that were not otherwise widely available, including contraception and abortion. Their willingness to provide these services ultimately left midwives vulnerable to attack from the growing medical industry (Solinger 1994). The degree to which either birth control or intentional miscarriage was used by women remains part of the undocumented past. Archaeology can provide some insight into midwives' involvement in family planning practices.

Before exploring these issues further, it is important to clarify the terms that I am using in this chapter. I am using "birth control" as an encompassing term for any practice or technique used to avoid giving birth to a live baby. Both intentional abortion and contraceptive methods fall under birth control. By "intentional abortion," I am referring to practices, be they mechanical, chemical, or otherwise, designed to prevent the birth of a live child. Most of the abortion methods that I will discuss in this chapter were chemical in nature, and served to expel uterine products from the womb. If the woman was pregnant at the time of using these methods (as she would have suspected she was, if using these practices), the products of conception would be expelled. Women did chemically abort later in pregnancy, with the ensuing birth resulting in a stillbirth of a nonviable fetus. I am using "contraception" to refer to any methods or practices that prevented conception from taking place. In most cases, even when abortifacients are employed, "birth control" is probably the most suitable term to use. For the women who regularly used chemical abortions as family planning, in their constructions of their reproductive bodies, the fetus did not exist until what is now referred to as the second trimester of pregnancy (12–24 weeks of gestation). This is an issue that will be explored further shortly.

Pregnancy and Birth Control in the Nineteenth Century

The nineteenth century brought with it rapid advances in allopathic medicine, ultimately establishing it as the dominant medical paradigm of American medicine (Armstrong and Armstrong 1992). Advances in anesthesia and the introduction of forceps increasingly enticed women of the upper classes to abandon midwives in favor of physician-directed births (Leavitt 1986; McMillen 1990; Scholten 1984; Wertz and Wertz 1979). Their ability to numb suffering during labor and birth quickly drew a following of women physicians newly interested in obstetrics. Women often paid with their health for this newfound birth style, as forceps-caused uterine ruptures and vaginal tears brought painful deaths or invalidism (Leavitt and Walton 1984). Though physician-directed births remained out of financial reach for most women, medical technological advances dealing with pregnancy and birth would come to affect women of all races and classes in the United States.

Women's health had traditionally been left in the hands, literally, of women. For the diagnosis of pregnancy, this was particularly true. "Quickening," or the time at which fetal movement became apparent to the mother, was the point when a woman confirmed her pregnancy. Quickening generally does not occur until the fourth or fifth month of pregnancy, although other symptoms of pregnancy would have been apparent to the woman. The notion of quickening was derived from British colonial common law, and remained legally in effect as the recognized beginning of life in most of the United States through 1860 (Mohr 1984:118). It was during this time, after conception and before first fetal movement, that women seem to have exercised the choice as to whether or not to continue a pregnancy. The cessation of menstrual bleeding, while often an indication of pregnancy, can also be caused by other health conditions. Treatment to release the menses commonly employed herbal remedies. Often the herbs worked by stimulating contractions of the uterus. By today's medical standards, successful attempts to force the resumption of the monthly cycle probably resulted in the miscarriage of early-term fetuses.

The dominant male ideology of the nineteenth century asserted that the natural proclivities of women's nature led them to be mothers, and birth control was not part of public discourse until early feminists like Sarah Grimké raised the notion of "voluntary motherhood" in the 1850s (A. Davis 1990:15, 18). Women learned about family planning from one another and through experience. Contraceptive methods were limited to a few tried and true techniques, such as male withdrawal (coitus interruptus), abstinence, douching, and barrier methods employing sponges, "womb veils" (a form of diaphragm), ointments, or herbs. The 1873 passage of the Comstock Act made it illegal for doctors to provide advice on birth control, and though this legislation may not have succeeded in preventing doctors from offering information on the subject, the anti–birth control movement more broadly prevented the development of new techniques among the medical profession (Reed 1984:126).

The nineteenth century in Europe and the United States was characterized by an increased concern over the morality and legality of abortion. In 1803, administering drugs leading to the abortion of a quickened fetus became a criminal act in Ireland and Britain; France had criminalized abortion in 1791; and in the United States, Connecticut became the first state, in 1821, to outlaw abortion of quickened fetuses; other states soon followed. The laws almost universally targeted the providers of abortions, and provided exceptions in cases where the mother's life or health was endangered (Riddle 1997:206–209).

Complicating the enforcement of these laws were the general acceptance of abortion of pre-quickened fetuses, and the difficulty of determining post-facto whether a fetus had or had not quickened. Physicians remained dependent upon women's truthfulness in indicating whether they believed themselves to be pregnant. The herbal remedies used to cause chemical abortions were widely available and well known. It was with the advent of better pregnancy diagnosis that physicians came to exert greater control over women's reproductive choices. By the mid-nineteenth century, doctors were aware of the early signs of pregnancy: the enlargement and softening of the cervix and uterus, swelling of the breasts and the deepening of nipple color (Mohr 1984). These are visible within the first months of pregnancy. With the invention of the stethoscope in 1818 by Théophile-René-Hyacinthe Laënnec, physicians were able to detect fetal heartbeat. By the mid-nineteenth century, doctors were able to detect fetal heartbeats at four months—as many as four to six weeks before quickening (Riddle 1997:221). Physicians had become possessed of technology that could contest assertions of women claiming not to be pregnant. In an 1872 [1974] monograph, physician Ely Van De Warker recounted in detail how to diagnose pregnancy through external and internal examination. The focus of Van de Warker's monograph was the detection of "criminal abortion." He details evidence that could be used to detect "illegal abortion" from the expelled products of conception, the areola and breasts, body temperature, and vaginal and uterine exams.

The outlaw of abortion seems to have done little to reduce the number of women who turned to chemical abortifacients. In 1870, during an address to the Philadelphia County Medical Society, Dr. Andrew Nebinger lamented that abortion was so rampant among women that from 1809 to 1868, the rate of still-births in New York had increased from 1 in 37.6 to 1 in 10.5 (1870 [1973]:6). He attributed the difference to intentional miscarriages—stressing that the statistics tracked only those stillbirths that had occurred after the period of quickening. Even more shocking to Nebinger was that women of all social classes were engaged in procuring abortions. Nebinger recounted the experience of a colleague who told him: " 'I have been often called upon by ladies of the most undoubted character, who very innocently suppose that it cannot be wrong to produce abortion, so long as there is no quickening. I have learned from undoubted sources, that many ladies of elevated standing in society and even in the church, are in the habit of having abortion produced without the least hesitancy as to any impropriety in the procedure.'" (16). While Nebinger and other doctors who wrote against abortion cited their desire to protect human life from the beginning of conception as their goal, their writings also demonstrate their desire to maintain and enrich their still-new gynecology practices. In 1891, Dr. H. S. Pomeroy published an essay in the *Andover Review* that argued against population control. In Pomeroy's opinion, it would be impossible for the United States population to increase enough to deplete available space or natural resources (1891 [1974]:2–25). It is hard to believe that his position was not at least influenced by a concern for a large thriving practice for obstetrics. Eugenic attitudes shaped anti-abortion writings as well. Nebinger, for example, observed in his essay that anecdotal evidence suggested Catholics were less likely to abort than Protestants—thus explaining the larger families of Irish immigrants. He also extensively quotes from an 1869 *Harper's Weekly* article that concluded that foreign-born populations were growing more quickly than "native-born American stock" (7–8). He concludes that the differences in birth rate could be attributed solely to the practice of abortion.

With growing legal proscriptions against aiding abortions, doctors found themselves increasingly unwilling to provide medicines that might induce a miscarriage. Women turned to druggists, folk medicine, traditional healers such as midwives, and to commercially produced medicines that promised to restore menses. Patent medicines designed to restore menses or deal with "female problems" became increasingly important through the nineteenth century. Pennyroyal, ergot, tansy, cotton, and rue, abortifacients that had been used for centuries, remained popular and readily available for women seeking to terminate pregnancies (Mohr 1984; Riddle 1997).

How prevalent birth control was remains an issue open for speculation—sex is often a subject surrounded by silence in the documentary record, with the most extensive discussions of the subject reserved for happenings or practices perceived to fall outside the realm of normative, or for men writing of what they perceive women's proper behavior to be. Certainly, during the second half of the nineteenth century, the average family size in the United States dropped considerably. In her study of domesticity and family life in Oneida County, New York, Mary Ryan (1981) reports that the generation of native-born women whose fertility cycle began in 1830 bore an average of 3.6 children, compared to the average of 5.08 for women 10 years older (155). Family planning methods had to be involved in this shift. Ryan has proposed that withdrawal, patent medicines, abortion, and abstinence to assure female purity were among the methods of birth control employed by middle-class Protestants of upstate New York (156–157). Likewise, Drew Gilpin Faust (1996) has presented letters between southern elite couples demonstrating that the women would avoid sexual contact with their husbands to avoid the risk of additional pregnancies.

While the seemingly extreme practice of abstinence during marriage may have provided additional status within middle-class communities engaged in elevating the "cult of true womanhood," it is unlikely to have been a normative practice. Archaeologists have remained surprisingly quiet on this topic, even in contexts in which one might expect the subject to be more fully explored, such as in brothels. Donna Seifert's (1991; Seifert, O'Brien, and Balicki 2000) discussions of brothel life in Washington, D.C., focus more on ceramic assemblages than sex, with no mention of what practices may have been used to prevent pregnancy, abort, or protect women from venereal diseases.

Period newspapers were filled with advertisements, some blunt and others subtle, promoting birth control (Mohr 1984; Ryan 1981; Riddle 1997). As late as 1907, abortifacient drugs provided as much as $50,000 in advertising revenue per newspaper in Chicago (Mohr 1984:120). Likewise, consumer catalogs provide some insight into the products available for use as birth control. As the provider of so many consumer goods for rural America, Sears, Roebuck, and Company is worth considering for representations of birth control and abortifacient products in its catalogs. A brief sample of catalogs demonstrates the quickly changing attitudes related to abortion versus contraception at the turn of the century. The earliest catalog listings are forthright in their descriptions, but they become increasingly ambiguous and veiled through time. In the 1897 Sears, Roebuck catalog, the copy for a product under the heading of "Female Pills" reads: "These pills are a combination of Pennyroyal, Tansy, Cotton root Bark in a concentrated form with other ingredients which increase the peculiar effect of these medicines. They are very powerful and require to be used cautiously, but if the very complete directions which can be found separately in each box, will be followed closely, all will be well" (Israel 1997:27). At 85 cents a box, Dr. Beaumont's Pennyroyal Pills were the same price as a pint bottle of Kidney and Liver cure sold on the same catalog page. If one desired, one could buy, for $8.50, a dozen treatments. That consumers were thought to be interested in purchasing in bulk may say something about how this product was used—with great regularity. The 1897 consumer could also procure Lydia Pinkham's Vegetable Compound from Sears. This famous patent medicine, which had many uses, was believed to be useful in terminating pregnancies. This medicine could be obtained for $1, or alternately, a no-name variety of Pennyroyal pills sold for $2 (Israel 1993:29). Despite growing legal proscriptions against abortion, the cost of controlling one's own reproductive health was less expensive than a visit to a physician and was only a mail-order catalog away.

By 1900, advertising copy in the Sears catalog had become less overtly descriptive of the use of female pills. Dr. Worden's Female Pills for All Female Diseases promised to cure a laundry list of symptoms that could be caused by pregnancy, but buried "leucorrhoea, tardy or irregular periods, and suppression of the menses" until the middle of the text. The advertisement included a disclaimer making it clear that "these female pills are not a purgative medicine," although the subtext of the copy indicates that they were (Schroeder 1970:16). "Blood Pills," advertised next to Dr. Worden's product, also promised to treat suppression of the menses and tardy menses, but like Worden's, ran a disclaimer denying that their product was a purgative. "Brown's Vegetable Cure for Female Weakness," however, provided no such caveats. The medicine promised to cure "Irregular and painful menstruation, inflammation and ulceration of the womb, flooding and ALL FEMALE DISORDERS" (emphasis in original, Schroeder 1970:17). The body of the product's text read:

> WOMEN DO NOT SUFFER SO! Brown's Vegetable Cure will cure you. In all female disorders it is the greatest remedy of the age. If you have any of the following symptoms take this remedy at once and be cured: Nausea and bad taste in the mouth, sore feeling in lower part of the bowels, an unusual discharge, impaired general health, feeling of languor, sharp pain in the region of kidney, backache . . . a desire to urinate frequently, a dragging sensation in the groin, courses irregular, timid, nervous and restless feeling, a dread of some impending evil, temper wayward and irritable. . . . If you have any of the symptoms send to us for Brown's Vegetable Cure and be cured at once. Doctors may not help you, other remedies may have failed, but Brown's Cure will cure quickly, pleasantly and permanently. (Schroeder 1970:17)

The symptoms described above summarize the experiences of many women's first trimester of pregnancy, making it very clear what the intention of this product was. One cannot help but be affected by the ominous nature of the line "Doctors may not help you" and the insight it provides into the fear and despair of women turning to these nostrums. Pennyroyal, a well-known and effective abortifacient, was not in the catalog in 1900, leaving women to struggle with deciphering the advertising text, which sent mixed messages and provided no list of ingredients. The 1902 catalog still includes Dr. Worden's Female Pills and Dr. M. Bain's Famous Blood Pills, bearing the same ambiguous text. Brown's product is not included. By 1902, however, Ladyline's Antiseptic suppositories, for "local treatment for the cure of inflammation, congestion and falling of the womb, antiversion, retroversion and prolapsus, dropsy of the womb, ulceration, polypus, tumor, leucorrhoea (whites), profuse, difficult and delayed menstruation" were now available (Amory 1969:463), as were a range of women's syringes for douching. Women's bulb syringes promised to "cleanse the vaginal passages thoroughly of all discharges" (Amory 1969:455).

By 1933, douching as a contraceptive measure seems to have become the dominant mode of birth control, with vaginal creams, antiseptics and suppositories and vaginal syringes filling a page (Sears Roebuck 1933:443), although an explicit use is not described for the products beyond the euphemism "feminine hygiene." Some evidence of possible abortifacients is still visible.

Lydia Pinkham's is still available, as are two other "vegetable compounds." One of these, "Cardui," touts itself vaguely as "a purely vegetable medium found by women to help overcome some of the simple female disturbances" (Sears Roebuck 1933:441). Likewise, Senna, an herb most often used to cure constipation but sometimes used as an abortifacient, was also sold as leaves (440).

How effective some of these products were remains a question. Brown's advertising press certainly suggests that product failures were not unknown to women. Dr. Van De Warker (1872) in presenting his research on abortifacient drugs, found that rue, pennyroyal, tansy, savin, aloes, and cottonwood did produce miscarriage in pregnant dogs, but he expressed doubt that the oils used in many of the commercially produced "female pills" were strong enough or pure enough to be effective. His gravest concerns surrounded what he referred to as "periodical drops," which contained strong enough mixtures of the herbs to be a risk to a woman's health (Van De Warker 1872:85). In the case of these mixtures, Van De Warker accused chemists (druggists) of providing them or the necessary ingredients for them over the counter to their customers.

> In the matter of the detection of the criminal use of those mixtures prepared by the druggist himself, and sold over his counter, much would depend upon the dose given. It is usual in these mixtures to give prominence to some one ingredient. Tansy, savine, or ergot would thus occupy a leading place,—the other drugs which may be present being thrown in with a vague idea that they would in some way aid to bring about the desired result. Iron, in some form, is added very often, from an imperfect knowledge of the action of iron in irregularity of the menstrual function. Powerful cathartics, either in infusion or solid form are also placed in the mixture with a better-defined idea. When the druggist gives the applicant either of the oils of savine or tansy, singly, it is generally in simple syrup or in mucilage.... These oils are sometimes prescribed in such minute doses that no effect would be evident from their use. Those men who thus prescribe have the very best of intentions to aid their customer, but are too timid in the use of the instruments. (87)

At several points in his text, Van De Warker complains of pharmacists who sold well-known abortifacient herbs to their customers. Yet his text also demonstrates that even when pharmacists were willing to sell such herbs, the consumer could not be assured that the medicine she had received would be effective.

African-American Midwives and Birth Control

In a context of changing attitudes regarding birth control—one in which contraception and intentional abortion were increasingly differentiated—midwives and other traditional healers, as well as pharmacists and quacks, became important alternative providers of reproductive care. In Western societies, the persecution of midwives for purported activities as abortionists has a long history, dating back to the medieval period (Riddle 1997). In the United States, the movement to abolish lay midwifery was in part justified by the American Medical Association as a means to halt what was perceived as an epidemic of abortion in American society (Fraser 1998:90–91).

W. W. Kerns, a Virginia doctor, raged in a 1927 editorial, "Lectures are given to midwives by county nurses, teaching negro women (unknowingly) how to produce abortion. No negro midwife should be taught the anatomy of the genital organs. I have had twenty-seven abortions within the past seven months. The majority of these cases had consulted some negro granny, who told them how to do the work" (369).

A dissenting view defended rural midwives from charges of being abortion providers. A 1950 article describing the regulation and licensing of midwives in Mississippi, wrote, "The less sophisticated rural midwife never acquired the reputation of abortionist as did her urban sister. In 1914 in Newark, New Jersey, thirteen of the city's ninety-odd midwives were being watched as abortionists. The abortionists of today in New Orleans keep an unbroken succession of beds in the Charity hospital occupied with critically infected women" (J. Ferguson 1950:85). In Fraser's view (1998:91), constant objectification of African-American midwives as immoral and unsanitary is the result of the close association of these women with the "dirty" work of abortion. In her interviews of African-American midwives, their descendants, and women who had relied upon them, Fraser found that midwifery and its associations remained topics that women were uncomfortable discussing.

Enslavement provided myriad incentives to avoid childbearing. A lessening of civil rights following Reconstruction created further cause to control fertility for some women. Enslaved women had no assurances that they could provide for the needs of any child they bore, or even that they would be allowed to see the child grow to adulthood. Other women resented being exploited as human reproductive machinery to increase the wealth of their enslavers (Giddings 1984). Pregnancy often provided no relief from labor demands for women, nor did it always provide a release from dehumanizing and life-threatening punishments (A. Davis 1983). While too horrific to be believable, the practice of digging holes in the ground to support a pregnant woman's belly during a whipping is described too often in the ex-slave narratives to be anything but true (e.g., Rawick 1973; Clayton 1990). Regarding abortion practices among minority women, Angela Davis (1990) has observed,

> When Black and Latina women resort to abortions in such large numbers, the stories they tell are not so much about the desire to be free of their pregnancy, but rather about the miserable social conditions which dissuade them from bringing new lives into the world. . . . Black women have been aborting themselves since the earliest days of slavery . . . refus[ing] to bring children into a world of interminable forced labor, where chains and floggings and sexual abuse for women were the everyday conditions of life. (17)

The desire to have children, to have the normalizing experience of constructing a family life outside of the fields, was starkly balanced against quality-of-life issues that shaped the everyday experiences of enslaved people. That women would choose to avoid pregnancy is none too surprising. Just as midwives provided the service of supervising births during and after slavery, there is ample evidence to suggest that they aided family planning practices as well.

The line between abortion and birth control is often difficult to draw. Agents that bring on "late menses" would by today's standards be classified as abortifacients, whereas means to prevent conception are seen as birth control. Products such as the "morning after" pill blur the line somewhat, since the drug causes an expulsion of the contents of the uterus, which may or may not include the products of conception or may expulse a fertilized egg before implantation—the medical criterion for pregnancy (Norsigian 1990:198). Such differentiations are the product of medical technology that allows a woman to identify a pregnancy as early as the first day of a missed menses, and a political environment that is determined to exert control over women's bodies. The differentiation between abortion and birth control seems itself to be a product of the modern birth control movement led by Margaret Sanger, who claimed to despise abortion but supported birth control (Riddle 1997). As I will explore a bit later, African-American midwives' beliefs and practices were not complementary to the early-twentieth-century birth control movement.

The degree to which enslaved women used birth control and abortion to regulate their reproduction remains a matter of debate (e.g., A. Ross 1993; White 1985; Roberts 1997; Bush 1990); scholars seem to agree that means of aborting pregnancies and preventing conception were known to African-American women during the period of enslavement. Most commonly, these scholars refer to the accounts of period doctors, who complained that enslaved women must have had means of limiting their reproduction, for on some plantations, barely any children were born (e.g., Sheridan 1985; White 1985; Bush 1990). These accusations must be taken with a measure of salt, for they may be as representative of the doctors' racist views as they are of family planning practices. For instance, at least one physician accused enslaved women of using abortion so that they could avoid a disruption of their ravenous sexual lives (e.g., Bush 1990:139). Other factors would have also influenced birthrates among enslaved women: poor nutrition, heavy workload, prolonged lactation, and endemic diseases such as yaws, syphilis, and elephantiasis, and epidemics of measles, smallpox, and scarlet fever would have increased rates of miscarriage and stillbirth among enslaved women (Sheridan 1985:246).

Though it is impossible to determine the extent to which low birthrates among enslaved women are attributable to health difficulties or birth control practices, there are convincing historical descriptions supporting the stance that enslaved women did use abortifacients. The limited historical descriptions available from the period of slavery suggest that chemical abortions were the most commonly used form of birth control. Physicians such as John Morgan wrote in published venues about the means that enslaved women used to effect miscarriage. The herbs he mentions—cotton plant seed, pennyroyal, cedar berries, and camphor (White 1985:85)—are all well-known herbal abortifacients. In his study of slave illnesses, Todd Savitt (1989) described amenorrhea, or lack of a menstrual cycle, as an affliction suffered by enslaved women. As discussed above, the cessation of menses has several possible causes, such as overwork, malnutrition, tight corsetting, and of course, pregnancy. Among southern white women (McMillen 1990), bringing forth delayed menses was a means of aborting pre-quickened fetuses. Perhaps some of the amenorrhea reported in the historical record reflects enslaved women's use of unknowing physicians to achieve abortions. In the Caribbean, planters accused enslaved women of taking "specifics" that induced miscarriage (Bush 1990). In his study of health care in the colonial British West Indies, Richard Sheridan (1985:244) recounts the report of a Jamaican doctor that midwives provided abortion services to young women. In this instance, the abortifacient used was wild cassava.

Often, remedies used as birth control, such as particular herbs, were just as useful as abortifacients (L. Ross 1997:263). Ex-slave narratives (e.g., Rawick 1974a, 1974b, 1977), while usually not expressly dealing with the topic of birth control, do mention a number of herbs used as medicines that are also known as menstrual regulators. Asafetida, quinine, rust of iron, cinnamon, nutmeg, juniper, and snakeroot (birthwort) are all examples of well-known abortifacients (Riddle 1997) that were used in other medical contexts by African Americans. Black and white women alike would have kept information about these medicines quiet as abortion became increasingly criminalized during the second half of the nineteenth century. For enslaved women, who often did not enjoy control over the sexual access to their bodies, the ability to have some control over the outcome of sexual assaults would have filled a particularly desperate need.

Giddings (1984) found references to enslaved women using camphor as a contraceptive in the 1860s; the drug was reported to have been taken just before or after menstruation, "in quantities sufficient to produce a little nervousness for two or three days" (46), after which time it was believed to have been effective. Older slave women were reported to supply herbal remedies for contraceptive use (46). Such knowledge was carefully guarded, however, for prevailing attitudes among the white population stereotyped black women as overly sexually active and more likely to have abortions (L. Ross 1997).

Though chemical abortions were favored among African-American women, the same results were sometimes achieved through mechanical means. Sharp objects inserted into the womb could cause a spontaneous miscarriage but could be dangerous to the mother. Barbara Bush (1990:140) refers to the Ghanaian practice of placing a Jatophra twig tied to a string in the womb, and then causing a miscarriage by jerking the twig out by the string. The *Baltimore Afro-American* newspaper reported in 1940 that pencils, nails, and hatpins were commonly used to self-induce abortions (Roedrique 1990:335). Mechanical abortions were much more dangerous to women than chemical abortions because they created greater risk of hemorrhage and infection.

Birth Control and the African-American Community

Birth control was a divisive issue in the black community in the first half of the twentieth century (Roberts 1997:56–103). For some, birth control was a means to regulate family size and ensure a more financially secure future for members of a family; others saw birth control as a tool of the dominant culture, encouraged to eventually eliminate African Americans.

Activists within the black community were split on the issue. W. E. B. Du Bois's *Crisis* ran several editorials promoting the use of birth control to ensure that the race remain healthy and strong. Du Bois (1922) wrote: "Parents owe their children, first of all, health and strength. Few women can bear more than two or three children and retain strength of the other interests of life" (250). Continuing on this theme, Du Bois wrote in 1933, "Our solicitude is not for the number of children, but their quality, their health, the provision of their up-bringing and education" (44). Despite Du Bois's support for black birth control, however, his editorials on the subject are also rife with classist and almost eugenicist overtones. For instance, in a 1932 essay, "Black Folk and Birth Control," appearing in *Birth Control Review,* he stated: "The mass of ignorant Negroes still breed carelessly and disastrously, so that the increase among Negroes, even more than the increase among whites, is from that part of the population least intelligent and fit, and least able to rear their children properly" (167). He suggests that Christian beliefs are in part to blame: "After Emancipation, there arose the inevitable clash of ideals between those Negroes who were striving to improve their economic position and those whose religious faith made the limitation of children a sin" (Du Bois 1932:167). Similarly sentiments underlie the text of an editorial Du Bois wrote on the subject for the *Crisis* in 1933. In that piece he writes, "Most of our increase today comes from the thoughtless peons of the black belt, while the better educated and most prosperous city groups are not reproducing themselves" (44). Given that forced sterilizations were all too frequently forced upon rural black women during this period (Roberts 1997; A. Davis 1983), Du Bois's sentiments seem callous. I bring attention to Du Bois's derogatory remarks about rural African-American populations because the Perrymans, although landholders, were not of the urban elite black populations with whom Du Bois aligned. As such, the Perrymans, with their large family, would have been part of the peons to whom Du Bois distastefully refers.

In contrast, political writer Marcus Garvey was opposed to African-American birth control. For Garvey, and others of his mind-set, political social strength could only be attained through strength in numbers. A black population that vastly outnumbered a white ruling class would be impossible for the elite to ignore (Roedrique 1990). In 1934, the same year that Du Bois and the NAACP were advocating birth control, Garvey's Universal Negro Improvement Association condemned birth control as contrary to the purpose of God in its annual convention (Roberts 1997:84).

In the African-American community, abortions and contraceptives were available from conjurers, root doctors, and midwives. Conjurers and root doctors were often, but not always, distinct practitioners. Conjurers tended toward treating spiritually based or caused disturbances experienced by the body, and root doctors generally treated illness and discomfort through pharmacological means. While conjurers might find a magical cause for gynecological illnesses, they seem to have employed herbal and medicinal remedies for a range of women's illnesses. While collecting African-American ethnomedical data between the world wars, Harry Middleton Hyatt (1970) encountered a woman whose menses had been stopped by a jealous rival. The rival stole the woman's menstrual rag and buried it in a graveyard. To restore her menses, the conjurer had the woman boil down Jamaican ginger (commonly available through druggists) into a tea "as hot as she could drink" to be taken three nights running while soaking her feet in water containing saltpeter and cayenne (375). The woman's period returned, but was a deep black in color—thus confirming that her illness had been the result of a trick.

A woman spiritualist who worked in New Orleans explicitly acknowledged the abortifacient properties of ginger to Hyatt: "And they say you can take ginger root. Have you ever heard of that? If you breedin' and done got caught [pregnant]—well, you can take ginger root and that makes you have a miss, you see. A hot, hot tea and you drink it at bedtime, and you get into bed and cover up and that begins to make your blood hot and you begin to sweat, and then the next morning, everything there what you looking for" (Hyatt 1970:496). The two ginger cures are remarkably similar, each relying on the root being delivered in a hot beverage as well as raising the body temperature through other means. Immersion in hot water is today recognized as being a potential cause of spontaneous abortion. Hyatt also found dirt dauber tea being prescribed by conjurers and root doctors to bring on menses or relieve uterine cramping during labor and menstruation (1970:432).

Another intriguing phenomenon described by conjurers that deserves some comment is the condition of "frogs in the stomach." Invasion of the body by animals such as snakes, turtles, and amphibians, in either whole (and moving) form or in a ground form is an often-recorded cause of illness in African-American ethnomedical taxonomies (e.g., H. Mathews 1992a). The cause of these infestations is typically conjure; however, I have found two descriptions of treatments for the removal of a frog from a woman that have raised my suspicions that there may be an additional level to this curse in some cases. One practitioner told Hyatt that to remove frogs from a woman's stomach, one should boil sassafras, put it in a bottle with whiskey, and have the woman take that for

9 mornings, followed by asafetida, then for the next 9 days, the woman should take dime scrapings with milk. After 18 days the frog will be removed (Hyatt 1970:234). Asafetida and sassafras are each believed to have some abortifacient properties.

I find the second description even more striking: "Then I seed a woman taking a frog from a woman. She got some peach tree leaves and she boiled them until they was real, real strong, and then she'd taken table salt and put in it and salt peter and bathed her. And she put 20 drops of turpentine in that and give a dose of caster oil behind in and it passed through her" (Hyatt 1970:463). After a request for clarification, the root doctor explained that the woman suffering from the frog in her stomach was required to drink and bathe in the peach leaf-turpentine tea. Turpentine is a known abortifacient, although I have not yet identified other uses for peach leaves. When reading these two descriptions, I could not help but wonder if they were describing an abortion, and if the "frog" was an expelled fetus. Neither description indicates from what orifice the frog was passed. For a woman to feel something moving in her stomach would mean that the time of quickening had occurred. Perhaps the "frog" was a code word for a late-term abortion. Certainly for a woman fearing she was experiencing an unwanted pregnancy, a diagnosis of a frog that could be removed may be a relief. There are fewer moral considerations when removing a foreign species from one's body than might be entailed in deciding to abort a pregnancy. Of course, this is merely conjecture on my part, but seems worthy of further consideration.

How widely birth control and abortion were available through African-American midwives versus other African-American healers is open to debate. Both Onnie Logan and Margaret Smith, Alabama midwives whose narratives have been published, practiced after the regulation of midwifery. By the period of their practices, abortion had become firmly criminalized within the United States and various religious organizations had taken firm stances against the aborting of any age fetus. Their opinions on the matter are going to represent their unique contextual experiences.

Intriguingly, in her research, Beatrice Mongeau (1985) encountered midwives and physicians who used ergot, a well-known abortifacient, to aid in the expelling of afterbirth. Ergot, along with Lydia Pinkham's Compound, turpentine, quinine, and caster oil were among the forbidden items often found by public nurses in African-American midwives' medical bags (Mongeau 1985:84–87). Each of these products is known to have abortifacient properties, or at least to have been popularly used for such a purpose.

Likewise, reports of what midwives may or may not have done from the communities who lived with them are similarly shaped by time and memory. For instance, in Ruth Schaffer's (1991) study of African-American midwifery in the Brazos Bottom of Texas, she found that although none of the 24 midwives she interviewed admitted to ever providing abortions, of the 179 other community members she questioned, 75 percent reported that abortions could be obtained from midwives. Clearly, there is some sort of disjuncture between the results of the two sets of interviews. It may be that some of the community members have internalized anti-midwifery propaganda as memories of actual practice—a phenomenon that Fraser encountered in her Virginia study (1998).

Sufficient evidence exists in the ethnographic record to suggest that African-American midwives did provide abortion services. Several of Schaffer's (1991) community informants were able to provide her with enough specific details of abortion practices to convince her that abortions were available to the community. In her study of midwives, Marie Campbell (1946:35) recorded that traditionally African-American midwives used tansy tea to induce miscarriage, demonstrating continuity in knowledge about this long-used plant. Mirroring information found in Hyatt, one Alabama midwife reported that hot ginger was believed to bring on late menses (M. Smith and Holmes 1996:39).

Onnie Logan was adamant in her interview that she opposed abortion on religious grounds. She recalled a midwife who on her deathbed worried she wouldn't make it to heaven because of all the little babies she had miscarried. Logan (1989:116–117) also remembered that the board of health had seized the licenses of older midwives believed to be offering abortion services. This latter piece of information suggests that anti-abortion sentiments were stronger among younger licensed midwives than among their elders. In her narrative, Logan also felt it necessary to dispel the notion that African-American women were more likely to abort their pregnancies than white women, stating that more white woman approached her for abortions than black (112).

Margaret Smith's brief discussion of birth control in her narrative clearly illustrates the ambivalence surrounding these practices. She stated:

> When we were having babies, there wasn't birth control. If there was, colored people didn't know anything about it. But some people just took things to keep from getting pregnant. They have taken gunpowder out of a gun. I just didn't approve of that. But I do remember them giving them teas to make their period come, and when they have cramps. They got some sort of root and gave it to them, but I never had complications with it. (Smith and Holmes 1996:48)

In this passage Smith manages to both disassociate herself from the practices, to deny their existence, and then to recount specific remedies she employed for those very uses. Smith's reference to using teas to "bring on menses" suggests that midwives may have continued to use the standard of "quickening" to confirm pregnancy. The application of this standard would have allowed midwives to help women terminate pregnancies while maintaining religious objections to intentional miscarriage. Until quickening had taken place, no pregnancy was present. Also noteworthy, for Smith, "birth control" seems to have a specific meaning for her—one that differs from "keeping from getting pregnant." This duality may reflect a division made by some birth control activists regarding "scientific birth control" versus "folk tradition." A passage from George S. Schuyler's

"Quantity or Quality," an essay that appeared in *Birth Control Review*, provides an example of this division. He writes: "If anyone should doubt the desire on the part of Negro women and men to limit their families, it is only necessary to note the large sale of preventative devices sold in every drug store in the various black belts and the great number of abortions preformed by medical men and quacks. Scientific birth control is what is needed" (1932:166).

Whatever the personal stance of an individual midwife regarding birth control and abortion, she would have had in her medical repertoire the ability to provide such services. Many of the herbal remedies used early in pregnancy to terminate a pregnancy were identical to remedies used late in pregnancy to induce labor or to speed contractions, because the medicines served to stimulate uterine contractions. The question is not whether the midwives possessed the knowledge but whether they chose to dispense it.

In a revealing evaluation of floral remains recovered from African-American slave cabins in the American Southwest, Mark Groover and Timothy Baumann discovered that plant species associated with birth control were recovered from archaeological deposits in greater numbers than would be expected from documentary sources, such as the ex-slave narratives. Groover and Baumann (1996:24–25) first reviewed ethnohistorical sources related to herbal medicinal practices recorded in South Carolina. They found that bitter root (*Apocynum cannabinum*) and cotton root bark (*Gossypium herbaceum*) were specifically named as abortifacients. Blackroot (*Pterocaulon pycnostachyum*), life everlasting (*Gnaphalium polycephalum*), and red oak (*Quercus falcata*) were named as relief for menstrual pains.

Although not named in the ethnohistorical literature reviewed by Groover and Baumann for that purpose, the list of species they compiled also includes aloe (*Agave virginica*), basil (*Ocimum basilicum*), bloodroot (*Ceanthus ovatus*), catnip (*Nepeta cataria*), honeysuckle (*Lonicera*), horehound (*Eupatorium hyssopifolium*), Jimson weed (*Datura stramonium*), parsnip (*Pastinaca sativa*), pennyroyal (*Hedeoma pulegioides*), pomegranate (*Punica granatum*), sassafras (*Sassafras albidum*), and four species of snakeroot—all of which have been recorded in other contexts as abortifacients. In the cases of aloe, pennyroyal, and cotton, their uses as abortifacients were so well known that physicians lectured on how to detect their uses in "criminal abortions" (Van De Warker 1872). The ethnohistorical literature reviewed by Groover and Baumann most frequently lists these plants as being used for "colds or fever," for "diarrhea," or in the case of parsnip, as having "no recorded use." In his 1872 lecture titled "The Detection of Criminal Abortion," Dr. Van De Warker warned his colleagues of women who, trying to hide pregnancies, might seek relief for delayed menses, claiming their condition had been brought on by extended illness. Unfortunately, from the archaeological assemblages studied by Groover and Baumann (1996) cotton was the only abortifacient recovered. Given that the leaves and roots were the portion of the plant most commonly used in these medicines, their presence in the archaeological record is most likely to be detected through specialized ethnobotanical analyses, such as phytolith recovery, rather than as macrofloral remains.

The willingness of African-American midwives to aid women in aborting pregnancies, despite the growing political effort to limit that practice in the late nineteenth century, became part of the focus of the American Medical Association's campaign against them. Writing about the 1940s, Rickie Solinger (1994) provides examples of court transcripts against midwives in abortion cases. In one case, a court psychiatrist described a midwife as an emotionally distorted female: "an unethical type with a strong need to be punishing, domineering and even sadistic towards members of her own sex" (349). In one instance, a midwife was described in a court case as having an unnaturally shaped clitoris—emphasizing her role as an unnatural woman (349–350).

Archaeology of Birth Control in Lucrecia Perryman's Practice

What, then, if anything, does the Perryman assemblage reveal about African-American birth control and abortion? As is the case with so many archaeological materials, there are no clear answers to be had, but interesting possibilities are raised. Based on the spacing of her own children, it seems unlikely that Lucrecia Perryman herself practiced birth control to limit family size, but she may have exercised some control over birth spacing. Lucrecia's children with Marshall were born in 1866, 1869, 1872, 1874, 1877, and 1879. Her children prior to her marriage to Marshall were born in 1852, 1858, and 1862. According to the census, Lucrecia had given birth to at least two more children. Overall, her children were spaced two to three years apart. Prolonged breast-feeding, a practice reported among black women in Africa, the Caribbean, and the American South (e.g., Sheridan 1985; White 1985; Bush 1990), would have provided one means of spacing births to these intervals.

In contrast, Lucrecia's surviving adult children tended toward much smaller families, if they had children at all. Daughter Caroline had only one child, as did Marsoline and Kate. Emma had three children—one with her first husband and two with her second. None of Lucrecia's sons, Frank, Marshall and Walter, had any children. Sally, whose life was cut short in 1894, was the most prolific of the Perryman family, having six children. Lucrecia's grandchildren, Susie Butler, Charles Perryman, and Eloise Douglas, reversed the pattern of their parents' generation and had larger families—eight, seven, and six children respectively. If birth control was being practiced to any great extent, the generation of Lucrecia's children would be the most likely candidates. For the most part, these family members' reproductive years coincided with the period that their mother was working as a midwife. If the small families of the Perryman children were the result of family planning practices, their birth control practices would have preceded attention to this issue by black activists such as W. E. B. Du Bois. It is also possible that the small family sizes of Lucrecia's children represented health problems. Marshall Sr., Frank, and Sally each died from complications of tuberculosis. Pregnancy and childbirth were seen as particularly dangerous for women who had tuberculosis, and it has been reported that women chose to forgo having children rather than risk the consequences of their disease (Leavitt 1986).

It is the grandchildren's generation—the generation that had larger families—who were having children at the time of birth control debates between Du Bois and Garvey in the black community. Though Du Bois clearly associated smaller family sizes with the adoption of middle-class values and ambitions of upward mobility for black families, at least three of the Perryman grandchildren did not. Nor does their abandonment of smaller family size represent a lack of class ambition. The children and grandchildren of Susie and Wiley Butler include businessmen, doctors, university professors, and schoolteachers. Their children credit their parents for instilling the importance of education into their children. Whether the decision to have a large family represents, in part, a politically influenced choice is intriguing to ponder.

The medical assemblage left behind by Lucrecia Perryman is the most fertile, so to speak, source of potential information regarding family planning services she may have provided (Table 6.1). For this discussion I will focus on the

Table 6.1 Products Containing Ingredients Believed to Cause Intentional Miscarriage Recovered from the Site*

Product	Ingredients Believed to Cause Miscarriage	Number Recovered from Site
Dr. Charles Fletcher's Castoria	senna	1
Dr. S. Pitcher's Castoria	senna	3
Dr. Grove's Tasteless Chill Tonic	quinine	1
Minard's Liniment	turpentine, camphor, ammonium hydroxide	1
Burnett's Cod Liver Oil	cathartic properties	1
Hamlin's Wizard Oil	ammonium hydroxide, turpentine	1

*It is notoriously difficult to identify ingredients in patent medicines at any time. These products represent only those with ingredients listed either in government documents or advertisements. Probably more of the patent medicines could be included if their contents were better documented. Likewise, it is possible that mineral/soda waters from the site could have included ginger or quinine, two commonly used abortifacients.

materials that were recovered from the well—the archaeological feature that dated to the period of Lucrecia's work as a midwife. The largest portion of this assemblage consists of glass medicine bottles, jars, and vials. A minimum of 122 glass medical containers were recovered from the site. Glass containers for medicines came to have fairly standardized shapes and colors, which allows for a certain amount of educated guessing regarding contents. In addition, 83 of the bottles were embossed with brand names, allowing for further identification of their contents. Many of the products represented are well-known patent medicines for which good documentary data are available (e.g., Fike 1987; Devner 1968; Baldwin 1973).

As will be discussed in later chapters, a number of the products recovered from the site clearly relate to the care of infants and expectant and nursing mothers. There were, however, no clearly identifiable "women's problems" products—no Lydia Pinkham's Vegetable Compound or Dr. Beaumont's Female Pills, no bottles that once contained prophylactic douche. Several of the bottles contained generic embossing for companies that produced a range of products. For instance, "Dr. Shoop's Family Medicines," "W. Wood," "Homeopathic Pharmacy of Kansas," and "Kellogg AME & Co" were producers of a variety of medical products, which were sold in identical bottles with differing labels. Not surprisingly, paper labels did not survive in the well. W. Wood of Trenton, New Jersey, manufactured soothing syrups for babies as well as a "female medicine" (Devner 1968:102), either of which may have been attractive to a midwife. Shoop's Family Medicines seems to have marketed a drug for any need.

Vaseline, which has a myriad of medical and beauty uses, was recovered in abundance from the site, represented by 10 jars. Vaseline could be used as a barrier method of contraception by applying it over the mouth of the cervix (L. Ross 1997:263). Similarly, it could be used to affix diaphragms and sponges. Douching was a popular method of contraception among African-American women in the 1930s (Roedrique 1990:334–335). One vaginal pipe for a syringe kit was recovered from the Perryman well. Ross (L. 1997:263) reports that quinine, teas of rusty nails, and turpentine were among the douches used as home measures. The recovered pipe was made from a white (probably zinc-based) metal compound, a more durable material than the hard rubber pipes often advertised in catalogs. Several recorded treatments for postpartem contractions (after pains) used by African-American midwives required douching. Lucrecia would have been capable of instructing her clients in proper technique, if needed.

Several of the products recovered from the well included products that, if taken in a large enough quantity, could have caused an abortion. Quinine was the active ingredient in the "Dr. Grove's Tasteless Chill Tonic" found at the site. "Dr. Fletcher's Castoria" and "Dr. S. Pitcher's Castoria" are both purgatives marketed for children that contain senna, an herb sometimes used to initiate miscarriage. Medical historians have noted that even these purgatives designed for children contained high enough doses of senna to cause painful bowel contractions (Young 1961). Castorias or Caster oils are reported in the ethnographic literature as being used to bring on contractions when labor is stalled (e.g., M. Campbell 1946), so its potential for stimulating the uterus was known to midwives. However, the amount of castoria necessary to bring on an intentional miscarriage may have been considerable.

"Minard's Liniment," which was sold as an internal and external cure-all, contained 10 percent turpentine, 5.45 percent camphor and 2.3 percent ammonium hydroxide (alum) (Canadian Government 2000). Enslaved women reportedly used these three ingredients separately as abortifacients (L. Ross 1997; Giddings 1984). Turpentine alone was used as an abortifacient in Mississippi and Alabama. In his study of the African-American birth control movement, Jesse Roedrique (1990:335) observes that "the use of turpentine as an abortifacient is significant since it is derived from evergreens, a source similar to rue and camphor, both of which were reported by a medical authority in 1860 to have been used with some success by southern slaves." The combination of these three ingredients in one medicine is somewhat suspicious and does make one wonder whether one of the unadvertised uses for this product was to induce miscarriage.

A final suspect as a potential abortifacient is "Ducro's Elixir Alimentaire," which was advertised as a cure for blood disturbances. Certainly, based on the advertisements we have seen for other "female pills," blood trouble seems to be a coded term for ceased menses. Despite the suspicious nature of some of these products, given their ingredients, as far as I have been able to learn from period advertising, none of these products presented themselves as cures for female problems. Their use as such would have been the result of long-retained folk knowledge and experience.

We must also consider that the presence of birth control products would be muted in the archaeological record. According to Dr. Van der Warker (1872), at least at the time of his writings, female pills were discretely packaged. "Their appearance is characteristic, being the result of an apparent attempt to conceal the nature of the contents of the bottle or box when in use. Thus they are put up in small and partially opaque glass bottles, in square tin boxes, or in small cylindrical tin boxes, covered by a wrapper, but having no label pasted directly upon the box" (85). Twelve plain medicine bottles were recovered from the site, but they are diverse in color, form, and size, and are not suggestive of the use of a single, unmarked product.

While we may never know whether any of the patent medicine products were used to bring on an intentional abortion, clearly a range of products used at the site had that potential. Given the tendency of archaeologists to lump patent medicines in reports under a single heading, rather than by product,

Table 6.2   Local Pharmacy Bottles Recovered from Perryman Well

Pharmacy Name	Pharmacy Location	Dates of Operation	Number of Bottles Recovered
G. Van Antwerp	2 S. Royal Street	1885–at least 1925	27
Bienville Pharmacy	164 St. Francis	1906–1918	2
Dave S. Bauer	320 Dauphin	1893–1924	2
A.J. Hamilton		not available	1
J. N. Hamilton		not available	1
J.G. Hulsbush	161 Dauphin, 57 Government and 251 S. Broad	1898–1907	1
West Ward Drug	St. Louis and Spring Hill Road	1890–1903	1

reconstructing the relative abundance of these products at other sites is difficult to do. Until contraception and abortion and their associated material culture receive greater attention within archaeology in general, and historical archaeology specifically, it will be difficult to assess how much of any typical medical assemblage were products related to reproductive health and control.

   Although the analysis of the patent medicines was more tantalizing than conclusive regarding birth control, druggists' bottles from the site are also promising. Thirty-five local pharmacy bottles were recovered from the well, representing seven different local pharmacies (Table 6.2). Six of the pharmacies were represented by no more than one or two bottles, but Van Antwerp's Pharmacy is represented in the assemblage by 27 bottles. In counting reconstructed bottles from analysis sheets, I was so surprised to see such a high number of Van Antwerp bottles that I pulled all of the artifacts from their drawers and lined the reconstructed bottles on a table together for recounting. The result remained the same. Twenty-one of the Van Antwerp bottles were clear glass, four were light blue, and two green. Whether this represents a difference in type of medicine contained within or simply variation within the assemblage is not known. The embossed panels do vary slightly, sometimes including "& Son," sometimes listing "Mobile," and alternating between "Chemists," "Apothecaries," and "Druggist" (Figure 6.1). Such variations are not surprising, for many druggists charged deposits on their bottles to ensure their return and reused the same bottles for many years. In terms of bottle size, the bottles are remarkably uniform, with all but four examples being a 3-ounce size.

   Garrett Van Antwerp first opened his Mobile Pharmacy in 1885, facing competition from already established druggists like B. Ward. Van Antwerp's pharmacy thrived, and he quickly became a wholesale and retail drug supplier.

Figure 6.1   Examples of local pharmacy bottles recovered from the well

With his wealth he was able to replace his original pharmacy building on Royal Street with Mobile's first skyscraper, a 10-story building constructed from 1905 to 1908 (Culpepper 2001:73). Based on city directories, Van Antwerp's son, Andrew, was a partner in the business in 1900, providing some evidence that the various bottles represent a certain amount of time depth.

The most obvious reason for the inclusion of so many pharmacy bottles at the site would be that the Perrymans were using these products in health care and discarding the empty bottles at the site. Before returning to this interpretation, it is worth briefly considering other ways the bottles may have arrived at the site. The 1900 census lists Walter Perryman's occupation as a "bottle peddler." It could be suggested that the bottles are the result of his work. After 1903, with the advent of the automatic manufacture of bottles, the cost of bottles dropped and resale was less lucrative (Busch 1983). As a result, Walter Perryman could have abandoned his useless inventory at his mother's home. By the time of the 1910 census, Walter was no longer working in this trade. The relative uniformity of the assemblage, however, suggests that it was not created as the result of salvage behavior. One would also expect a salvage assemblage to contain a greater variety of bottle size and less variation between the relative abundance of different pharmacies. Similarly, if Lucrecia were collecting bottles for reuse to bottle medicines she derived herself, one would not necessarily expect such uniformity in the bottles. Given this, I favor the interpretation that these bottles represent the acquisition and use of the products they contained by the Perryman family.

That said, do the bottles represent the medical needs of the family, or are they related to Lucrecia's midwifery practice? This is an issue I will consider again in regard to the types of patent medicines being used, but for now, I will focus on the pharmacy bottles. First, it is surprising to find such a large concentration of druggist bottles at a single house site. Paul Mullins (1999), in his study of middle-class African-American families in nineteenth-century Annapolis, found patent medicines at the site rather than pharmacy bottles. When dealing one-on-one with white merchants, be they grocers or pharmacists, African-American consumers were not always assured of receiving the same quality of product as white customers, and they selected national brands instead (Mullins 1999). We have seen that the Perryman assemblage contained a sizable number of nationally known patent medicines. I will suggest, however, that the patent medicines represent part of Lucrecia's indoctrination of new mothers into scientific mothering, and her training them in what products to use for their children. In other words, when she used medicines that she intended for her clients to procure themselves in the future, she selected national brands. I will elaborate on this point in the next chapter. In contrast, I think that the pharmacy bottles represent a different aspect of Lucrecia's practice.

But I digress. Let us return to the question "For whom are these pharmacy products intended?" One interpretation could be that the deposited assemblage is the result of an extended illness that required extensive medical treatment. Both Frank Perryman and Sally Cunningham endured wasting diseases that prompted consultation of a physician, for the death certificates of each indicated that each victim had been visited shortly prior to death. While this is certainly a plausible interpretation, one reason I will argue against it is simply ease of access. Of the pharmacies represented archaeologically, Van Antwerp's, is located farthest from the Perryman land, and was founded in that location before the expansion of Mobile's electric streetcar line. John Hulsbush Drugs and West Ward Drugs (Figure 6.2) are both located closer to the Perryman home. According to the Mobile city directory, West Ward Drugs was in operation at the time of Sally Cunningham and Frank Perryman's deaths. Dave S. Bauer's pharmacy, which provided two of the recovered bottles in the assemblage, was also slightly closer to the Perryman home and in operation at the same time.

To shop at Van Antwerp's required one to travel nearly to the riverfront portion of Mobile. Marshall Perryman would have made this trip each day to reach his place of employment, at 72–74 Dauphin Street, but Van Antwerp's opened after his death. Beginning in 1893, Mobile began its first electric streetscar service. The fare cost 5 cents, and the single line took a passenger from a stop at Dauphin and Jackson to Virginia and Marine (C. Mathews 1941:27). By 1911, streetcar service was available in most of the city, and when the location of the pharmacies patronized by the family are plotted against the 1911 streetcar system, there is reason to believe that access to streetcars shaped the family's consumer habits in part (Figure 6.2). Though the Perrymans would eventually be able to take a streetcar from a stop two blocks from their home, traveling to Van Antwerp's would have required transfers between lines. Seemingly on the same

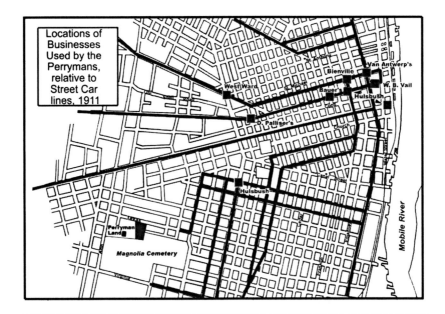

Figure 6.2 Location of pharmacies used by the Perrymans, as related to 1911 streetcar routes

street car route as Van Antwerp's was the Davis Street business district, where African-American–owned businesses, including pharmacies, were located. Yet no products from any of the African-American pharmacies were recovered.

Now, Van Antwerp was a very successful pharmacist, and perhaps part of his success arose from aggressive pricing strategies—the documentary evidence I have found is inconclusive. Given the quantities in which the products seem to have been purchased, any difference in price could have been important for Lucrecia. I suspect, however, that the distance of Van Antwerp's from her neighborhood, and presumably much of her clientele, was one factor that made this particular pharmacy attractive to the midwife. It may be that she avoided black-owned pharmacies for a similar reason.

Recall that physicians accused pharmacists of providing women with medicines and oils that could be used to induce miscarriage. Perhaps Van Antwerp's Pharmacy was Lucrecia Perryman's source of medicinal ingredients for certain remedies. Oral histories from midwives in Alabama (e.g., Logan 1989; M. Smith and Holmes 1996) illustrate that midwives prided themselves on creating their own unique tonics and remedies. Midwives and other African-American healers built reputations for themselves based upon the efficacy of their cures and remedies. In his interviews with traditional healers, Hyatt (1970) often found that he would be provided with vague ingredient lists. Midwives typically served their immediate geographic communities; therefore, the distance of Van Antwerp's from her home was likely to have lessened the chance of Lucrecia's patients observing her or one of her family members purchasing the raw ingredients for her remedies.

Perryman was certainly involved in the preparation of medicinal products and food medicines, as I discussed in an earlier chapter. By procuring medicinal ingredients elsewhere, and then recombining and mixing them into her own remedies, Lucrecia Perryman would be serving as a gatekeeper for knowledge regarding what herbs served which functions. Further, midwives were notoriously poorly compensated for their work. By producing and selling her own cures, whether they be abortifacients or other female or child-oriented cures, Lucrecia could have found another way to supplement her income.

Another important consideration: in the case of morally sensitive health decisions, such as the termination of pregnancy, by maintaining control over the effective ingredients, Lucrecia could serve as a moral gatekeeper. Given the differing views of midwives about the morality of ending pregnancies, particularly depending upon at what stage the pregnancy was, this would be an important control to maintain. If, like so many American women of her time, Lucrecia used the standard of quickening for diagnosing pregnancy, she could, by providing medicines that relieved menstrual amenorrhea, aid women fearful of experiencing unwanted pregnancies while not providing abortion services. Further, if she only provided access to these products in her home (dosing patients herself), she could ensure that both the product and the knowledge remained with her. Based upon the decoration of the Perryman home, which clearly emphasized themes of mothering and domesticity, as well as the example of other midwives' practices, there is reason to believe that Perryman saw some patients in her home.

Of course, what we are lacking in this analysis is any kind of a smoking gun, so to speak. There is no explicit evidence that any of the remedies Lucrecia Perryman prepared were used for abortion or birth control. While it would be more satisfying to provide a definitive answer in one direction or the other, the ambiguity is more appropriate. Abortion then, as today, was a controversial but commonly employed method of birth control for women of all races and classes. Any woman attempting to chemically abort would need to be discreet. The public controversy over whether Lydia Pinkham's Female Cure was intended to be an abortifacient or a health tonic exemplifies the intentional vagueness and ambiguity that surrounded these products and their uses (Riddle 1997). Doctors described abortifacient drugs being packaged in containers with no labels so that even in use, the function of the contents would remain quiet and unobtrusive. Given the political and social climate of their time, midwives would have maintained an ambiguity regarding what birth control services or advice they may or may not have dispensed, carefully evaluating which clients to aid and trust. Why should we expect Lucrecia Perryman to easily provide an answer to us—nosey strangers digging through her trash?

Narrative Interlude V

Liza Peters

Molly Givens

Mt. Zion Baptist Church, corner Grove Street and Jefferson, Turnerville
Interview Date: July 1, 1937
Interviewed by: Hazel Neumann

"Miss Neumann, yoo-hoo, Miss Neumann, over here! It's me, Christine Freeman!" Mrs. Freeman hurried across Grove Street to catch me, her parcels coming perilously close to toppling. I was not sure which surprised me more, the great vigor she exhibited for a person of her great age, or the enthusiasm with which she greeted me.

"Remember how I told you about my midwife deliveries? Well, just happens that the midwives have their club meeting today at the church. I know at least two of the old aunts were catching babies in slave times, and several had mothers who did, too! They usually have some tea and pastries, so if you take a sweet, I'm sure you can talk to a few and fit right in!"

So once again, I found myself bearing groceries in hopes of earning an interview or two. The Mt. Zion Baptist Church is a clean white structure sitting on the corner of Grove Street and Jefferson and has a meeting room in the back. The church is a simple white building, constructed in the 1890s, with glass that has been painted to look like leaded glass. The interior is clean and simple, with lines of wooden pews that serve as desks for the children who attend the church school. The meeting room is simply furnished, and painted white. Although designed for use by the ministers before service, it is clear that the room is used for a variety of community services.

The public nurses who lead the midwives' club meeting were just finishing up the business part of the meeting when I arrived. Since the 1920s, Negro midwives are required to be registered and licensed by the state to practice. Attendance was required at monthly meetings where they hear lectures about hygiene and other topics related to their practices. Their midwife bags are examined for evidence that the midwife is using old-time remedies. The midwives seem to enjoy the opportunity to mix with others in their field, and seem to like the refreshments following the meetings best.

While sipping on lemonade, I was able to introduce myself to Liza Peters and Molly Givens. The women are old friends but, living on opposite sides of Turnerville, see each other only at the meetings. The two are so similar in appearance and mannerisms that they could easily be mistaken for sisters. I mention this to them, and they laugh, remarking that all old women look alike. Both women were young girls when slavery ended. Miss Givens remembers hearing the booming of the gunboats on the Mississippi during the siege of Vicksburg, while Mrs. Peters remembers her mother helping to bury the planter family's silver when the Yankees came marching through their plantation. The two women are excited to see my increasingly visible "condition," and not surprisingly, the talk turns to babies.

"When are you due?" asks Miss Givens.

"You don't need to ask that," scolds Mrs. Peters. "You can see she's at the five month mark."

"You've obviously seen a lot of pregnant women," I comment, agreeing with her assessment.

"I have had the privilege of bringing over 300 babies into this world. With the help of God, I haven't lost one baby or mother."

"And that includes babies born before the New Law,"* added her friend.

"That's right," the woman agreed, "they can't say my practice got better with the new rules, it was already perfect."

"Has regulation changed your practice much?" I inquired.

Both women suddenly looked worried, as if perhaps I might be a representative from the state Board of Health. Miss Givens piped up, "I'm speaking for the both of us when I say that we both follow the New Law completely, and do not do anything besides what we are allowed."

"Well, it's clear that you are both very responsible and professional women," I assured them. "I'm interested, though, in any of the old practices you might remember, so I can record them. I know that people don't use those practices anymore, but I was hoping you might have heard about how things used to be done."

This was greeted with great enthusiasm. The two women were obviously more comfortable talking about the old ways when it was clear we were discussing the long ago past. I told the women about what Christine Freeman remembered about her births.

"Oh, the hat! You know, hats are powerful in the birthroom, they bring the father into the room and help ease the mother's misery. I know lots of women who used axes or knives, too," Miss Givens explained. "Those are things that bring spiritual comfort, you know, like reading certain Bible passages, or praying."

"Molly, you remember that midwife who used to use chicken feathers? She would burn the chicken feathers and say the smoke would ease contractions."

"Well, I never saw the sense of that. I mean, what's the connection between a woman and a chicken?"

"But the mole's foot always worked for teething babies, and apart from the fact that both crawl around in the dirt, I don't see a connection there."

Mrs. Peters turned to me. "The thing about the old ways, they worked not because some doctor said they should, they worked because midwives had been

---

* Editor's note: Midwives often refer to the period prior to regulation as the "Old Law" and regulation as the "New Law."

using them and found them to work. They were ways that were tried and true. It didn't matter whether you understood how they worked, just that you had the faith that they did. There were lots of good medicines made in those days. Some used spirits, some used herbs and roots. Some of the medicines they sell today aren't any different from the old medicines, they just come in jars and bottles and cost more. In the old days, different women had different medicines they would make for different problems. A midwife built her reputation with her medicines."

"I knew a woman," said Miss Givens, "who was so secretive about what went in her tonics, that she only collected her roots at night when others couldn't see what plants she was using. Another woman had an arrangement with a druggist who would get her certain ingredients for her tonics."

Mrs. Peters began to laugh. "Do you remember ol' Jinny on Long Neck Plantation? She would go buy Lydia Pinkham's women's tonic, add a little whiskey to it and rebottle it in Mason jars to sell it to her clients. She used to sell that stuff and say that Pinkham had stolen her recipe from her, that's why they tasted the same. Finally, she was caught burying a bunch of empties!" The two women laughed at the memory.

"Back in the old days, there were more midwives. They didn't all do it to make a living; some did it because they felt God's calling, some wanted the respect that goes with being a midwife. There was a lot more competition between women. Even now, there are midwives who start rumors about other midwives to get their licenses revoked," explained Miss Givens.

"Since you ladies know a lot about pregnancies and babies, I was wondering if you could clear something up for me." I recounted the story told to me by Olive Johnson and asked what they knew about herbs and roots to end pregnancies.

Miss Givens looked concerned, motioned to me to come closer and spoke in a lowered voice. "Oh honey, you know midwives can't give you nothing for that. Besides, you are too far gone, that baby must be kicking."

I quickly assured them that I was very happy to be pregnant, I was just curious. Mrs. Peters quickly stated she knew nothing about such things. Miss Givens was more open.

"Any woman can tell you that there is a world of difference between being with a child you want and a child you don't want. A baby can't grow right if a mama doesn't love it. Now, these doctors today say a lot of things that make no sense. First, and you remember this when your time comes, there is nothing sickly or unnatural about having a baby. Second, they seem to think they can tell you when you have a baby growing in you long before you would ever know. How can they know first? You don't really know there's a live baby in you till it kicks, that's when you know you have a baby with a soul, when it quickens. That's God's way of saying, you have three or four months to get ready, here it comes. Now, sometimes a woman's cycle stops, and the blood collects inside. There are teas made of certain plants that a woman can take so that her monthlies resume. They won't work if she has a living baby in her, so if they work, it means her blood was off, and now she's right. Those medicines are not used so much anymore, so I'm not going to tell you what they were. In the old days a lot of women, Negro and white, would go to midwives and root doctors to get them, because the white doctors wouldn't help them because they don't think bad blood happens. But no, those medicines aren't around like they were."

"And we wouldn't use them if they were," Mrs. Peters quickly added.

I decided to redirect the conversation, asking, "What do the two of you find the most different about midwifery now versus the old days?" This time it was Mrs. Peters who spoke first.

"I miss the feeling of knowing that whatever happened, you had the power to save the mother and baby because God was there with you, guiding your hands and mind. You gave yourself to Him, you trusted Him to bring you through. Now instead of calling on God, you call on the doctor. God was more reliable, and I know He has more experience than me."

Miss Givens nodded, then said, "When I was made an apprentice, I felt like, here I am, right at the center. A long line of midwives stretching back to the continent of Africa came before me, and after me will be a long line of future midwives, taking us who knows where? That connection is gone. I'll never hand down my practice to anyone. It's like I've lost my place in things, like we all lost something."

A younger midwife soon joined our group, and the conversation drifted away from the past. I watched the two old midwives leave the church, heading for the bus station. As they left, I couldn't help but feel I had lost something as well.

July 2, 1923

Dear Sweet-Pete,

Are you missing me, with there being so much more to miss? I suspect that very soon my position here will come to an end. My field supervisor is traveling next week to Turnerville to check on my progress, little knowing what kind of progress I am actually making! You would think that the 1920s had never happened, the way some people behave. Having conducted these interviews, I can see why the Abolitionists and Suffragists allied together in the early days. Perhaps Stanton was too quick to sever those ties.

I think you will be amused to hear about my interviews yesterday. I met by chance in the street one of my earlier informants, the woman who first recognized my condition. She encouraged me to attend a midwife's meeting. The midwives, all Negro, are required to attend monthly meetings led by the public health nurses to ensure that they are not performing secret "hoodoo" rites on their patients. So there I am, trying to minimize attention to my condition, surrounded by women most likely to spot it. You can imagine that I was the subject of much attention, as well as forecasting. Based on the height of my increasingly visible swell, we are assured of having a son to pass on your family name. This was the overwhelming sense of the women there, so I suggest we begin to think of boy's names in earnest. I make light, but the reality is, I would feel as safe in the hands of these women, particularly the older ones, as I would the hands of the doctor I have been seeing here. Why it is necessary for him to prod me in numerous indelicate ways when a granny can merely look at me, feel my stomach, and make the same recommendations, I simply do not understand. Truly, I had always expected the eyes to most closely observe my greatest intimacies to be my husband's, not my physician's. There is something to be said for some kinds of Victorian moralities!

I am in a "wordy" mood tonight, a circumstance increasingly evident in my interviews as well. I feel that my writing is beginning to flow more freely, and that I am less afraid to inject more of myself into it, to, as you fondly say to your students, "allow the reader to appreciate the unique perspectives the writer brings to our understanding of the world." For the first time, I begin to think I have something of worth to contribute. Even if I am sent home tomorrow, this venture will have been a success.

With my greatest love,
Hazel (and your son)

7

Midwifery and Scientific Mothering

Rapid advances in science and technology accompanied the last quarter of the nineteenth century. Science was increasingly viewed as a means of improving the quality of everyday life. In medicine, new hope for controlling the transmission of diseases came from increased understandings of microorganisms like bacteria and viruses. Collectively, these microorganisms came to be known by the public as "germs," and medical practice in the home turned toward an increased vigilance in combating these invaders of the domestic realm. "Germ theory," or the notion that contact with germs leads to illness, became quickly entrenched in much of American society after its introduction in 1870 (Tomes 1997:37).

An increased emphasis on the importance of sanitation, clean water and food, and personal hygiene (and associated rituals of good hygiene) characterized this period of American society. These practices were part of a growing movement of preventative medicine, intended to stop disease before it developed, rather than merely treat symptoms and illnesses already suffered. Reform physicians like Elizabeth Blackwell were at the forefront of the preventative medicine movement, which ultimately led to improvements in women's and children's health (Wood 1984:233). Scientific housekeeping promoted new standards of cleanliness, and emphasized women's role as sentries against the invasion of germs into their home (Tomes 1997).

As scientism became a larger part of daily practice, a new mothering ideology developed, that of "scientific mothering." Initially, scientific mothering was an empowering ideology that stressed the ways knowledgeable mothers could use scientific findings to better care for and raise their children. Like any professional, the woman who worked as a mother was supposed to be "up to date," in the parlance of modernity, so that she could create the safest, most efficient environment in which children could be raised (Apple 1997; Litt 2000). Information about the most modern practices could be found in etiquette and household management books, in child-care volumes, newspapers, and magazines, and could be gotten from doctors. Women would use these sources to inform their child-rearing practices. Domestic scientists like Ellen Richards, the first female faculty member at MIT, saw the increased emphasis on household sciences as ultimately leading to greater employment opportunities for women (Stage 1997). Nutrition, food chemistry, and sanitation were all elements of the new home economics, and ultimately, scientific mothering.

Perhaps one of the best-known examples of this early manifestation of scientific mothering is found in Catharine Beecher and Harriet Beecher Stowe's *The American Woman's Home: or, Principles of Domestic Science.* This volume was first published in 1869 but was reprinted regularly. Unlike the later work of Richards, household sciences for Beecher and Stowe were firmly embedded in the cult of domesticity. The book was dedicated to "The Women of America, in whose hands rest the real destinies of the Republic, as moulded by the early training and preserved amid the maturer influences of home" (1870). Beecher and Stowe compiled the volume upon sensing the imbalance between the ways that men were trained for professions versus the lack of formal training for woman running households. At 38 chapters (500 pages) in length, there were few topics not discussed by the authors. In addition to the expected subjects of child care, cooking, manners, and oversight of servants, a good amount of space was allotted to the necessities of exercise and healthy diet. The importance of cleanliness and the proper lighting, ventilation, and modes of heating a house were just a few of the topics covered.

Beecher and Stowe's volume is remarkable in a number of ways. Upon perusing the book, I was struck by the level of detail provided. For instance, the chapter on cleanliness begins with a discussion of the scientific treatment of the skin.

> Fig. 57 is a very highly magnified portion of the skin. The layer marked 1 is the outside, very thin skin, called the *cuticle* or *scarf skin.* This consists of transparent layers of minute cells, which are constantly decaying and being renewed, and the white scurf that passes from the skin to the clothing is a decayed portion of these cells. This part of the skin has neither nerves nor blood vessels. (1870:150)

The chapter continues to discuss other aspects of the skin's physiology before providing information regarding the best skin care for individuals of varying ages. In a chapter on infant care, they write:

> Be very careful of the skin of an infant, as nothing tends so effectually to prevent disease. For this end, it should be washed all over every morning, and then gentle friction should be applied with the hand, to the back, stomach, bowels, and limbs. The head should be thoroughly washed every day, and then brushed. (269)

Contrast this level of detail to a passage from Lydia Child's popular 1831 *The Mother's Book* regarding skin washing:

> Bathing the hand and feet, or combing the hair gently, will sometimes put a sick person asleep when he can obtain rest in no other way. An experienced and very judicious mother told me that, in the course of twenty years' experience, she had never known washing the face and combing the hair, fail to soothe an angry and tired child. But then it must be done gently. The reason children frequently have an aversion to being washed is that they are taken hold of roughly, and rubbed very hard. (1989:25)

Where Beecher and Stowe see the need for sanitation, Child looks for means of comforting a child. The language of Beecher and Stowe is very much that of capitalist America, with infants being "trained" to set sleep schedules and bowel movements, the exercise activities of children being "managed," and children learning the personal discipline of amusing themselves. Child uses anecdotes from experienced mothers; but in Beecher and Stowe, we see the appeal to the "professional" as they cite specific research case studies and particular physicians publications. That said, it is important to stress that the intent of Beecher and Stowe was not to replace the authority of mothers over their children, but rather to educate and train mothers in the most scientifically endorsed practices of child care and household management. They are not condescending in their presentations, but fully expect women to understand and consider the material they are presenting intelligently. Women are advised by the authors to strictly follow doctor's orders, once the reasoning behind the doctor's recommendation has been explained. As we shall see, as scientific mothering ideologies develop through time, blind adherence to doctor's orders becomes expected (Apple 1997).

Although Beecher and Stowe's book is one of the most widely available example of the late-nineteenth-century "new home economics," scientism and its companion, "scientific mothering," are clearly seen in other works. Helen Campbell's 1881 *The Easiest Way in Housekeeping and Cooking* also emphasizes the importance of ventilation, drainage, and lighting in the construction and arrangement of a home. Though Campbell's work is lacking in the scientific illustrations of anatomy found in Beecher and Stowe, she includes pages of tables documenting the elements of the human body and their relative abundance. In her discussion of sickroom cookery, she admonishes the reader, "Let ventilation, sunshine, and absolute cleanliness rule in the sickroom. Never raise a dust, but wipe the carpet with a damp cloth, and pick up bits as needed" (253).

Writing in a home economics guide, Maria Parloa (1910) explained her understanding of disease transmission for her readers:

> Under some conditions which are not thoroughly understood the air becomes badly contaminated by the decomposition of animal and vegetable matter. Air thus contaminated may cause specific diseases, and some of these are spoken of as being caused by *malaria,* a word which signifies simply bad air. What it is in this bad air which causes these diseases has not yet been determined but it seems probably, from researches on other diseases, that there are in the air microscopic germs which have the power to develop in the body and then to cause the symptoms which are referred to as malaria. (58)

Parloa also recommends polished floors to her readers, for such floors could be cleaned with the minimal use of water, an advantage because "moisture is one of the conditions favoring the growth of bacteria" (268).

Scientism in the household initially provided women with a means of expressing their expertise in the realm of mothering and domesticity. As such,

scientific mothering and the home economics movement began as a reification of the cult of true womanhood. Initially, scientific mothering provided
a means for African-American women to challenge mothering as an exclusive domain of white women. If good mothering was a matter of practice and
learning, African-American women could appropriate these behaviors as their
own, providing through practice a counter-image to the racist stereotypes. As
scientific mothering evolved from a woman-centered practice to one that was
physician-centered, however, scientific mothering became an ideology that reified whiteness and wealth. Litt (2000) has charged that because scientific mothering was born in a discourse that defined good mothers as white and middle
class, the ideology was "constituted as a site of heightened ethnoracial and class
differentiation among women. As their material resources, status needs, and
social networks differed, so did the ways these women took up the dominant
medical discourse of mothering" (4). Litt's study focuses on the experiences of
African-American and Jewish mothers who raised their children in the 1930s
and 1940s, and explores how the medicalization of motherhood was differentially constructed along ethnoracial lines. Mothers in her study engaged with
scientific mothering once it had been established as a realm in which mothering
experience was devalued in the face of scientific "professional" expertise. This
incarnation of scientific mothering demanded mothers to submit to constant
surveillance of their practices by physicians, and required them to engage in
what Sharon Hayes (1996) has called "intensive mothering," whereby women's
lives became child-centered to the exclusion of other interests, obligations, or
desires. Alternative approaches or models of mothering were constructed as
deviant, thus automatically denoting working mothers as inherently "bad."

Through the material culture recovered from the Perryman site, we can
investigate the ways that the Perryman family articulated with this ideology as
a part of their everyday household practice and as part of midwifery practice.
Scientific mothering was still seen as a means for African-American women to
publicly assert their worthiness as mothers. Perryman's adoption of scientific
mothering practices would have been, at this time, an act of political optimism
and part of a quest for self-improvement.

Scientific Mothering in the African-American Community

Scientific mothering was embedded in larger African-American social movements striving to improve public health. By establishing women's clubs that
focused on serving particular communities or causes, African-American women
embraced what was known in domestic science circles as "municipal housekeeping" (Stage 1997:30). The community existed as an extension of the household.
Through club work and church work, African-American women were able to
participate and shape changes in public health policy (Higgenbotham 1993;
Neverdon-Morton 1989; S. Smith 1995; Cash 2001).

Women's voluntary groups took the form of church groups, female aux-
iliaries, and women's clubs (S. Smith 1995:1). Through their volunteerism,

African-American women from both the middle and working classes built schools, hospitals, and day-care centers, and provided support for working women. So instrumental were women's clubs to reform and political movements that the National Association for Colored Women was founded in 1896 to represent the network of women's clubs. For middle-class African-American women, improvements in public health represented another avenue of social uplift for the poorer classes. Through the efforts of church groups, working-class African-American women also participated in the Progressive movement. The "politics of respectability" became a means of contesting and resisting the dominant culture (Higginbotham 1993). Their efforts were doomed to failure, as physicians began in the 1930s to assert their own exclusive control of authority over child care, naming maternalists themselves as one of the dangers facing the welfare of children. Established pediatricians advised their colleagues that part of a doctor's responsibility was to instruct mothers of their shortcomings (Litt 2000:31).

African-American women's clubs and church groups highlighted hygiene and sanitation in their public health movements. Sanitation represented not just a cleansing of environment but a cleansing of the soul. In 1904, Fannie Barrier Williams wrote of the club movement:

> The fact is that the colored race is not yet sufficiently aroused to its own social perils. The evils that menace the integrity of the home, the small vices that are too often mistaken for legitimate pleasures give us too little concern. The purpose of colored women's clubs is to cultivate among the people a finer sensitiveness as to the rights and wrongs, the proprieties and improprieties that enter into—nay regulate the social status of the race. (100–101)

By cultivating social niceties, she promised, club women would "become the civic mothers of the race by establishing a sort of special relationship between those who help and those who need help."

Williams's equating the role of club women to that of mothers is not surprising. Progressive-era reform movements often had children at their center. It is also evident, from some of their writings, that the educated middle-class women of the clubs sometimes fell into the trap of considering impoverished African-American mothers as childlike. Certainly, monetary poverty was often equated with moral poverty and ignorance, even in the minds of other African Americans. Sylvanie Francaz Williams (1904) wrote, "As a proof of the moral progress of the colored woman all down the line is the fact that we find families of six and seven children who are the offsprings of the same father, and the celebrations of silver wedding anniversaries among the lowly are quite frequent" (299). Her statements suggest that she assumes such family circumstances were a new phenomenon.

The Tuskegee Institute conducted some of the earliest and most visible public health events, particularly with the staging of its "Negro National Health Week" beginning in 1915. The institute's "movable school," an outfitted wagon, traveled through the rural areas surrounding Tuskegee in 1906 (T. Campbell 1969:92). In addition to teaching up-to-date agricultural techniques, the movable school provided personal hygiene and sanitation information. Thomas Campbell (1969), who had served in the movable school at its inception, recalled in his memoir the unsanitary conditions he encountered on rural plantations, "At most places where I stopped, the farmers lived in unscreened houses. Many, many times I was forced to eat food over which flies had crawled and these flies had equally free access to open privies, near-by barns, and pig pens. In most cases I either had to drink water from polluted surface streams or shallow wells that were little more than cess-pools, or drink none at all." Mothers were taught how to feed and bathe their children, the importance of cleaning, and the importance of individual drinking cups rather than communal dippers for the consumption of beverages.

Margaret Washington, the spouse of Booker T., was an influential club woman, serving as the president of the National Association of Colored Women in 1898, and the president of the Alabama State Federation of Colored Women's Clubs in 1900 (S. Smith 1995:25). Club women were responsible for providing much of the organization and implementation of Tuskegee public programs. The institute's philosophy was, in the words of Susan Smith (1995), to "support a racial uplift agenda that called for people to be clean in mind, body, and soul" (25). Women were primary targets of this movement, and Washington was noted to remark upon her frustration with the mothering skills of rural women. Washington (1904) described, in *The Voice of the Negro,* how Tuskegee Institute had provided models of proper living and behavior in the rural communities of Alabama, encouraging marriage and suitable housing (the institute advocated a three-room cabin with separate sleeping quarters for parents and children). She stated, "We firmly believe that these plantation colored women will prove not 'a menace' to the race, but a deliverer, for through her will come the earnest, faithful service for the highest development of home and family that will result in the solution of the so-called 'race problem' (294).

By focusing on hygiene and sanitation, club women were able to direct their attention to two ongoing health problems within the African-American community: high incidences of tuberculosis and infant mortality. As I explored in the previous chapter, high infant mortality rates were one of the reasons that birth control use was supported by black activists. Training that emphasized proper baby care and diet attempted to increase the overall health of African-American children. Proper hygiene, such as the brushing of teeth, hair, and nails, and regular bathing were all emphasized. The clubs were particularly remembered in some areas for their distributions of toothbrushes and toothpaste. Women's clubs also sponsored milk drives, providing impoverished families with milk for their children (S. Smith 1995).

Tuberculosis was recognized in the public health industry as one of the greatest threats to African Americans. In 1920, the tuberculosis rate per 100,000 was 85.7 for the white population, and 202 for the black population (Gamble

1989:1). Reasons for the difference in mortality rates were debated among physicians of the early twentieth century, whose explanations ranged from differences in the lung structures of African and European peoples to outlandish claims that African Americans did not have the mental fortitude necessary to thrive in freedom, therefore they were left physically and mentally vulnerable to diseases such as consumption and insanity (Gamble 1989:4). Alcoholism, abortion, and sexual immorality were cited by other white physicians as causes of high tuberculin infection among African Americans (e.g., E. Jones 1907; Northern 1909). Seale Harris, writing in the *Journal of the American Medical Association,* exemplifies these attitudes: "The fact that there were so few cases of tuberculosis among the negroes while they were slaves was a great triumph of intelligent, though enforced, hygiene, and it also proves that tuberculosis is a preventable disease" (1903:834). Among other factors, tobacco had a role to play in the spread of consumption, Harris suspected.

> The filthy habit of spitting shows its highest development among the colored population. Nearly all the men chew tobacco and their women use snuff, and the healthy and the tuberculous alike spit on the floors of many of their homes and churches. The best of their churches are provided with boxes filled with dry sand or sawdust into which they expectorate. The sputum, either on the floors or in the boxes, becomes dry and gets into the dust of the atmosphere, and the bacilli are inhaled in large numbers, and lodging on lung tissue already weakened from the causes of which I have spoken. (1903:836)

As a native white southerner, Harris could be expected to be biased in his portrayal of relative tobacco use between black and white southerners. The American passion for spitting—excuse me, expectorating—was often commented upon by visitors from abroad, and seems to have been a practice that crossed ethnoracial and class lines.

Thomas Campbell, who worked with Tuskegee's movable school in the early twentieth century, also observed the practice of spitting into sawdust piles. This young, middle-class African-American student was obviously shocked by the poverty he encountered, and even 50 years later, writing his memoirs, could not hide his horror at the conditions some tubercular patients lived in: "From the fact that the windows were shut—it was late in the afternoon—and appeared not to have been opened that day, I surmised that no fresh air had been let into the room during the day . . . on the floor by the bedside was a pile of sand into which this young man expectorated. The sand had not been changed during the day and was covered with flies" (1969:105). Campbell explained that he took no food or rest at that house because of his concern over the unsanitary conditions.

The close quarters in which many African-American families lived and worked made transmission between an infected and healthy person more likely, a point made by African-American activists. W. E. B. Du Bois and other African-American scholars and physicians argued that social conditions like segregation, poverty, and poor access to health care were responsible for the high mortality rates. In an address to the American Anti-Tuberculin League, John Hunter, a physician of African-American descent, declared environment, not heredity, to be the cause of high incidences of tuberculosis. One circumstance he identified as leading to transmission of the disease was child care and diet.

> The feeding period in poor children, with a large number of our race, is the time when the tubercular foundation is laid. Working mothers leaving their babes at home to be cared for by other children only a step higher in the family, depending for nourishment on a crust of bread dipped in "pot liquor" and coated with the dust of the floor, bad milk, if any at all, that has passed through a warm bottle of germs, likewise open the way for the enemy. (Hunter 1905:252)

African-American activists turned their attentions to strengthening black hospitals and improving medical training at black colleges (Neverdon-Morton 1991; C. Smith 1995; Cash 2001). In the South, nursing programs were among the earliest training opportunities available to young African-American women. Spelman opened its training school for nurses in 1886; Hampton in 1890; Tuskegee in 1892 (Neverdon-Morton 1991). Community training was an outgrowth of these efforts and was seen as the social responsibility of educated black women.

Black publications show some influences of scientific mothering—though because the consumers of these publications were assumed to be educated (and therefore, already informed in these matters), this kind of information is more limited. In the March 1911 edition of the *Crisis,* Mrs. John E. Milholland's "Talks about Women" draws upon some of the teachings of scientific motherhood. She introduced her column as being on hygiene and dedicated to homemakers and mothers. In the column, she advised mothers to teach their children proper hygiene, to breathe properly through the nose to purify the blood, to engage in daily exercise. She emphasized that a strong healthy living body led to strong morality (29). *Half-Century Magazine* emphasized the domestic sciences in a regular column, typically focusing on recipes. The March 1917 column focused on introducing more varied ways of cooking vegetables and fruits, illustrating the scientific mothering emphasis on good family diet (Porter 1917:13). Advertisements for food products, such as canned fruits and vegetables and baking powder, emphasized the high quality and purity of their products, demonstrating the influences of the hygiene movement. The journal regularly announced the dates of National Negro Health Week and provided brief updates of prominent women's clubs. It is clear from a review of journals such as these that the authors and editors assumed that their readers were already indoctrinated in the realms of domesticity and scientific mothering.

Lucrecia Perryman and Scientific Mothering

Lucrecia Perryman had good reason to be attracted to changing ideas regarding disease transmission and sanitation, as her family had been dramatically

Table 7.1 Food Medicines Recovered from the Perryman Well Feature

Product	Number Recovered
Mellin's Infant Food	1
Horlick's Malted Milk	1
Malt extract	1
Leibig Malt Extract	4
Johan Hoff Malt Extract	2
Peptonoid's	1
Sweet oil (olive oil)	5
Burnett's Cod Liver Oil	1

touched by the horror of tuberculosis. When Marshall died of a form of tuberculosis in 1884, the knowledge that this disease was transmitted by bacteria, rather than through heredity, was only two years old (Tomes 1997:38). Ten years after Marshall's death from this disease, two of Lucrecia's children died from the disease in close succession. Statistics drawn from five southern cities demonstrated that African Americans in Mobile suffered both a higher mortality rate overall and specifically from tuberculosis, than the white population. In 1890, the mortality rate was 21.5 per 1,000 for the white population, compared to 34.5 for the black population. Tubercular diseases accounted for 6.08 African-American deaths per 1,000, versus 3.04 for the white population. By 1900, the African-American death rate had declined slightly to 32.5 per 1,000, but the tubercular rate had increased slightly to 6.09. The white statistics demonstrated a similar trend (S. Harris 1903:835).

Among the medicine bottles recovered from the site were a number of products that served as food medicines (Table 7.1). These medicines assured users of greater strength and muscle tone, better color, and more vigor. They were recommended for invalids and young children. These products could have been used in the Perryman households to supplement children's diets, or as part of Lucrecia's midwifery practice. Yet consumption, as tuberculosis was more commonly known, was aptly named, and these drugs could also represent desperate attempts by the family to halt the wasting away of young bodies ravaged by this disease. Death certificates recorded for Frank Perryman and Sally Cunningham each suggest that death had come slowly but predictably, each being visited by a physician a week before their deaths.

Though the use of the nutritive medicines is ambiguous, perhaps the presence of two bottles of "Allen's Lung Balsam" and three bottles of "Piso's Consumption Cure" recovered from the Perryman well are more forthright in their meaning. "Burnett's Cod Liver Oil" was another product that claimed, among its other uses, to treat consumption. Consumption cures offered empty hope of a reprieve from the disease, while lung balsams promised to treat the lung congestion and chronic cough that characterized the condition. The porcelain spittoon that we admired in the Perryman's assemblage takes on an additional meaning when we consider the incidence of tuberculosis in the household. The vessel was a sanitary item, whether used for containing expectorant from the recreational habit of using snuff or chewing tobacco. The household wares recovered from the well included 13 commercial tumblers. These items would have been purchased initially for their contents, then reused as drinking vessels after they were emptied. While we are most familiar in today's markets with jelly tumblers, in fact, snuff was (and is) one of the products sold in commercial tumblers. The tumblers recovered from the site can as easily be evidence of snuff consumption as of jelly eating. Their presence means that we cannot simply attribute the presence of the spittoon to use by the tubercular family members. Whatever the cause of expectorating at the site, the spittoon would have safely contained exuvia, and could be washed with antiseptic, bleach, or boiling water to disinfect it.

Based upon what we can glean from the documentary record, Frank Perryman returned home from Chicago in the final stages of his illness. At this point in his illness, he would have been at his most virulent. Tuberculosis is transmitted through the air, and an ill person can infect others through coughing and sneezing. These others breathe the bacteria, which through the lungs enter their bloodstream. In 90 percent of the cases, the immune system is able to prevent the bacteria from forming the disease tuberculosis; this is particularly true of individuals who are not suffering from malnutrition or other immune system suppressions. An infected person can develop the disease years after initial exposure. Given these statistics, and the number of people living on the Perryman property in the early 1890s—at least four adults and at least 10 children—if everyone was infected, we would expect at least one person to develop the disease. That only Sallie is known to have become ill may suggest that the family members were generally healthy and well nourished, or that they were successful in minimizing exposure, or a combination of the two. It is easy to understand how this disease came to ravage urban African-American populations.

In addition to the Perrymans' spittoon, other aspects of their household lives that we have already mentioned may also indicate a concern for sanitation. For instance, the family's use of pitchers and individual tumblers can be seen as both an embrace of the values of domesticity and as part of hygienic practice. The use of communal water dippers, which threatened to aid transmission of communicable diseases among family members, was one of the unhygienic practices targeted by reformers. Serving beverages from a communal pitcher would limit such transmission. Only one example of an embossed "antiseptic" product was recovered from the well, "Dr. Tichenor's Antiseptic," but at least four other bottles recovered are of the shape that typically contained antiseptics such as witch hazel, microbe killer, ammonia, carbolic acid, or boracetine (Israel 1997; Amory 1969).

A final set of artifacts is worth consideration in regard to sanitation and hygiene. While preservation of organics was not great at the well site, 152 fragments of shoe soles and leather, as well as a stacked heel and brass eyelets, were found, as was one rubber shoe sole. The fragments, based on size and shape, seem to indicate the presence of women's, children's, and men's shoes. Shoes were not inexpensive commodities, and keeping a family as large as the Perryman's shod would have required some expenditure on the family's part. An infants' booties might be had for as little as 18 cents, but children's shoes were more often in the range of 80 cents to $1.40. Adults' leather shoes were seldom available for less than $1.50; most styles found in the Sears catalog went for $2 to $3 (Israel 1997:191–206).

A review of photographs taken by the Farm Security Administration during the 1930s and 1940s demonstrates that adults and children alike in rural areas often went shoeless in the warm weather of the South. In the photographic collection of William E. Wilson, who photographed daily life in Mobile during the late nineteenth and early twentieth centuries, African-American children wear no shoes in roughly 50 percent of the photographs (Culpepper 2000). In part, shoelessness in the South led to an enduring health problem—vulnerability to hookworm.

Hookworm, introduced to southern North America from West Africa, thrives in feces and dirt. The larvae enter the skin, often between the toes, infiltrate the bloodstream, lungs, and throat; they are then swallowed and enter the gastrointestinal tract. There they embed in the intestine, feeding on blood. An adult hookworm can live five years; eggs are passed through the feces. The host is said to have a hookworm infection until the worm load causes iron deficiency anemia, which marks hookworm disease. The warm climate, combined with the barefoot, privy-less lifestyle lived by many rural families, allowed hookworms to thrive; as much as 40 percent of the South's population was believed to have been infected with hookworm by end of nineteenth century (Ettling 1981:2). The parasite went undiagnosed, although the symptoms—a gaunt appearance, tiredness, earth-eating, and a shambling gait—were well known. Diagnosis tools were first developed in 1878 in Europe, and Charles Wardell Stills began to draw attention to the problem in the 1890s, although it was 1909 before the situation drew much public health attention. Nicknamed "the laziness germ" by a journalist, this parasitic infection is what caused the behaviors that came to be seen by the public as typical of the white southern sharecropper. In 1901, Stills's work drew the attention of John Rockerfeller, who donated $1 million to establish the Sanitary Commission for Eradication of Hookworm Disease (Ettling 1981:35–38).

Though Rockerfeller's commission disseminated information to black and white populations alike, there was a sense within the scientific community as early as 1902 that African Americans had more bodily resistance than the white population to hookworm, despite a lack of systematic supporting evidence.

The abundance of traditional vermifuges described in the ex-slave narratives suggest that African-American families were aware of and treating a variety of parasites. Interestingly, one remedy for worms was to steep a rusty (therefore, iron) nail in vinegar or whiskey (Clayton 1990). The resulting tea could be consumed. By the 1960s, iron supplements were used to treat the anemia caused by hookworms. The combination of traditional remedies employing iron and dietary iron derived from simmering meals in cast iron pots may have provided some mitigation for hookworm anemia for rural African Americans.

Hookworm had become one of the foci of both white and black women's reform clubs by 1910, and women who failed to take precautions for their children were deemed to be "bad mothers" (Ettling 1981:136). Despite the perception that they were less affected by hookworms, African Americans were targeted by the white press as the source of the hookworm scourge, blamed as carriers of the disease who should be treated to protect white interests. Public health solutions for the problem of hookworm focused on treating extant cases and preventing reinfection. Shoes and the construction of privies that would not allow for contaminants to filter into the soil were the commonly touted solutions (Ettling 1981; T. Campbell 1969; S. Smith 1995).

Now, I do not mean to suggest that the Perryman family wore shoes simply to prevent hookworm infection—in fact, they probably did not, given that hookworm had only just begun to receive great attention at the time when the well was filled. Protecting the feet of family members would have been a statement of affluence and respectability, not just practicality. For women who had been keeping their children's feet shod, learning that this practice had been protecting them from hookworm would reaffirm their status as good mothers. In such a way, scientific mothering reified middle-class values, even in revisionist ways. The construction of proper domesticity and scientific mothering was ongoing, and subject to elaboration, just as were other aspects of middle-class etiquette.

Scientific Mothering and Midwifery

Scientific mothering offered women who followed its principles of proper nutrition, health care, exercise, and hygiene the outcome of a healthy, thriving baby. This was not a promise to be taken lightly, and for less affluent families it was frequently a promise outside their anticipated experience. As a midwife, Lucrecia Perryman was in a position of considerable influence. Since midwives helped to shape the early mothering practices of the young women they delivered, Perryman could introduce women to practices and treatments that would improve the health of a child long after the child and mother ceased to be her patients. The principles of scientific mothering are evident not just in Lucrecia's home, but also in the materials likely to have been used in her midwifery practice. In many instances, the incorporation of scientific mothering practices could be accomplished in ways that were complementary to existing African-American medical traditions.

To Breast-feed or Hand-feed

How to best nourish a baby, particularly in situations in which mothers and infants might be separated from each another, has long been a subject of intense debate (Golden 1996; Maher 1992; Scheper-Hughes and Sargent 1998a). An infant can obtain nourishment through its mother's breast milk, a wet nurse's breast milk, or from a breast milk substitute, through a process known as hand- or bottle-feeding. It is not until the twentieth century that hand-feeding had much success. Most milk substitutes used a base of cow's milk, which is hard for some infants to digest, leading to diarrhea, dehydration, and death. In addition, cow's milk, prior to pasteurization, was a primary source of tuberculosis (Cox 1996). Infants ran the grave risk of being infected from their formula, or from unsterile water or bottles. The examination of human remains from a mid- to late nineteenth century church graveyard in Spitalfields, England, revealed high incidence of tubercular lesions among young children, possibly a result of their middle-class parents hand-feeding them according to the period's fashion (Cox 1996). Wet nurses were also suspect, being of the lower classes and possibly infected with tuberculosis, syphilis, or other communicable diseases (Grulee 1916). Still, there are a number of reasons to forgo breast-feeding one's infant in favor of alternative methods.

Marylynn Salmon (1997) has noted that fear of breast-feeding-related illnesses and conditions encouraged some women to seek wet nurses. Chapped and cracked nipples, infected mammary glands, and plugged ducts were chronically suffered by nursing women and were significantly more difficult to treat before the introduction of antibiotics. For women who worked outside the home, hand-feeding was necessary. Likewise, hand-feeding was necessary for women with low milk production or who had tested positive for diseases such as open tuberculosis (manifested by sores), pneumonia, or syphilis. The practice of hand-feeding became more popular with the end of the nineteenth and beginning of the twentieth century. As awareness of the role of cows in the transmission of tuberculosis increased, however, mothers were often reluctant to feed their children fresh, and possibly contaminated, milk. Canned milk, particularly sweetened condensed varieties, became incorporated into feeding regimes.

Pediatricians, practitioners of a growing subdiscipline of medicine by the early twentieth century, were anxious to cement their roles as authorities in child-care matters. Dr. Clifford Grulee's book *Infant Feeding*, originally published in 1912, and then republished in 1914 and 1916, is an example of one such attempt. His study is worthy of our consideration, for his intended audience was fellow physicians, not mothers. Thus we are allowed a peek into the kinds of information physicians communicated amongst themselves. In his introduction, Grulee (1916) writes:

> The successful combating of infant mortality can only be brought about by the education of the mothers in the essential facts of the science of the nourishment of the infant. In the future, however, there must be facts, and not unproved theories. At present the most glaring example of the harm that may be done by well-intentioned but uninformed individuals is that of public officers of health, whose continual cry has been to kill the bacteria, and this without any reference whatever to the composition or amount of food given the individual infant.... [I]t is the duty of the physician to see that his community is properly informed. (19)

Grulee (85–87) advised that breast-feeding was the best option for babies when at all possible, but he recognized instances in which the child was not thriving (failing to gain weight), as well as in those in which the mother suffered from acute infectious diseases, exhibited inverted nipples that could not be corrected with shields, or developed cracked and painful nipples that made feeding too uncomfortable. For sore nipples, Grulee suggested that a compound tincture of benzoin should be used, and the breast surface and child's mouth should be cleaned to avoid transmission of infection. All nursing mothers were recommended to clean their breasts with a boric acid solution between feedings.

Grulee recognized that artificial feeding, as he referred to it, was an established practice and could not be avoided. He recommended cow's milk, but advised his colleagues that the cleanest of milks would not be accessible to "more ignorant classes (therefore those to whom the most infants belong)" (1916:117), and recommended that doctors attempt to encourage their poorer patients to use milk, even if not the purest. He expressed his reservations regarding pasteurization, convinced that the process was used only on the dirtiest of milks, thus making them less desirable than unsterilized milk from healthy cows. Condensed milk was suspect for similar reasons—to be profitable the canners had to use a very low grade of milk. Grulee cited experiments that suggested that traces of cow manure and tubercle bacilli were found in condensed milk. Proprietary infant foods could be used, Grulee advised, but only if prepared with milk. He observed:

> There is no question that, in spite of the efforts of eminent pediatricians to decry them, the proprietary infant foods have been the mainstay of the general practitioners.... So long as such foods are used by the physician with definite indications and with definite ends in view, and so long as their composition is definitely known and, again, provided they are to be used in connection with milk, then we may say that their chief dangers are eliminated. (135)

There is little evidence of hand-feeding of infants in the Perryman assemblage. Cans were not well preserved in the site, with only 18 of the 713 can

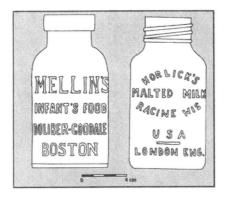

Fig. 7.1 Infant food bottles recovered from the well

fragments recovered identifiable as to can form. Six of these fragments could have been lids from milk cans. One glass milk jug was recovered from the site, and the presence of two stoneware butter churns suggests that dairy products were prepared at the site. Buttermilk was reportedly used to feed infants. Two bottles of proprietary infant food, one labeled "Mellin's" and the other "Horlick's Malted Milk," are the only evidence found (Figure 7.1; Table 7.2). Mellin's Infant Food was sold as a milk replacement for infants and invalids and was established in 1882 (Fike 1987:57); Horlick's was a nutritional food supplement sold for all ages starting in 1875 (Devner 1968:46). Each could be mixed with water, but preferably with milk. These companies are just two examples of what was a thriving late-nineteenth and early-twentieth-century market for milk substitutes. Nine different baby food companies were advertised in the 1897 Sears, Roebuck, and Company catalog (Israel 1993:28).

Apart from these two products, there is no evidence of the paraphernalia that would be expected to accompany hand-feeding. By the 1880s, nursing bottles were widely manufactured and available in a variety of distinctive forms, as

Table 7.2 Nutritional Values of Infant Foods Recovered from Perryman Well (after Grulee 1914: 136)

	Mellin's Infant Food	Horlick's Malted Milk
Protein	11.5	16.5
Fat	.2	9.0
Sugar	80.0	68.0
Starch	—	—
Salts	3.6	2.5
Caloric Value Per Ounce	120.0	135.0

were rubber nipples (Figure 7.2). Bottles that had broader necks, were clear in color (so that contamination could be detected), and could be easily cleaned with a bottle cleaner were recommended by physicians (Grulee 1916:142). In 1897, nursing bottles could be obtained for 60 cents a dozen (Israel 1993:28). They often were graduated so that the amount of food being consumed could be measured, for ensuring that babies were fed exactly the proper amount was part of the scientific mothering paradigm. Rubber nipples could be easily sterilized, and came in a variety of shapes and sizes; some promised easy nursing, while others claimed to reduce the symptoms of colic by minimizing the intake of air. Some were designed to fit over the top of the bottle, while others were inserted inside the neck. A dozen could be obtained from the Sears catalog for 20 cents to 60 cents (Israel 1993:28).

The absence of nursing bottles from the site is not necessarily indicative of a lack of bottle-feeding. The average size for nursing bottles was between 6 and 12 ounces, a size range that was typical for many bottles manufactured for uses other than nursing. A visual inspection of rubber nipples suggests that some varieties could have been used over the neck of larger prescription finish medicine bottles, or even over the bead finish of a long-neck soda or beer bottle. It is possible that the inclusion of so many mineral bottles at the well site is actually the result of their use in hand feeding. What dissuades me from this interpretation, however, is the accompanying lack of rubber nipples. Rubber did survive in the well context, as evidenced by, among other artifacts, the recovery of a hot-water bottle and medical appliance tubing. If any number of children were being hand-fed, either by the family or as part of Lucrecia's midwifery practice, I would expect rubber nipples to be present. These items were notorious for their short life span and their tendency to crack with use, so they would have been discarded and replaced often.

As an alternative to formulas, some mothers used thicker gruels, referred to as "pap," to feed their children. These mixtures, commonly of barley water, ground-nut water, or cornmeal and water, were fed out of infant feeders resembling modified teapots. These vessels were also used to feed invalids. Cornmeal pap was frequently used to wean enslaved babies, and was blamed for nutritional deficiencies in children (Corruccini et al. 1985). One of Jacquelyn Litt's (2000) informants recalled breast-feeding her child for two years, after which time the child was weaned to whatever food she was eating. Another remembered during her childhood in the South that older people would chew table food then feed it to weaned children. Her recollections of greens and pot liquor suggest that such a diet was richer in nutrients than could have been derived from conventional infant foods. Lucrecia Perryman would have experienced problems of nutritional deficiencies in children as an enslaved mother, and it is likely that these experiences influenced her attitudes towards infant feeding. There is little evidence to suggest the hand-feeding of infants played any large role in the Perryman family or in the midwifery practice. Given the

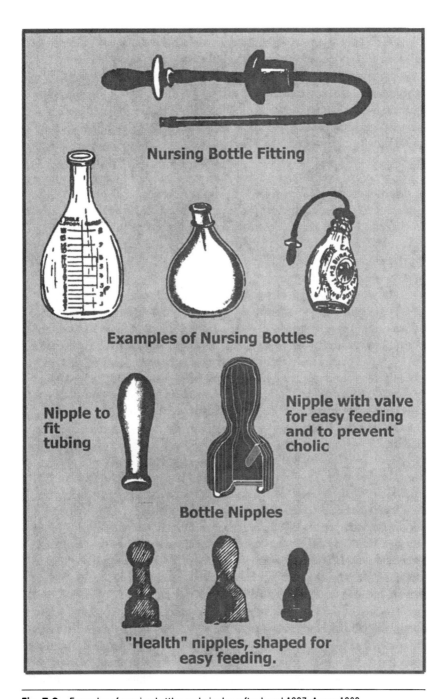

Fig. 7.2 Examples of nursing bottles and nipples, after Israel 1997; Amory 1969

high incidence of women suffering from tuberculosis, Lucrecia may have had patients suffering from this disease, who would not have been the best candidates for breast-feeding. There is certainly not enough archaeological evidence to suggest that infant foods were used in any abundance at the site.

Also missing from the site is any unambiguous evidence of equipment that might accompany breast-feeding. The recovery of breast pumps from archaeological contexts is not unknown (Costello 2000). We were not so blessed. The rubber tubing from the site could have been used with a breast pump, an enema kit, or with a vaginal syringe. Nipple shields and breast pumps are usually composed of both glass and rubber parts, but in no instance were we able to identify any of our fine, thin, clear glass as part of anything but lamp chimneys. Breast pumps are generally used to pump excess milk from the breast to relieve the discomfort of overfull breasts. The milk may be discarded or saved for later. The same effect can be achieved through manual expression. In fact, the manual expression of milk from the breast can often serve to minimize conditions such as infections from impacted milk glands.

The mechanical contraptions of motherhood, like breast pumps and nursing bottles, seen as commonplace among white mothers, were unnecessary, and probably not part of the mothering experiences of enslavement. In some ways, the breast pump can be seen as an elaboration of scientism in mothering, one that encouraged distance between a woman and her own anatomy. For obstetrics to thrive, it had been necessary for doctors to convince women that pregnancy and birth were unnatural, or pathologies requiring treatment (Bullough and Voght 1984). Gynecological and obstetrical practices were shaped by what was convenient for the doctor, not the female patient. Any practice or treatment that created distance between a woman and her body enforced the professionalization of these medical practices.

One product recovered from the site may be related to one of the discomforts that can accompany breast-feeding—cracked and sore nipples (in this case, the human kind, not the rubber!). As we have already discussed, Vaseline, in its many forms, was a useful salve for many conditions. Among the examples recovered from the site were jars that once contained carbolized Vaseline, which were in distinctive blue jars (rather than the clear or brown used for other varieties). The addition of carbolic acid to the Vaseline was believed to speed the healing process. As many young mothers have learned, nursing is not an instinctual behavior, but one learned by an infant. Improper attachment, gnawing, and other breaches of nursing etiquette by a newborn can leave nipples cracked, peeling, and even bleeding. The frequency with which newborns nurse leaves little recovery time. Generally, ointments and salves that provide a moisture barrier for the nipple are most soothing, and ingestion of small amounts of Vaseline would not be harmful to a nursing infant. While I have not found specific reference to Vaseline being used to treat sore nipples, of the products available at the time, it would have been my most likely choice.

Interviews with midwives who practiced during the period of regulation emphasized the importance of breast-feeding. Augusta William supervised her last birth in 1965; she recalled doctors trying to stop mothers from breast-feeding. "I always encourage all my mothers, the ones that wanted to—and a lot of 'em didn't want to. But I encouraged them and they did. At least, I tell 'em, they should nurse their babies a month . . . Mother's milk always better for a baby! And then it makes you closer to your baby when you nurse your baby. You are closer to your baby. You loves it. You learns to care for it. And then the child is closer to you" (quoted in Susie 1988:80–81).

Breast milk was not only an important source of physical nourishment but a powerful substance through which mothers could transmit knowledge and talent to their children. Gertrude Fraser (1998:197–198) said in her study of Virginia midwifery that "mother wit," or the common sense and shrewdness that allows one to thrive in the world, was transmitted through breast milk. One informant said that the increase in formula use and abandonment of breast-feeding had led to a communal loss of mother wit, leading to the loss of traditional medical practices.

Two other artifacts recovered from the well may be related to infant feeding. The only way to ensure a child was receiving enough nutrients from its food, be it breast milk or other source, was to regularly weigh the child. Two lead weights, intended for use with a balance scale, were found. The larger weight was 16 ounces, the smaller one was 4 ounces. It is tempting to consider that perhaps these were used to weigh infants or ingredients for medicines.

Maintaining the Bowels

The maintenance of the bowels became part of the ideological package of "germ theory." Irregularity was believed to cause many bodily discomforts:

> The undue retention of excerementitious matter allows of the absorption of its more liquid parts, which is a cause of great impurity to the blood, and the excretions, thus rendered hard and knotty, act more or less as extraneous substances, and, by their irritation, produce a determination of blood to the intestines and to the neighboring viscera, which ultimately ends in inflammation. It also has a great effect on the whole system; causes a determination of blood to the head, which oppresses the brain and dejects the mind, deranges the functions of the stomach, "causes flatulency" and produces a general state of discomfort. (Dr. Burne, quoted in Beecher and Stowe 1870:336)

Any impurities or germs contained within the food being digested had a greater opportunity to develop into illness the longer they remained in the body. Unstable bowels were particularly problematic for young children. Beecher and Stowe (1870) recommended a diet that included whole wheat bread, no animal food, and scheduled, structured meals to ensure regularity (276).

Despite the teaching of the pro-cereal movements led first by self-help guru Sylvester Graham (inventor of the Graham cracker) and later by John Harvey

Kellogg, one of his followers (A. Ross 1993), the average diet remained woefully lacking in the levels of fiber necessary to ensure regularity. Cathartics and enemas became the constant companions of constipated Victorians. Enema kits were sold equipped to serve entire families, with a collection of adult rectal and vaginal tubes, and smaller children's rectal tubes (Israel 1993). Even infants were subjected to colonics to treat cholic, for it was believed that imbalances to the gentle digestive systems of infants was a leading cause of high infant mortality (Grulee 1916:147).

Cathartics advertised specifically for use in children were abundant. The products promised to be gentler on small digestive systems than those formulated for adult use. Castroline, the product most promoted by the Sears, Roebuck catalog, was typical of the genre, promising, "Castroline will destroy worms, allay fever, prevent vomiting, cure diarrhoea and wind colic, relieves teething troubles. Cures constipation and flatulency. It assimilates the food, regulates the stomach and bowels and gives to the child a natural and healthy sleep (Israel 1993:39). Among the medicines recovered from the well were two of the most popular castorias, Dr. Charles Fetcher's Castoria, represented by a minimum of one bottle, and Dr. S. Pitcher's Castoria, represented by a minimum of three examples. Olive oil, or "sweet oil," as it was also known, was also used to relieve constipation. The olive oil recovered from the site could have been used in this way. Cod Liver Oil, also recovered from the site, was popularly used as a digestive regulator and, as we have seen, a consumption cure. Dr. Grulee (1916:137) also recognized cod liver oil as a food medicine to treat rickets as well as increasing the resistance of infants to respiratory infections. "Dr. Grove's Tasteless Chill Tonic" was used to treat malaria, but was more regularly used as a "spring tonic" to cleanse the systems of children at the end of winter. Given that quinine was one of the major ingredients of the medicine, it may be that the intent of this medicine was to prevent children from catching malaria in the first place. "Allen's Lung Balsam" is another medicine that appealed to mothers. Although we have discussed it as a consumption remedy, by the 1890s the product's makers advertised it as a cure for croup.

Collectively, these artifacts reflect items specifically designed and marketed to mothers to use for their children. Rima Apple (1997) has discussed the ways that advertisers of proprietary and patent medicines sought to appeal to mothers as knowledgeable consumers of scientific information as they selected products. The medicine trade cards from the 1880s included elaborate "scientific" details, describing the uses and advantages of their particular product. The fronts of cards used to promote children's medicines often featured images of beautiful, rosy-cheeked, white children embodying perfect health. In teaching her patients to use these products, Lucrecia was introducing them to discourses on sanitation, hygiene, and good, informed, mothering. As a midwife and a successful mother, Perryman was in a position to instruct her patients on how to best raise healthy children. In effect, Perryman was encouraging her patients to appropriate as their own the right to raise a beautiful, healthy child—a right that the dominant society communicated was the sole privilege of white women. In this aspect of her mother work, Lucrecia Perryman was as much involved in racial uplift as any of the women's clubs.

Scientific Mothering and the Demise of Midwifery

By the 1920s, the AMA, hoping to expand opportunities for the overabundance of doctors being trained in the United States, targeted midwives as undesirable competition for patients in the new fields of gynecology and obstetrics (Kobrin 1984; Susie 1988; H. Mathews 1992b). The AMA successfully waged a smear campaign in the northern United States against European immigrant midwives, leading to the eradication of their practices. As I have already discussed in the previous chapter, midwives' role in providing access to abortions was one realm focused upon by the medical industry.

After this success in the North, the AMA directed its efforts to the South, where the vast majority of practicing midwives were of African-American descent. The AMA helped with the preparation of state reports alleging that African-American midwives were unsanitary, superstitious, and dangerous to their patients, citing unsubstantiated reports of high infant mortality. Southern states began to require that midwives gain state training, supervision, and licenses, thus forever altering African-American midwifery. The scale of change inspired by the elimination of midwives can be seen in birth statistics from the era. Midwives in Birmingham, Alabama, for example, attended 968 births in 1917; in 1924, following regulation, that number had dropped to 10 (Litoff 1978:8).

Midwives were a casualty in what was a larger struggle between physicians, nurses, and public health officials for control in the professionalization of medicine. Carolyn Conant Van Blarcom (1914) is credited with beginning in earnest the campaign against midwives. Blarcom accused midwives of being ignorant, superstitious, untrained, unsupervised, and dirty. She elaborated:

> The extreme ignorance of some of the more unfit of these women is suggested by the superstitions which they foster; one, for example, will advise the mother to wear a string of bear's teeth to make the child grow strong; another that in cases of tardy labor it is beneficial to throw hot coals on hen feathers and place them under the patient's bed; another that it is flying in the face of Providence to bathe the infant before it is two to three weeks old; while others recommend that such articles as cabbage hearts, bacon rinds, beer, etc. should be included in the baby's dietary. (198)

While it was Blarcom's critique of midwives that captured public attention, she was equally critical of physicians, proclaiming, "However, bad as the midwife is, we are sorry to have to admit that on the whole a patient is often better off in her hands than in the care of many of the physicians who compete with her" (198). Perhaps more relevant to understanding of this trained nurse's anger is the fact that she wondered at nurses needing two to three years of hospital training before being competent to take orders from doctors who required only two to four years of training in all. In light of this comment, Blarcom's call for the elimination of midwives, or at least for their training and licensing, can be seen as a means of further legitimating the position of trained nurses. Because midwives served a rural clientele outside the interest area of many physicians, doctors tended to favor the gradual elimination of midwives until such a time when the number of rural physicians had increased (e.g., J. Ferguson 1950; Baughman 1928).

Midwives were targeted in particular for two perceived wrongs: their unwitting contribution to high maternal and infant death rates through the spread of childbed fever (puerperal infections) through unsanitary tools; and the incidence of childhood blindness (Fraser 1998). Though infant mortality was high during the late nineteenth and early twentieth centuries, there is little statistical evidence to suggest that midwives were less successful than physicians. Fraser (1998:79) found that in 1923 Virginia, one study cited the infant mortality rate for babies delivered by African-American midwives as 67 per 1,000, while the rate for physician-attended hospital births was 78 per 1,000. The study's authors had adjusted the rate to favor physicians by not counting in their number infants who died in the hospital after first being attended by midwives elsewhere. These statistics suggest that hospital birth was not safer than home birth.

Evidence used against midwives came from yet another faction—African Americans engaged in public health. Booker T. Washington was among those responsible for the "germs know no color line" campaign, which was directed toward raising white interest in African-American public health problems. Washington emphasized that African-American cooks, laundresses, and nannies could bring germs into the households of their white employers; therefore it was in the best interest of the white community to become involved in solving the health problems that plagued the black community. In telling anecdotes to enforce his theme, Washington often portrayed black women, particularly rural black women, as agents for the spread of disease (S. Smith 1995:40). The campaign was successful in gaining white attention, but it ultimately reinforced the white community's worst stereotypes of black womanhood as tainted. As we have already seen, this same kind of reasoning was used to blame African Americans for the spread of hookworms.

Ultimately, the accusations that African-American midwives were unclean and unsanitary may have been part of the reason that middle-class African Americans never defended their cause or livelihood. The NAACP, which lauded itself as a defender of workers' rights, never addressed the midwife controversy in the *Crisis*. Indeed, the magazine encouraged women to seek hospital births. W. E. B. Du Bois (1933:44) advised "the systematic use of physicians, dentists and hospitals' not simply to recover from disease but to prevent illness, especially the use of hospitals for births, severe illnesses and necessary operations." In the same issue, the *Crisis* provided a biographical piece on a medical school–trained African-American woman doctor (33).

There were other reasons for the black elite to ignore the situation of African-American midwives. As discussed earlier, nursing programs were among the earliest college educational programs developed for women at black institutions of higher education. The training of African-American nurses and doctors was seen as a way of addressing the public health issue. As the twentieth century progressed, the health industry began to mimic changes in scientific mothering paradigms, with nurses and mothers (both groups being women) expected to defer to the greater scientific authority of physicians (who were almost exclusively men). Midwives did not fit into this hierarchy. They were autonomous health care workers who trained themselves experientially. Their science was based upon established, experiential, successful practice. Their laboratory was the birth room, not the hospital, and, as a result, they did not fit into the dominant medical paradigm. Midwives perceived birth not as an illness, but as a natural event, a perspective that further placed them outside the dominant medical discourses. Midwives saw their authority as partly arising from a spiritual calling, and as such, they were a compelling, less expensive, and successful alternative to physician-assisted hospital birth. In every way, the existence of the midwife was a threat to the professionalization of medicine that both the elite white and black populations were invested in promoting.

In 1921, the United States Congress passed the Sheppard-Towner Act into legislation. This act provided funding until 1928 for states to develop programs for improved infant and maternal health. In many southern states, the Sheppard-Towner Act led to midwife retraining, registration, and licensing programs designed to bring lay midwifery under government control and regulation. Most states followed a similar procedure. First, the midwives were located and listed in a register. Many midwives responded to requests to identify themselves, and were eager to participate in educational opportunities. They quickly learned that their participation subjected them to limitations on what they could do for their patients, searches of their equipment, bureaucratic paperwork, and the ever-present threat of being retired (Fraser 1998; Susie 1988; Montegeau 1985; Campbell 1946).

The midwifery regulations emphasized hygiene, mandated that midwives call physicians in high-risk births, outlawed midwives' own medicines, and required record keeping for generating statistics. The regulations tightly scripted what midwives could and could not do, and violation of these regulations could lead to the immediate loss of one's license. Susan Smith (1995) found that competing midwives would sometimes inform on the violations of others to shore up their own practices. In many instances, regulations would require action (or

Table 7.3   Example of Midwife's Medical Bag, Post-Regulation (after Ferguson 1950:95)

Inner bag of white washable material
Cap, mask, gown
hand brush
wooden nail cleaner
blunt scissors
bottle of Synol soap
bottle of Lysol
Silver nitrate, 1% in ampules
Sterile tape to tie cords
sterile eye wipes
mouth thermometer
funnel with rectal tape
manual for midwives
midwife permit pinned on last page
birth certificates
leather bag to keep inner bag clean
sterile band and cord dressing

non-action) that contradicted generations of tradition and established practice. For instance, Fraser (1998) observed that requiring midwives to fill out birth certificates with the child's name on it at the time of birth contradicted African-American traditions that delayed naming until as late as the ninth day following birth. The contents of medical bags were scrutinized, and the use of traditional medicinal preparations banned. Contents were strictly regulated and limited to particular products (Table 7.3).

Marie Campbell (1946), a public health nurse who supervised African-American midwives during the period of regulation, described searches of midwives' bags:

> Nurses also watch for contraband in the midwife bag, because the grannies used to carry little or nothing in the way of supplies except patent medicines, pills, brew of roots, herbs, etc.; homemade salves, all sorts of "remedies" with which they dosed their patients. They are now forbidden to do this. Nurses have learned to look under the removable lining of the bag. There may be found such things as coins tied into the corners of a handkerchief, a piece of rope, a box of snuff, a bottle of homemade tonic or "bitters," a rabbits foot, or some other good luck charm. (27)

As I discussed in the previous chapter, African-American medicine recognized the importance of maintaining spiritual and mental balance for healthfulness. Midwives were bearers of communally constructed, negotiated, and performed medical beliefs, a role that regulation diluted if not eradicated. Midwives resisted regulation when possible, particularly when it contradicted communal standards. Some midwives circumvented control of their tool kits by keeping two medical bags, "one to show and one to go" (S. Smith 1995). As we have seen from Margaret Smith's (Smith and Holmes 1996) recollections of her midwifery practice, she was called upon to provide herbal treatments to her patients after regulation, stopping only once she feared her reputation had grown too large to be safe. Likewise, midwives, when faced with emergency delivery situations and convinced that a physician would not arrive in a timely manner, broke the prohibition against penetrating the birth canal (Mongeau 1985; Logan 1989). Still other midwives continued to practice without licenses (Dougherty 1982).

Many of the changes to midwifery were as much concerned with appearances as practice. James Ferguson (1950:86), a doctor who supervised midwife regulation in Mississippi, exulted: "The old Negress in dirty nondescript dress, a pipe stuck in her mouth and a few odds and ends of equipment thrown into a paper shopping bag or a drawstring sack began to be replaced by a cleaner woman in a white starched dress and a white cap carrying a neat black leather bag which contained a carefully scrutinized set of supplies." For physicians and public nurses, it often seemed that the appearance of professionalism was most important to them.

Midwives worked to the best of their abilities within the parameters of regulated practice. They used their authority within their communities to enhance public health opportunities, to demand physician care for needy patients, and to encourage health education. Midwives remained established and trusted figures within their communities, as vividly illustrated by *Life Magazine*'s 1951 pictorial essay about the daily routines of African-American nurse midwife Maude Callen (Smith 1951). Though Callen had been trained in nursing, the role of nurse, comforter, adviser was no different than the role performed by lay midwives prior to regulation.

Despite their best intentions and conformance to licensing and regulation, lay midwives were not permitted to continue their practices. Midwives found themselves unexpectedly retired, with surprise celebratory parties at monthly midwife club meetings. The presentation of the retirement certificate was little recompense for having a life's work taken away. By the 1970s most states were no longer issuing lay midwife permits, and the remaining numbers practicing were negligible (S. Smith 1995).

The loss of lay midwifery had profound consequences for African-American medical traditions and community. To illustrate some of these consequences, it is worth considering Litt's (2000) study of African-American women's medical experiences in the North and Fraser's (1998) study of Virginia midwifery. Litt's informants had moved from the South in the teens and twenties of the twentieth century. Their migration corresponded with the implementation of regulatory midwifery programs in the South. Lay midwifery had already been abolished in the North, and as a result these women had not necessarily been exposed to the public health rhetoric condemning midwives. Several of the women had experienced midwife-directed births before migrating from the South; others remembered midwife deliveries experienced by their mothers or other family members.

Litt (2000) found that her African-American informants remembered with greater acuity and respect the medical traditions of their past than did her Jewish informants. Traditional remedies and the medical/caretaking authority of the women who created them were held in esteem and at times still employed. She observes, "These women were oriented toward the knowledge, values, and traditions of trusted individuals and in their practices they supported not a fracture between the generations but a continuing process of weaving the generations together" (77). We have seen in the previous chapter the ways that midwives actively combined innovation and tradition in their practices to make the birth experience relevant and understandable across generations. Litt's informants demonstrate that this attitude was carried to the North. While a number of Litt's informants admitted that they no longer used traditional remedies, they did not denigrate the traditional practices but, more typically, revered them as evidence of a sense of community and mutual caring missing in their new homes. Their memories and relationship to traditional healing stand in contrast to Fraser's experience.

Fraser (1998) found women hesitant to discuss their experiences with midwives and were reluctant to express agreement or support for their practices. Fraser observed, "It was unwise to accentuate past cultural beliefs and practices and ways of living that fell too far outside the normative standards of what would be considered appropriate cultural and social behavior in today's world" (148). The rhetoric used to cast doubt and suspicion on midwives had relegated their history to a site of community silence. Most fascinating, from this perspective, is the way that older women, who had relied upon midwives, rationalized their disappearance. They asserted that old medicines would not work on new, modern bodies. Instead, African-American women's bodies were conceptualized in their communities as having changed in fundamental ways through the generations (164). Grandmothers no longer found the bodies of their granddaughters intelligible. The sense of generational connection, fostered in part by lay midwives and their approach to multigenerational participation in birthing, had been fractured by medicalization. The communal body had been ruptured.

Perhaps one of the saddest ironies is that by appropriating ideologies of modernity, like scientific mothering, African-American midwives had partially played a role in their own demise. They were positioned in public health debates as unclean and unsanitary—yet the archaeological evidence of Lucrecia Perryman's midwifery practice suggests the opposite. Perryman seems to have been aware of public health and scientific mothering discourses of her time and actively incorporated them, and the emancipatory power they offered mothers, into her practice. Taken out of the context of communal continuity and strengthening, traditional practices were rendered unintelligible to the younger generations, and came to be seen as outdated, or even embarrassing. As one of Litt's informants stated when asked about the use of traditional remedies, "You get modern, I guess. I mean you go and buy, you don't make, you don't bother with all those remedies. You go and buy" (2000:145).

African-American midwifery was left unprotected by the African-American middle class as it sought to create new opportunities for blacks in the medical fields. Affluent African-American club women may have adopted the ideologies of scientific mothering as a way of combating racism, but ultimately, the ideology shifted in ways that further rewarded white motherhood and denounced the experiences of black motherhood as peripheral to the dominant discourse. In the process of attempting to appropriate scientific mothering for the black community, activists and reformers sacrificed the much-needed health care and cross-generational community building provided to rural African-American women by lay midwives.

Narrative Interlude VI

Marsoline Collins

Tressa Burns

18 Jefferson Street, Turnerville, Mississippi
July 7, 1937

Well, Independence Day for me has come a bit late. My field supervisor was appalled to learn that a woman "in-the-family-way" has been in his employ, and has demanded that I return to my husband and allow another (a man) to take my place in the project. I am idling along Jefferson Street, delaying the task of preparing my interviews to be sent to Jackson and packing for the return to Oxford. Whether my feet have intentions of their own, or it is merely a random circumstance, I find myself in front of the home of Marsoline Collins. Well, I think to myself, Mrs. Collins did indicate I should return to talk with her, and it would be remiss of me to not complete my duties before leaving. I climb the porch and ring the bell.

From inside I hear voices debating whose turn it is to answer the door, shuffling and thumping, and then the door swings open with great energy. A young woman who looks strikingly like Marsoline Collins stands in the doorway. I quickly introduce myself and explain why I have come, and inquire as to whether I might speak with Mrs. Collins.

"Oh, nana spoke of you. She said she enjoyed remembering the old days, so I suspect she would like to visit some more." She showed me inside to the familiar parlor, and introduced herself as Tressa Burns, Mrs. Collins's granddaughter. She went to tell her grandmother of my arrival, and returned with a cup of hot tea.

"My grandmother is insisting that she be properly dressed to receive a visitor—she'll be just a moment, why don't we share a cup of tea while we wait." She then smiled, "Given both of our conditions, it might be best if we sit next to one another rather than at the table!" It indeed appeared that Mrs. Burns and I were expecting babies on a similar schedule (and now that I am no longer hiding my pregnancy, I am amazed how large I have become).

On my previous visit, Mrs. Collins had mentioned a granddaughter who had attended Dr. Washington's Institute at Tuskegee, and I inquired if that were she, and she confirmed this was the case. Tressa's husband owned one of the few black-owned enterprises in Turnerville—a pharmacy. We chatted for a few moments about the problems of running a business, then, as is typical for women in our state, our discussion turned to the topic of birth.

"Will you be using a granny?" I inquired.

Tressa looked at me and laughed, "You have been spending a lot of time speaking with our older people! Oh no, I'll be going to the hospital in Jackson when the time comes. After all, won't you be having a hospital birth?" I recognized the challenge in her tone, and suspected, just as in my first interview, that I had inadvertently stumbled again. I perhaps answered more stiffly than I intended.

"I planned to have a hospital birth, but I must say, I understand the attraction of using a midwife. I have been impressed by the devotion to their work exhibited by the midwives in town."

"The old dears mean well," she agreed, "there is no doubt of that. They love their patients and their work. Love alone, however, cannot save a baby with an infection. The world has moved on. We know so much more about medicine, and hygiene. It would be irresponsible to deny our babies anything but the most modern and up-to-date care. It's only a matter of time until professionally trained nurses and doctors are available to care for rural people. The midwives can then enjoy happy retirement."

"Don't you think it would be sad for those traditions to fade away? After all, midwives are part of a long folk heritage. Their techniques may not be modern to our thought, but they seem to be very effective . . ."

"Well, it is the role of people like yourself to record that heritage. I can appreciate the role of the midwives in the past without subjecting myself to their potions and notions," she asserted. "The idea that Negroes are backward and superstitious has done much to impede my people's progress." I had to agree with her statement, but felt that perhaps some common ground could be reached. I was unable to pursue the conversation further, for Mrs. Collins (whom I had quite forgotten!) entered the room and greeted us.

"I see you have met my wonderful granddaughter," she smiled. "The two of you are a delightful sight, solving the world's problems over a big belly and cup of tea."

I reminded Mrs. Collins about our last talk, and her memories of growing up during and after slavery.

"I probably talked your ear off! I love remembering those days with my mother, father, brother, and sisters. Those were some of my happiest days to date. I expect to have more soon, though, with a great-grandchild in the house," she said. "I raised Tressa. Her mother was my daughter. My daughter and her husband had a hard time making a go of it. Work was hard to come by, and Jane, my daughter, had to work to help support their three children. Even when it's hard for the men to get work, there is always work for women, cleaning and washing. Jane's husband was a good man, but a weak one. He didn't think it right to have a woman earning more money than a man, and they'd fight over her job."

"Now, Nana," Tessa interrupted, "you're not being fair to daddy. He didn't like mama working in those kinds of conditions. She was always spending time raising someone else's children and was left no time to spend with us. There was always some white employer ready to abuse her, whether it was a white woman thinking her worn clothing was suitable payment instead of money, or her husband wanting to corner her alone. How is a man supposed to have a sense of dignity when he cannot even feel that he can protect his wife?"

"Your mama was working to make sure you children could eat good food, and go to school, and marry college graduates. She sacrificed, but she was protecting you. Your father should have seen that and respected her for that. A woman isn't less a wife or mother just because she washes some other family's clothes. But he fought and fought with her to quit and let him do the work. Does that make sense? How would you have lived? He drove her into the ground." She now turned to me.

"My daughter died of tuberculosis, leaving little Tressa, the baby of the family. I took her in, as I knew my daughter would want me to. I told you how lucky my family was. My father supported our family. My husband supported my family till he died. My sisters had to work, and work hard. Domestic service, mainly. It can be insulting work, scrubbing and bowing to some person who doesn't see you as fit to be in their house. Working for miserable pay for long hours. But when you get home, and you've brought your baby some milk or a new lesson book for your child, you know you've done the right thing. Last thing you need is your man telling you that you're a bad wife because you aren't home waiting on him. That's one thing about slave times, men and women understood what work had to be done. They understood compromise."

I glanced at Tressa, whose jaw was set as she stared past the front door. I could tell she was withholding a response. She had the expression of one who has spent a long time listening to the complaints of her elders about the "younger generations." This was clearly a new version of an old disagreement between the two—with the difference that my presence gave the older woman a new verification of her authority. I had the sense, and not for the first time, that I had never been the one leading these interviews.

The tenseness passed, and the conversation wandered aimlessly through various avenues of pleasantries and small talk. I stayed longer than I had intended, and longer than I could justify, given I was no longer in our government's service. I thanked both women and wished them well, I advised Mrs. Collins that a new interviewer might be visiting Turnerville at some point and want to speak with her further. As the door of Mrs. Collins's house shut behind me, I knew my WPA-funded career had also come to a close.

July 9, 1937

Dear husband,

    I hope this finds you well. I am finishing my tasks in Turnerville, and will travel tomorrow to Jackson to file my interviews. I am planning on staying with my friend Eliza for a few days before returning to Oxford. Soon we will be together again, though I suspect you will find me much changed! My increased appetite, along with continuous offers of good "home-style" cooking has enhanced my changing silhouette. I wonder how pleased you will be to see such a wife.

    While excited to see you and home again, I am also sad to leave this place; this experience has been so much more than I had ever anticipated. I have truly led a sheltered existence, behind the walls first of my family home, then of your ivory tower. I have met so many people whose experiences I could not have ever imagined. While my intent may have been to practice my writing and search for "character" material, the experience has been so much more profound. I expected simple folks living simple ways, yet found such profound depths of reflection. The pain, both physical and psychological (how modern I sound), endured by these people is voiced so eloquently that attempts to edit or rephrase their sentiments only serves to destroy them.

    I have enclosed in this letter, dear husband, a handful of interviews I have decided not to file with the state. I do not believe that I have done the people they recount any great justice in my writing. It may merely be a reflection of my current state (and associated sensitivity), but I also feel that these interviews stand apart from the others. They say too much. They arise too much from these people's hearts. Released to the world, these words may take on a life of their own and come back to harm the people who first spoke them. Their stories are important, but I believe they can be told in other ways. Perhaps that was the reason for this journey. I give them to you, my love, because these interviews tell stories of mothers, fathers, children, wives and husbands, love and regret. As we come to this great new adventure of ours, I think we will find lessons we can take from them.

I will be with you soon.
With my greatest love,
Hazel

8

Conclusions: The Many Ideologies of African-American Motherhood

African-American women found their social identities constantly shaped by dominant discourses on race, gender, and class, a phenomenon that Collins (2000) has referred to as intersecting oppressions. Ideologies defining what constitutes good and bad mothering are embedded within these same discourses. An archaeological exploration of mothering, then, provides an opportunity to meaningfully discuss the convergence of class, race, and gender identities in African-American communities without reverting to privileging one aspect of social identity over another. In this work, I have attempted to present what I see as two differing scales of agency. African-American activist organizations combatted stereotypes about black mothering and womanhood, through their writings and through collective political action. These discourses influenced, directly and indirectly, the experiences and attitudes of families and individuals and helped shape the ways they acted on behalf of their families and communities. The mothering and the motherwork performed by the Perrymans was part of a politicized and, I would argue, transformative agency exercised by African-American families who saw claiming their privileges of parenting as a means of staking a claim for other social and political rights.

Recent works in historical archaeology have attempted to construct interpretations that meaningfully recognize in a multidimensional way different aspects of social identity, with mixed results (e.g., Delle et al. 2000; Orser 2001; Wilkie 2000a). In many instances, class becomes the social identity given preferential treatment (Wurst and Fitts 1999). One of the important issues to arise out of feminist thinking has been the critique of the centrality of white, middle-class women's experiences to feminist discourses (Spelman 1988; Collins 2000; Giddings 1984; A. Davis 1983). Historical archaeologists often replicate this bias by assuming that families think about class identity in similar ways, despite differing experiences of race and gender. By drawing on feminist theory, particularly critiques of feminism that focus on the experiences of women dealing with poverty and racism, I have tried to counter this tendency. By taking this approach, I find that the archaeological evidence seems to suggest that the Perryman family selectively appropriated those aspects of white middle-class ideology that emphasized their commitment to family life and the importance of personal hygiene, sanitation, and health. They do not seem to have adopted those aspects of white middle-class ideology that favored individualism over family connections (segmentation), or deprivation over pleasure (temperance movements). Similarly, while the family supported their kin and community through their motherwork, they do not appear to have adopted consumer habits that ensured the economic success of the black bourgeois businessmen of Mobile. The lack of any medicinal products from the site that could be linked to any of the three black-owned pharmacies in the city illustrates this point. This is not evidence of a lack of activism on the family's part, but indicative of the kinds of social discourses in which they chose to engage. Family, stability, educational opportunity—not the accumulation of wealth or conspicuous consumption—seem to have been the foci of the family's efforts to socially situate themselves.

One of the strengths of historical archaeology is its ability to contribute to history's understanding of the diverse ways that families and groups navigated through the tangle of conflicting norms, views, and practices of the societies in which they lived. As Angela Davis's (1998) study of the blues has demonstrated, mothering and domesticity were not every African-American woman's primary concern or interest. In the case of the Perryman family, mothering and how to mother are themes that linked multiple generations of the family and shaped their lives together. In this particular archaeological assemblage, it was only once I considered the ideas of other mothering and motherwork developed by feminist theorists (e.g., Collins 1994, 2000; Stack and Burton 1994; Scheper-Hughes 1992; Glenn et al. 1994; Giddings 1984) that a coherent narrative for the archaeological interpretation presented itself to me. Ideologies of mothering are pervasive; debates about proper mothering, ongoing. I do think that mothering and, more broadly, nurturing deserve greater attention in the future from archaeologists, no matter the time period of their focus.

Would it have been possible for me to construct a similar archaeological study with class, race, or gender solely as an interpretive entrée? I think not—the reason being that mothering is a socially constructed role that we tend to render invisible in our everyday lives. It is only when mothering is seen as deviant or poor that mothering becomes a focus of public scrutiny. As part of its invisibility, mothering is treated as a naturalized practice, not one that is socially situated and constructed. In vital ways, classic feminist theory (e.g., Chodorow 1978; Ruddick 1984) has contributed to that naturalization by deeming motherhood to be a universalizing experience that bonds women across different socioeconomic and racial lines.

Engendered archaeologies are still few in historical archaeology, even though more than a decade has passed since the publication of Donna Seifert's edited volume (1991). A surprisingly small number of those that have appeared explicitly engage in feminist theorizing (e.g., Beaudry, Cook, and Mrozowski 1991; Wall 1994; Yentsch 1994), with works by feminist historians being the most influential for historical archaeology. With a few notable exceptions (e.g., Franklin 2001; Joyce 2000, 2002; Meskell 1999, 2000), feminist approaches within text-aided archaeologies have not fully utilized critiques of feminist theory that question the centrality of white, middle-class, and heterosexual subject positions to the feminist agenda (e.g., Butler 1990, 1993; Collins 2000; Glenn et al. 1994). Given that archaeologies of the recent past have focused increasingly on racism and oppression, it seems that a consideration of these scholars' work can contribute to archaeological interpretation.

Final Thoughts on the Perryman Family

To mother, or more specifically what it is to mother well, is entangled in the center of American discourses about class, race, power, and gender, and has been so for the entire history of the Republic (Apple and Golden 1997). The myth surrounding American motherhood is that somehow it resides in the private sphere of the home, outside the realm of the public. Nothing could be further from the truth. Motherhood is publicly constructed and performed, and both publicly and privately practiced. For African-American women, the role of "good mother" was denied to them first by enslavement, then by continuing stereotypes and converging oppressions that limited their opportunities to mother according to shifting, white, middle-class, and elite standards (Giddings 1984; Feldstein 2000). Today, African-American women continue to be constructed as "bad mothers" in social discourses involving welfare, illegitimacy, and substance abuse (Glenn et al. 1994).

One way that African-American women combated oppressive stereotypes was by explicitly engaging dialogs on domesticity, femininity, and motherhood. Through their actions and words, African-American women contradicted the portrayals of them promoted in dominant, white, middle-class discourses. African-American women did not unconditionally embrace the complete ideological package associated with the cult of true womanhood. The complementary nature of male and female spiritual essence was well known in African-American communities and shaped interactions between the sexes. Perhaps this recognition facilitated the adoption of the separation of men's and women's spheres (when economically possible) by African-American families following the end of enslavement. This was a complementary gender relationship, however, forged during enslavement, not based on the patriarchal model of male dominance structurally reproduced in white households (A. Davis 1983). Black women, be they educated political activists (e.g., Cooper 1892; F. Williams 1904a, 1904b, 1906) or working class (Davis 1998), resisted attempts by African-American men to repress or control them on the basis of their gender. The aspects of domesticity that appealed to African-American women were those aspects that empowered them or elevated the status of black womanhood and motherhood.

Lucrecia Perryman, like so many women of her generation, was already raising a family when the end of slavery came. She would have known firsthand the fear of losing a child to unnecessary illnesses or sale; she would have known what it was to have control over raising your children taken away; she would have known the frustration of being limited in what you could provide your children. With freedom, she had the opportunity to assert more control over her family, more control over her mothering. In doing so, she may have found her decisions shaped not only by her own experiences of mothering during enslavement but, perhaps, also by the experiences of her own mother or other female relatives. The memories recorded by the WPA in the ex-slave narratives illustrate how profoundly enslavement influenced the ways that African Americans came to think about black womanhood and motherhood. Mothering had been a communal activity during enslavement, and that tradition continued in freedom, with women mothering on behalf of their own children and on behalf of their communities—past, present, and future.

It is less clear what Marshall Perryman's parenting experiences might have been during enslavement, just as it is difficult to know what he may have witnessed of his mother's experiences of slavery. Just as Lucrecia brought her three children to their marriage, Marshall brought his mother. Perhaps this action of Marshall Perryman, the bringing together into one household two women of obvious importance to him, communicates a great deal to us about his priorities and views. Each of these women, thanks to Marshall's paid labors, was able to avoid entry (at least for a significant amount of time) into the workforce. Caroline, Lucrecia's eldest daughter, likewise established herself as working only within the household. Caroline would work for her family her entire life, raising her siblings' children in addition to her own child, but she, by all accounts, never labored for another outsider after the end of enslavement.

White, middle-class, and elite America had constructed mothering as an exclusive site of white privilege and entitlement. In refusing to work for anyone other than their own families, African-American women who became full-time homemakers and mothers following freedom attacked that exclusivity. The actions of the Perryman family—the ways they organized their home life, their pursuit of stability and wealth, the materials that they chose to grace their home—can be seen as part of a larger African-American effort to claim domesticity as their own. Lucrecia's working for her family in the home while Marshall and Frank supported the family through their labor outside the home is clearly an appropriation of white, middle-class household organization. The Perrymans were actively pursuing what came to be known as the "American dream" of home-ownership, education, and upward mobility. The Perrymans' ambition to live as a "proper" family can be seen in their selective adoption in their material lives of middle-class ideals. The acquisition of ceramics that communicated the sacredness of the home and the use of glassware and ceramic vessels that reinforced the corporate nature of the family were recognizable statements to their contemporaries. The addition of decorative items to the household furnishings provided an additional space for the expression of individual taste and desires, establishing the unique history and style of the Perryman household. The limited material culture available from this period of the family's lives together communicates an appreciation for the sanctity of family and home life.

Interestingly, children's activities are not well documented by the archaeological record. In part, this is a function of the types of deposits recovered: both features are waste pits and include intentionally discarded materials. Child-specific materials, such as toys and clothing items, are often lost unintentionally and are found in yard middens during excavations. The items that were recovered include broken doll and toy teapot parts, and a single marble. Toys made of perishable materials would not preserve. Pencil fragments may also be indicative of the children's activities, since neither Marshall nor Lucrecia appear to have been literate. One type of item not recovered from the site but common to many Victorian homes, are child-specific food vessels. These items were made in children's sizes and were used to train children in proper table manners, and in notions of individuality and segmentation in the white middle class (Fitts 1999; Praetzellis and Praetzellis 1992). While the rest of the ceramic assemblage suggests an embrace of symbols communicating the sanctity of the family and domesticity, there is no evidence that children were treated differentially at the table. This may reflect a fundamental difference in the way that childhood was conceptualized within the family—children were not a distinct subset of the family, but rather an integrated part of the family whole. Children were contributing members of the corporate household, not merely contributors-in-training.

From 1869 until 1884, the Perryman family seemed to have succeeded in creating stability and security for themselves. The Perryman children were being educated, and unlike so many of their peers, were literate at a young age. The family had continued to acquire wealth in the form of property and goods. The eldest children were marrying, and grandchildren had begun to enter Marshall and Lucrecia's lives. Marshall had a stable income and a stable position, as did his stepson. His mother and wife lived and cared together for the Perryman children. The family lived in a small community, surrounded by diverse neighbors. Marshall regularly paid both his property taxes and his poll tax, asserting his economically demonstrated right to vote, even if the social reality was different. The family appears, from what we know of their actions, to have been expressing the optimism described by scholars as common among recently freed people— that if they could demonstrate they were good citizens, they would be rewarded with the rights and privileges that accompanied citizenship (A. Davis 1983; Giddings 1984). Even as he grew more ill, Marshall wrote a will and secured the support of influential white men to assure that his family's estate would remain intact. No matter how well Marshall attempted to assure the security and prosperity of his family members, however, his death would permanently alter their economic and home situation. The dream of domestic tranquility that the

Perrymans seemed to be building together was shattered with Marshall's death, just like the Rebecca at the Well teapots that lay broken along their fence line.

Lucrecia received her calling to midwifery presumably shortly after Marshall's death, for by 1889 she is listed in the city directory as a nurse/midwife. Perhaps a local midwife, even one who had supervised the birth of Lucrecia and Marshall's children, sought her as an apprentice. Marie Campbell (1946) recounted the experiences of a woman called to midwifery through a local doctor after the loss of her only child. However it happened, midwifery provided an opportunity for Lucrecia to work within her community with the skills of mothering she had honed during the birth, care, and raising of her own children.

Although Marshall was gone, the family continued to communicate its commitment to domesticity and mothering through its material culture. In some ways, with Lucrecia's taking up the occupation of midwife, this message seems amplified in the archaeological remains. Marie Campbell (1946), in her study of midwives in the 1940s, remarked that she never saw a midwife's yard that was lacking flowers or ornamentation. In one midwife's home, she found that "in the hallway and front bedroom was a large display of hobnail glassware— obviously a family treasure" (83), and in another instance, a midwife displayed in her parlor photographs of each of the 204 babies she had delivered (105).

While midwives as a rule would not deliver babies in their own homes, their homes did become centers of their practice. Prospective clients would come to the midwife's home to engage her services and consult her during pregnancy and after, and it was from her home that the midwife would be called when labor began. Midwives were selling their experience and their good mothering skills. In the case of the woman with the photographs, a visitor could not help but be impressed at the experience and knowledge held by a woman who had supervised so many births. Likewise, the presence of fine goods, a clean house, and a pretty yard attested to the gentility and propriety of the midwife. As scientific mothering ideologies became more entrenched in the public mind, cleanliness and tidiness increasingly were equated with morality and good housekeeping. The pair of cherub vases recovered from the site certainly evoke images of healthy, beautiful children. As discussed before, the ambiguity of their racial features suggests a direct contradiction to the dominant ideology of the time that equated the raising of healthy children only with middle-class white motherhood. During this time, the ceramic assemblage of the Perryman was enhanced in ways that may have been intended to build upon the existing set used by the family during Marshall's lifetime. Only in the teawares, a generally mixed and eclectic set, do we see a nod to current fashions and trends, such as the popularity of Japanese motifs or the increased popularity of decalcomania decorated wares.

Midwives made mothers, both through the transformative event of aiding birth as well as through the training of young women in infant care. Birth and child care were experiences that linked multiple generations of women. During enslavement, it was typically the oldest generation that cared for the youngest, with biological mothers forced to work in the fields away from their children. In such a system, generational ties grow strong, and generational memories are long. Birth involved the participation of multiple generations as well, with mothers and grandmothers often in attendance. Even though midwives viewed birth as a natural part of life, no woman would deny the potential danger associated with this event. For this reason, midwives had to comfort not only the laboring and birthing woman, but also her attending kin. Her approach and techniques had to be understandable across the generations to be meaningful.

Within Lucrecia's midwife practice, we see a combination of traditional and innovative practices. The presence of sulfur, cow's feet, pocket knives, and home-made medicines attests to the strong traditional element marking her midwifery practice. These products collectively suggest that like other recorded African-American midwives, Perryman offered spiritual and physical healing and treatment in her practice. Birth was a time when male and female spiritual essence converged in a powerful way, serving to provide comfort and courage to the birthing woman. Midwives, therefore, served as both gender and generational mediators for their communities. Other products, such as the Vaseline, castor oil, olive oil, food medicines, antiseptics, and the vaginal pipe, also attest to the incorporation of new products into the practice. Some of these products, such as the Vaseline and food medicines, represent functional substitutions—in this case, the replacement of traditional medicines with commercially produced equivalents. Other items, such as the pipe and the castorias, may represent the introduction of new ideas about the body and health care into the ethnomedical system.

Following the birth of a child, midwives continued to advise mothers as to the proper feeding and health care of the child. In these arenas, we can begin to see the influence of scientific mothering ideologies on traditional practices. Breast-feeding had been the preferred means of feeding infants during enslavement (Schwartz 2000) and remained so in Perryman's practice. Commercially produced infant foods seem to have been used only to a limited degree, perhaps in cases in which breast-feeding was not possible or needed to be supplemented.

Artifacts recovered from the well suggest that the sanitation gospel of scientific mothering was adopted within the midwifery practice as well as in family life. The spread of germs was contained through the use of antiseptics, or perhaps in the case of the family's brush with consumption, through controlled expectoration into a spittoon. Individual serving and drinking vessels would have minimized the spread of germs as well. Likewise, the adoption of Castoria use for children suggests submission to the cult of regularity, an outgrowth of germ theory that equated regular evacuation with a healthful cleansing of the body's systems. In particular, regulation of the bowels falls outside of African-American ethnomedical traditions, which tend to focus on treatment of blood ailments, and by association, organs such as the heart, liver, lungs, or kidneys

(Mathews 1992). The addition of the bowel emphasis represents an elaboration of the medical tradition rather than an abandonment of it.

Scientific mothering, in its early development, was an empowering realm for women, recognizing their expertise and the professional nature of their contribution to society. Scientific mothering ideology essentially promised that any woman, armed with proper information and common sense, was in a position to decide the best way to raise and care for her child. This assertion would be particularly appealing to mothers outside of the dominant middle-class discourse, for it suggested that motherhood was an achieved, not ascribed, status. Women who adopted scientific mothering practices in the mid- to late nineteenth century could not have anticipated that the co-opting of scientific mothering principles by an increasingly professionalized medical industry would ultimately strip them of their authority as mothers (Apple 1997).

In her selection of patent and proprietary medicines, Perryman opted for well-known brands that had identified themselves in consumers' minds as particularly safe and reliable for the treatment of children—again, reinforcing that through making the proper purchases, proper mothering could be recognized. Adoption of scientific mothering ideologies would allow Lucrecia to introduce her patients to "modern" health discourses and permit them to participate publicly in the performance of good mothering through their consumer habits.

The emphasis on scientific principles of mothering firmly aligned Perryman with the reform efforts of African-American women's clubs and church groups. The historical record does not provide us with any insight into Perryman's possible community activism through a church or other organization, but her material assemblage suggests that, at least in her medical practice and family life, she was engaged in work that would be perceived as part of a broader racial uplift movement.

Angela Davis (1998) has suggested that the ability to travel freely and the freedom to explore and control one's own sexuality were among the greatest changes to African-American life following the end of enslavement. Forced intercourse and pregnancies and arranged marriages were among the controls imposed upon women during slavery. It was only after freedom that they were free to explore their own individuality and expression of that individuality through their sexuality. Davis has described the musical tradition of the "blues" as one arena in which these explorations and negotiations can be studied. Sexual freedom is also related to reproductive freedom—whether or not to conceive or bear a child as a result of sexual activity. Roedrique (1990) has indicated that the twentieth century was marked by an increased interest in birth control among African Americans, citing as part of his evidence the ubiquitous contraceptive advertisements in African-American publications. Similarly, Loretta Ross (1997) has explored the role of abortion as both a forced and a freely chosen necessity in African-American women's lives since enslavement. As the twentieth century progressed, African-American activists were alarmed by high infant mortality rates among African-Americans. Birth control and the regulation of family size was one proposed solution, the idea being that having smaller families would allow each child greater resources, and therefore better health.

Constructions of pregnancy and the female body altered radically during the nineteenth century, with the increased sophistication of pregnancy detection methods in the medical industry. What had once been solely within the realm of women's knowledge and definition, the diagnosis of pregnancy, was usurped by the medical industry. Pregnancy, traditionally defined as beginning at the time of quickening, was now defined as beginning much sooner. Women who had formerly terminated suspected pregnancies with herbal teas and other remedies found themselves restrained by physicians and legislators who increasingly demanded to regulate and control the female body. Midwives were important keepers of knowledge regarding birth control, and as reliable chemical abortifacients became more difficult to acquire, midwives and other traditional healers found their services in greater demand.

Post-regulation midwives rarely discussed abortion, and when they did, it was typically to state their abhorrence to the practice. These responses are not surprising: part of the justification for regulating midwives was the accusation that they were responsible for providing illegal abortions; African-American midwives were typically devout and may have found performing abortions contrary to the teachings of their faith; and most important, midwives seemed to adhere to the alternative understanding of pregnancy diagnosis. Linda Holmes's comments that she didn't provide abortions but recalled using a tea to bring on the menses clearly suggests this last possibility. Delayed menses could be caused by a series of medical complaints, among which could be a pregnancy, though not necessarily. Halted menses were a blood complaint, which could be caused by both natural and supernatural means, therefore; to help a woman's cycle to resume had no causal relationship to the presence or absence of pregnancy.

Midwives, as part of their understanding of female reproductive biology, possessed knowledge necessary to bring about menses. A number of plants with abortifacient qualities are known from African-American medical traditions (Grimé 1976; Groover and Baumann 1996). These herbs, taken singly or in combination as a tea, could produce an intentional chemical miscarriage. Chemical abortion is safer and more sanitary than mechanical abortion, and a means through which women in many cultures have controlled their fertility. A number of patent medicines were recovered from the Perryman well that contained either singly or in combination well-known abortifacients, such as turpentine, camphor, and senna. While a number of these medicines were commonly used during birth, their potential use as abortifacients cannot be ruled out. Likewise, the medicinal tonics created by Perryman for her patients could have included abortifacients or menstrual regulators. Barrier methods of contraception were also known, and some included the use of products recovered from the site, such as Vaseline. While it is not possible to know whether birth control was part of Lucrecia Perryman's midwifery practice, the archaeological record does not rule out the possibility.

To mother was central to the social identity constructed for themselves by Lucrecia Perryman, Caroline Bowers Saunders, and Sally Cunningham. The 1910 census described Lucrecia as having borne 11 children during her lifetime, of whom only 5 were still living. The historical record provides an accounting of four of those lost children, Rachel, who died sometime between 1870 and 1880; Frank, who died in 1894; Sarah, who followed in the same year; and Emma, who died in 1897. Of these, only Rachel died before reaching adulthood. Based on birth spacings of two to three years for Lucrecia and Marshall's children, and Lucrecia's age at the time of Marshall's death, the remaining lost children must have been born during enslavement, possibly in the six-year gap between the birth of Caroline and Sarah.

Lucrecia would have given birth to five children in slavery, six in freedom. Two of her enslaved children died very young. Lucrecia outlived all but one of her children born in bondage—Caroline, her oldest. In contrast, four of her six freedom children lived to mourn her. The comparison is disquieting and underscores the horrible toll of enslavement on African-American mothers and families. The effects of the conditions of enslavement did not end with Emancipation, but affected children's health for a lifetime. Did poor childhood nutrition contribute to Sarah's and Frank's deaths from tuberculosis? Given the opportunity to give her attention to her children full time in freedom, Lucrecia was able to raise a larger family than she had during enslavement. Lucrecia's mothering extended beyond her own family, as her midwifery provided motherwork for her community. Sally Cunningham lived and worked full time as a mother, holding no outside employment. Caroline had the fewest biological children but raised the orphaned children of her siblings. In constructing their identities as mothers, the Perryman women reacted both in accordance with and in opposition to dominant ideologies of mothering, discounting racist caricatures of black womanhood while embracing domesticity and scientific mothering. The archaeological record provides material evidence of the ways that members of this family engaged with the mothering discourses of their time, both in their own families and, in the case of Lucrecia, in her midwifery practice.

The archaeological record also provides illumination of how lay midwifery became entangled in debates over medical professionalization and mothering. It is terribly ironic to learn that African-American lay midwives, who were driven from their practices with accusations of unsanitary and unscientific methods, were engaged in the same sanitation and hygiene discourses promoted by the public health officials that demonized midwives, at least as suggested by the evidence for Perryman's practice. Adherence to the same hygiene and sanitary principles taught by the midwives to their patients seems to have made abandonment of the midwives by the African-American populace easier.

Conclusions

An archaeology focusing on mothering has allowed us to explore African-American activism, consumerism, class negotiations, and family life from a perspective different from that generally presented. By placing the notions of mothering, motherhood, and motherwork at the center of these interpretations, it has been possible to explore individual personhood and decision making within the Perryman household during 30 years of the family's life course. What makes this study fundamentally different from other archaeological studies of African-American family life after freedom is my focus on African-American women and their position at the intersection of multiple oppressions—racism, sexism, and poverty. Acknowledging that African-American women occupy a unique social space has opened up the possibility of exploring through the materiality of everyday life how African-American families strove to reconstruct and resignify what it was to be a black woman following enslavement.

"Motherhood" and "mothering" are highly charged sites of cultural and social tensions. Perhaps for no generation of African-American women was this more amplified than for the women of Lucrecia Perryman's generation, who raised children both before and after enslavement. For these women, the hurt at having been denied control over the rearing and care of their children was raw, and the hope for a new future still untainted by the quick descent into the realities of Jim Crow life.

Through public performance and private practice, African-American women have consistently asserted their opposition to the notion that they are inherently not good mothers (and in doing so, contest all of the accompanying social oppressions that accompany that evaluation). Rooted in enslavement, the pervasive stereotypes of black womanhood have been actively combated continuously by African-American intellectual, social, and political movements, and by individual women as they have gone about their everyday lives.

This archaeological study has been at its core an archaeology of agency—agency from the bottom up—as exercised by a family establishing a social identity for themselves following enslavement. The family members were not actors performing in a vacuum, but constructed their social identities in a context of the collective experiences of family, neighbors, community, and national black political movements. These broader social networks and ideologies shaped their decisions and the ways they navigated freedom, but did not dictate them. Through the archaeological study of the Perryman family, we can see how, through its engagement with conflicting and changing mothering ideologies, the family asserted their right to be recognized as members of and contributors to Mobile's society, and as freed people. Finally, through the mundane objects of everyday routine, we can also see how one woman in particular, Lucrecia Perryman, strode into freedom with her arms firmly embracing the children of her family and the women and children of her community.

Bibliography

Abel, E. K. and M. K. Nelson (eds.) (1990) *Circles of Care: Work and Identity in Women's Lives*. Binghamton: State University of New York Press.

Alabama State Planning Commission (1941) *Alabama: A Guide to the Deep South, Compiled by the Workers of the Writers; Program of the Work Projects Administration in the State of Alabama*. New York: Richard R. Smith.

Alexander, A. L. (1991) *Ambiguous Lives: Free Women of Color in Rural Georgia, 1789–1879*. Fayetteville: University of Arkansas Press.

Allison, P. (ed.) (1999) *The Archaeology of Household Activities*. London: Routledge.

Amory, C. (ed.) (1969) *1902 Edition of the Sears, Roebuck Catalogue*. New York: Crown Publishers.

Amos, H. (1985) *Cotton City: Urban Development in Antebellum Mobile*. Tuscaloosa: University of Alabama Press.

Anderson, A. (1968) 'The Archaeology of Mass-Produced Footwear.' *Historical Archaeology* 2:56–65.

Apple, R. D. (1997) 'Constructing Mothers: Scientific Motherhood in the Nineteenth and Twentieth Centuries.' In R. D. Apple and J. Golden (eds.), *Mothers and Motherhood*, Columbus: Ohio State University Press.

Apple, R. D. and J. Golden (eds.) (1997) *Mothers and Motherhood*. Columbus: Ohio State University Press.

Armstrong, D. and E. M. Armstrong (1991) *The Great American Medicine Show*. New York: Prentice Hall.

Armstrong, D. V. (1990) *The Old Village and the Great House*. Urbana: University of Illinois Press.

Ascher, R. and C. H. Fairbanks (1971) 'Excavation of a Slave Cabin: Georgia, U. S. A.' *Historical Archaeology* 5:3–17.

Bagnell, A. (1999) 'Justus Von Liebig.' In *Liebig Company's Practical Cookery Book* (reprint of 1894 edition). Lewes, England: Southover Press.

Baldwin, J. (1973) *A Collector's Guide to Patent and Proprietary Medicine Bottles of the Nineteenth Century*. New York: Thomas Nelson.

Bankole, K. (1998) *Slavery and Medicine: Enslavement and Medical Practices in Antebellum Louisiana*. New York: Garland Publishing.

Banks, A. C. (1999) *Birth Chairs, Midwives, and Medicine*. Jackson: University Press of Mississippi.

Banks, I. (2000) *Hair Matters: Beauty, Power, and Black Women's Consciousness*. New York: New York University Press.

Bassin, D. M. H. and M. M. Kaplan (eds.) (1994) *Representations of Motherhood*. New Haven: Yale University Press.

Baughman, G. (1928) 'A Preliminary Report upon the Midwife Situation in Virginia.' *Virginia Medical Monthly* 54(12):749–750.

Beaudry, M. (1998) 'Farm Journal: First Person, Four Voices.' *Historical Archaeology* 32(1): 20–33.

Beaudry, M., L. J. Cook and S. A. Mrozowski (1991) 'Artifacts and Active Voices: Material Culture as Social Discourse.' In R. H. McGuire and R. Paynter (eds.), *The Archaeology of Inequality*. Oxford: Basil Blackwell.

Beausang, E. (2000) 'Childbirth in Prehistory: An Introduction.' *European Journal of Archaeology* 3(1):69–87.

Beecher, C. E. and H. B. Stowe (1870) *The American Woman's Home*. New York: J. B. Ford.

Beeton, I. (1907) *Mrs. Beeton's Book of Household Management*. London: Ward, Lock.

Blackwell, M. S. (1992) 'The Republican Vision of Mary Palmer Tyler.' *Journal of the Early Republic* 12:11–35.

Blakey, M., T. E. Leslie and J. P. Reidy (1994) 'Frequency and Chronological Distribution of Dental Enamel Hypoplasia in Enslaved African Americans: A Test of the Weaning Hypothesis.' *American Journal of Physical Anthropology* 95:371–383.

Blassingame, J. (1979) *The Slave Community: Plantation Life in the Antebellum South.* 2nd ed. Oxford: Oxford University Press.

Brodkin, K. (1997) *How Jews Became White Folks and What That Says about Race in America.* New Brunswick: Rutgers University Press.

Brown, K. and D. Cooper (1990) 'Structural Continuity in an African American Slave and Tenant Community.' *Historical Archaeology* 24(4):7–19.

Buchli, V. and G. Lucas (2000a) 'The Archaeology of Alienation: A Late Twentieth-Century British Council House.' In V. Buchli and G. Lucas (eds.), *Archaeologies of the Contemporary Past.* London: Routledge.

—— (2000b) 'Children, Gender and the Material Culture of Domestic Abandonment in the Late Twentieth Century.' In J. Sofaer-Derevenski (ed.), *Children and Material Culture.* London: Routledge.

Bullough, V. and M. Voght (1984) 'Women, Menstruation, and Nineteenth-Century Medicine.' In J. W. Leavitt (ed.), *Women and Health in America.* Madison: University of Wisconsin Press.

Burroughs, F. (1904) 'Not Color but Character.' *The Voice of the Negro*, July: 277–279.

Bush, B. (1990) *Slave Women in Caribbean Society 1650–1838.* Bloomington: University of Indiana Press.

—— (1996) 'Hard Labor: Women, Childbirth, and Resistance in British Caribbean Slave Societies.' In D. B. Gaspar and D. Hine (eds.), *More Than Chattel.* Bloomington: University of Indiana Press.

Butler, J. (1990) *Gender Trouble: Feminism and the Subversion of Identity.* New York: Routledge.

—— (1993) *Bodies That Matter: On the Discursive Limits of "Sex."* New York: Routledge.

Caback, M., M. D. Groover and S. J. Wagers (1995) 'Health Care and the Wayman A.M.E. Church.' *Historical Archaeology* 29(2):55–76.

Campbell, H. (1881) *The Easiest Way in Housekeeping and Cooking.* New York: Fords, Howard and Hulbert.

Campbell, M. (1946) *Folks Do Get Born.* New York: Rinehart.

Campbell, T. M. (1969) *The Movable School Goes to the Negro Farmer.* New York: Arno Press and the New York Times.

Canadian Government (2000) Drug Product Database. www.hc-sc.gc.ca/hpb/drugs-dpd/product/p61577.html

Cash, F. B. (2001) *African American Women and Social Action: The Club Women and Volunteerism from Jim Crow to the New Deal, 1896–1936.* Westport: Greenwood Press.

Chase, S. E. and M. F. Rogers (2001) *Mothers and Children: Feminist Analyses and Personal Narratives.* New Brunswick: Rutgers University Press.

Child, L. (1989 [1831]) *The Mother's Book.* Boston: Applewood Books.

Childress, A. (1986) *Like One of the Family: Conversations from a Domestic's Life.* Boston: Beacon.

Chodorow, N. (1978) *The Reproduction of Mothering: Psychoanalysis and the Sociology of Gender.* Berkeley: University of California Press.

Claney, J. P. (1996) 'Form, Fabric, and Social Factors in Nineteenth-Century Ceramics Usage: A Case Study in Rockingham Ware.' In L. DeCunzo and B. Herman (eds.), *Historical Archaeology and the Study of American Culture.* Knoxville: University of Tennessee Press.

Clark, C. E., Jr. (1987) 'The Vision of the Dining Room: Plan Book Dreams and Middle-Class Realities.' In K. Grover (ed.), *Dining in America, 1850–1900.* Amherst: University of Massachusetts Press.

Clayton, R. (1990) 'Motherwit,' *University of Kansas Humanistic Studies 57.* New York: Peter Lang.

Clement, C. O., R. M. Grunden and J. K. Peterson (1999) *History and Archaeology at the*

Mann-Simmons Cottage: A Free Black Site in Columbia, South Carolina. Columbia: South Carolina Institute of Archaeology and Anthropology, University of South Carolina.

Cody, C. A. (1996) 'Cycles of Work and of Childbearing: Seasonality in Women's Lives on Low Country Plantations.' In D. B. Gaspar and D. C. Hine (eds.), *More Than Chattel,* Bloomington: University of Indiana Press.

Coe, E. (1995) 'Granny Midwives: Grandmother to Nurse Midwives.' Paper presented at the American Anthropological Association Meetings, Washington, D. C.

Collins, P. H. (1994) 'Shifting the Center: Race, Class, and Feminist Theorizing about Motherhood.' In E. N. Glenn, G. Chang, R. Forcey (eds.), *Mothering: Ideology, Experience and Agency.* New York: Routledge.

—— (2000) *Black Feminist Thought: Knowledge, Consciousness, and the Politics of Empowerment.* 2nd ed. New York: Routledge.

Conkey, M. and J. Gero (1991) 'Tensions, Pluralities, and Engendering Archaeology: An Introduction to Women and Prehistory.' In J. Gero and M. Conkey (eds.), *Engendering Archaeology.* Oxford: Blackwell Press.

Cooper, A. J. (1892) *A Voice from the South: By a Black Woman of the South.* Xenia, Ohio: Aldine Printing.

Corruccini, R., J. Handler and K. Jacobi (1985) 'Chronological Distribution of Enamel Hypoplasias and Weaning in a Caribbean Slave Population.' *Human Biology* 57: 699–711.

Costello, J. (1998) 'Bread Fresh from the Oven: Memories of Italian Breadbaking in the California Mother Lode.' *Historical Archaeology* 32(1):66–73.

—— (2000) 'Red Light Voices: An Archaeological Drama of Late Nineteenth-Century Prostitution.' In R. A. Schmidt and B. Voss (eds.), *Archaeologies of Sexuality.* London: Routledge.

Cowan, R. S. (1983) *More Work for Mother.* New York: Basic Books.

Cox, M. (1996) *Life and Death in Spitalfields 1700–1850.* York: Council for British Archaeology.

Craton, M. and G. Saunders (1992) *Islanders in the Stream.* Athens: University of Georgia Press.

Crisis (1911) Advertisement for the Negro National Doll Company. August 2(4):174.

Culpepper, M. (2001) *Images of America, Mobile: Photographs from the William E. Wilson Collection.* Charleston: Arcadia Publishing.

Dalton, S. (2000) 'Nonbiological Mothers and the Legal Boundaries of Motherhood: An Analysis of California Law.' In H. Ragoné and F. W. Twine (eds.), *Ideologies and Technologies of Motherhood: Race, Class, Sexuality, Nationalism.* New York: Routledge.

Davis, A. (1983) *Women, Race, and Class.* New York: Vintage Books.

—— (1990) 'Racism, Birth Control, and Reproductive Rights.' In M. G. Fried (ed.), *From Abortion to Reproductive Freedom.* Boston: South End Press.

—— (1998) *Blues Legacies and Black Feminism.* New York: Vintage Books.

Davis, G. B., L. J. Perry and J. W. Kirkley (1983) *The Official Military Atlas of the Civil War.* New York: Random House.

Deetz, J. (1977) *In Small Things Forgotten: The Archaeology of Early American Life.* New York: Anchor Books.

—— (1993) *Flowerdew Hundred: The Archaeology of a Virginia Plantation, 1619–1864.* Charlottesville: University of Virginia Press.

Delle, J. (1997) *An Archaeology of Social Space.* New York: Plenum Press.

Delle, J., S. A. Mrozowski and R. Paynter (eds.) (2000) *Lines That Divide: Historical Archaeologies of Race, Class, and Gender.* Knoxville: University of Tennessee Press.

Derks, S. (ed.) (1994) *The Value of a Dollar: 1860–1989.* Detroit: Gale Research.

Devner, K. (1968) *Patent Medicine Picture.* Tombstone, Ariz.: Tombstone Epitaph.

DiQuinzo, P. (1999) *The Impossibility of Motherhood: Feminism, Individualism, and the Problem of Mothering.* London: Routledge.

Dolph and Stewart (1929) Map of Mobile and Environs, Alabama. Mobile Chamber of Commerce.

Dougherty, M. C. (1978) 'Southern Lay Midwives as Ritual Specialists.' In J. Hoch-Smith and A. Spring (eds.), *Women in Ritual and Symbolic Roles.* New York: Plenum Press.

—— (1982) 'Southern Midwifery and Organized Health Care: Systems in Conflict.' *Medical Anthropology* 6:113–126.

Douglass, F. (2001) *The Narrative of One Life of Frederick Douglass, An American Slave.* Edited by J. Blassingame, J. R. McKivigan and P. P. Hinks. New Haven: Yale University Press.

Du Bois, W. E. B. (1911) 'Violations of Property Rights.' *Crisis* 2(1):28–30.

——— (1922) 'Opinion.' *Crisis* 24(6):247–252.

——— (1932) 'Black Folk and Birth Control.' *Birth Control Review* 16(6):167.

——— (1933) 'Postscript.' *Crisis* 41(2):44.

——— (1970) *W. E. B. Du Bois: A Reader.* Edited by M. Weinberg. New York: Harper and Row.

Edwards-Ingram, Y. (2001) 'African American Medicine and the Social Relations of Slavery.' In C. E. Orser (ed.), *Race and the Archaeology of Identity.* Salt Lake City: University of Utah Press.

Epperson, T. W. (1997) 'Race and the Disciplines of the Plantation.' *Historical Archaeology* 24(4):29–36.

——— (1999) 'The Contested Commons: Archaeologies of Race, Repression, and Resistance in New York City.' In M. P. Leone and P. B. Potter (eds.), *Historical Archaeologies of Capitalism.* New York: Kluwer Academic/Plenum Publishing.

Ettling, J. (1981) *The Germ of Laziness.* Cambridge: Harvard University Press.

Ewert, G. (2001) 'The New South Era in Mobile 1875–1900.' In M. Thomason (ed.), *Mobile: The New History of Alabama's First City.* Tuscaloosa: University of Alabama Press.

Farnsworth, P. (1993) ' "What Is the Use of Plantation Archaeology?": No Use at All If No One Else Is Listening!' *Historical Archaeology* 27(1):114–116.

——— (2000) 'Brutality or Benevolence in Plantation Archaeology.' *International Journal of Historical Archaeology* 4(2):145–158.

——— (2001) 'Beer Brewing and Consumption in the Maintenance of African Identity by the Enslaved People of the Bahamas, 1783–1834.' *Culture and Agriculture* 23(2):19–30.

Faust, D. G. (1996) *Mothers of Invention: Women of the Slaveholding South in the American Civil War.* New York: Vintage Books.

Federal Population Census [FPC] (1820) Population Schedule of the Fourth Census of the United States, North Carolina.

——— (1850) Population Schedule of the Seventh Census of the United States, Mobile County, Alabama, Free Schedule.

——— (1850) Population Schedule of the Seventh Census of the United States, Mobile County, Alabama, Slave Schedule.

——— (1860) Population Schedule of the Eighth Census of the United States, Mobile County, Alabama, Free Schedule.

——— (1860) Population Schedule of the Eighth Census of the United States, Mobile County, Alabama, Slave Schedule.

——— (1870) Population Schedule of the Ninth Census of the United States, Mobile County, Alabama.

——— (1880) Population Schedule of the Tenth Census of the United States, Mobile County, Alabama.

——— (1900) Population Schedule of the Twelfth Census of the United States, Mobile County, Alabama.

——— (1910) Population Schedule of the Thirteenth Census of the United States, Mobile County, Alabama.

Feldman, L. (1999) *A Sense of Place: Birmingham's Black Middle Class Community 1890–1930.* Tuscaloosa: University of Alabama Press.

Feldstein, R. (1994) ' "I Wanted the Whole World to See": Constructions of Motherhood in the Death of Emmett Till.' In J. Meyerowitz (ed.), *Not June Cleaver: Women and Gender in Postwar American, 1945–1960.* Philadelphia: Temple University Press.

——— (2000) *Motherhood in Black and White: Race and Sex in American Liberalism, 1930–1965.* Ithaca: Cornell University Press.

Ferguson, J. H. (1950) 'Mississippi Midwives.' *Journal of the History of Medicine and Allied Sciences* 5(1):85–95.

Ferguson, L. (1992) *Uncommon Ground.* Washington, D.C.: Smithsonian Institution Press.

Fike, R. E. (1987) *The Bottle Book: A Comprehensive Guide to Historic, Embossed Bottles.* Salt Lake City: Peregrine Smith Books.

Fitts, R. (1999) 'The Archaeology of Middle-Class Domesticity and Gentility in Victorian Brooklyn.' *Historical Archaeology* 33(1):39–62.

Flamm, Wm. A., and Co. (1895) Map of the City of Mobile. Baltimore: Flamm and Co.

Fleming, W. L. (1911) *Civil War and Reconstruction in Alabama*. Cleveland: Arthur H. Clark.

Fontenot, W. (1994) *Secret Doctors: Ethnomedicine of African Americans*. Westport: Bergin and Garvey.

Foster, H. B. (1997) *New Raiments of Self: African-American Clothing in the Antebellum South*. Oxford: Berg.

Fox-Genovese, E. (1988) *Within the Plantation Household: Black and White Women of the Old South*. Chapel Hill: University of North Carolina Press.

Franklin, M. (1997) 'Out of Site, Out of Mind: The Archaeology of an Enslaved Virginian Household, c. 1740–1778.' Ph.D. dissertation, Department of Anthropology, University of California, Berkeley.

—— (2001) 'A Black Feminist-Inspired Archaeology?' *Journal of Social Archaeology* 1(1):108–125.

Fraser, G. (1998) *African-American Midwifery in the South*. Cambridge: Harvard University Press.

Fried, M. G. (ed.) (1990) *From Abortion to Reproductive Freedom: Transforming a Movement*. Boston: South End Press.

Gailey, C. W. (2000) 'Ideologies of Motherhood and Kinship in U.S. Adoption.' In H. Ragoné and F. W. Twine (eds.), *Ideologies and Technologies of Motherhood: Race, Class, Sexuality, Nationalism*. New York: Routledge.

Gamble, V. N. (1989) Introduction to V. N. Gamble (ed.), *Germs Have No Color Line: Blacks and American Medicine 1900–1940*. New York: Garland Publishing.

Gaspar, D. B. and D. C. Hine (eds.) (1996) *More Than Chattel: Black Women and Slavery in the Americas*. Bloomington: University of Indiana Press.

Gates, W. C., Jr., and D. E. Ormerod (1982) 'The East Liverpool, Ohio, Pottery District: Identification of Manufacture.' *Historical Archaeology* 16(1–2).

Gatewood, W. B. (2000) *Aristrocrat of Color: The Black Elite, 1880–1920*. Fayetteville: University of Arkansas Press.

Gero, J. and M. Conkey (eds.) (1991) *Engendering Archaeology*. Oxford: Basil Blackwell.

Gibb, J. G. (2000) 'Imaginary, but by No Means Unimaginable: Storytelling, Science, and Historical Archaeology.' *Historical Archaeology* 34(2):1–6.

Giddings, P. (1984) *When and Where I Enter: The Impact of Black Women on Race and Sex in America*. New York: William Morrow.

Gilchrist, R. (1994) *Gender and Material Culture: The Archaeology of Religious Women*. London: Routledge.

—— (1999) *Gender and Archaeology: Contesting the Past*. London: Routledge.

Gill, J. (1997) *The Lords of Misrule: Mardi Gras and the Politics of Race in New Orleans*. Oxford: University Press of Mississippi.

Ginsburg, F. (1989) *Contested Lives: The Abortion Debate in an American Community*. Berkeley: University of California Press.

Glenn, E. N. (1994) 'Social Constructions of Mothering: A Thematic Overview.' In E. N. Glenn, G. Chang, and L. R. Forcey (eds.), *Mothering: Ideology, Experience, and Agency*. New York: Routledge.

Glenn, E. N., G. Chang, and L. R. Forcey (eds.) (1994) *Mothering: Ideology, Experience, and Agency*. New York: Routledge.

Godden, G. (1964) *Encyclopaedia of British Pottery and Porcelain Marks*. London: Barrie and Jenkins.

Golden, J. (1996) *A Social History of Wet Nursing in America: From Breast to Bottle*. Cambridge: Cambridge Unversity Press.

Grimé, W. E. (1976) *Botany of the Black Americans*. Michigan: St Clair Shores Press.

Groover, M. and T. Baumann (1996) ' "They Worked Their Own Remedy": African-American Herbal Medicine and the Archaeological Record.' *South Carolina Antiquities* 28(1–2):88–32.

Grover, K. (ed.) (1987) *Dining in America 1850–1900*. Amherst: University of Massachusetts Press.

Grulee, C. G. (1916) *Infant Feeding*. Philadelphia: W. B. Saunders.

Gums, B. (1998) *The Archaeology of an African-American Neighborhood in Mobile, Alabama*. Mobile: University of Southern Alabama Center for Archaeological Studies.

Gutman, H. (1976) *The Black Family in Slavery and Freedom, 1750–1925*. New York: Pantheon.

Harris, S. (1903) 'Tuberculosis in the Negro.' *Journal of the American Medical Association* 41:834–838.

Harris, T. (1982) *From Mammies to Militants: Domestics in Black American Literature.* Philadelphia: Temple University Press.

Hays, S. (1996) *The Cultural Contradictions of Motherhood.* New Haven: Yale University Press.

Henry, S. L. (1987) 'Factors Influencing Consumer Behavior in Turn-of-the-Century Phoenix, Arizona.' In S. Spencer-Wood (ed.), *Consumer Choice in Historical Archaeology.* New York: Plenum Press.

Herskovits, M. (1962 [1941]) *Myth of the Negro Past.* Boston: Beacon Press.

Hewett, J. B. (1996) *The Roster of Confederate Soldiers 1861–1865, Vol. 15.* Wilmington: Broadfoot Publishing.

Higgenbotham, E. (1993) *Righteous Discontent: The Women's Movement in the Black Baptist Church, 1880–1920.* Cambridge: Harvard University Press.

Hodder, I., M. Shanks, A. Alexandri, V. Buchli, J. Carman, J. Last and G. Lucas (eds.) (1995) *Interpreting Archaeology: Finding Meaning in the Past.* London: Routledge.

Holloway, W. and B. Featherstone (eds.) (1997) *Mothering and Ambivalence.* New York: Routledge.

Holmes, L. (1984) 'Medical History: Alabama Granny Midwife.' *Journal of the Medical Society of New Jersey* 81:389–391.

hooks, b. (1992) *Black Looks: Race and Representation.* Boston: South End Press.

—— (1994) *Outlaw Culture: Resisting Representations.* New York: Routledge.

Hopkins, G. M. (1878) *City Atlas of Mobile, Alabama.* Baltimore: G. M. Hopkins.

Hunter, J. E. (1905) 'Tuberculosis in the Negro: Causes and Treatment.' *Colorado Medical Journal* 7:250–257.

Hunton, A. (1904) 'Negro Womanhood Defended.' *Voice of the Negro,* July: 281.

Hurston, Z. N. (1990 [1935]) *Mules and Men.* New York: Harper and Row.

Hyatt, H. M. (1970) *Hoodoo-Conjuration-Witchcraft-Rootwork, Vol. 1.* St. Louis: Harry Middleton Hyatt.

—— (1973) *Hoodoo-Conjuration-Witchcraft-Rootwork, Vol. 3.* St. Louis: Harry Middleton Hyatt.

—— (1974) *Hoodoo-Conjuration-Witchcraft-Rootwork, Vol. 4.* St. Louis: Harry Middleton Hyatt.

Israel, F. L. (ed.) (1997) *1897 Sears, Roebuck Catalogue.* New York: Chelsea House Publishers.

Jacobs, H. (2000) *Incidents in the Life of a Slave Girl.* New York: Penguin Books.

Jenks, B. and J. Luna (1990) *Early American Pattern Glass 1850–1910.* Radnor, PA: Homestead-Wallace Books.

Jones, E. H. (1907) 'Tuberculosis in the Negro.' *Transactions of the Tennessee State Medical Association,* pp. 175–182.

Jones, J. (1985) *Labor of Love, Labor of Sorrow.* New York: Basic Books.

Jones, S. (1997) *The Archaeology of Ethnicity: Constructing Identities in the Past and Present.* London: Routledge.

Joyce, R. (2000) *Gender and Power in Prehispanic Mesoamerica.* Austin: University of Texas Press.

—— (2002a) 'Dialogues Heard and Unheard, Seen and Unseen.' In R. Joyce (ed.), *The Languages of Archaeology: Dialogue, Narrative, and Writing.* Oxford: Blackwell.

—— (2002b) 'Introducing the First Voice.' In R. Joyce (ed.), *The Languages of Archaeology: Dialogue, Narrative and Writing.* Oxford: Blackwell.

—— (ed.) (2002c) *The Languages of Archaeology: Dialogue, Narrative, and Writing.* Oxford: Blackwell.

Joyce, R. and S. Gillespie (eds.) (2000) *Beyond Kinship: Social and Material Reproduction in House Societies.* Philadelphia: University of Pennsylvania Press.

Joyce, R. and R. Preucel (2002) 'Writing the Field of Archaeology.' In R. Joyce (ed.), *The Languages of Archaeology: Dialogue, Narrative, and Writing.* Oxford: Blackwell.

Kasson, J. F. (1987) 'Rituals of Dining: Table Manners in Victorian America.' In K. Grover (ed.), *Dining in America, 1850–1900.* Amherst: University of Massachusetts Press.

Kerns, W. W. (1927) 'Why Young Physicians Are Not Locating in the Country.' *Virginia Medical Monthly* 54(6):369–370.

King, W. (1996) ' "Suffer with Them Till Death": Slave Women and Their Children in

Nineteenth-Century America.' In D. B. Gaspar and D. C. Hine (eds.), *More Than Chattel.* Bloomington: University of Indiana Press.

Kobrin, F. (1984) 'The American Midwife Controversy: A Crisis of Professionalization.' In J. W. Leavitt (ed.), *Women and Health in America.* Madison: University of Wisconsin Press.

Kolchin, P. (1972) *First Freedom: The Responses of Alabama's Blacks to Emancipation and Reconstruction.* Westport: Greenwood Publishing.

Kovel, R. and T. Kovel (1986) *Kovels' Dictionary of Marks.* New York: Crown Publishers.

Kunzel, R. G. (1994) 'White Neurosis, Black Pathology: Constructing Out of Wedlock Pregnancy in the Wartime and Postwar United States.' In J. Meyerowitz (ed.), *Not June Cleaver.* Philadelphia: Temple University Press.

Ladd-Taylor, M. (1988) ' "Grannies" and "Spinsters": Midwife Education and the Sheppard-Towner Act.' *Journal of Social History* 22(2):255–276.

Ladd-Taylor, M. and L. Umansky (eds.) (1998) *"Bad" Mothers: The Politics of Blame in Twentieth-Century America.* New York: New York University Press.

Langdon, B. (1990) Edgefield County Marriages 1769–1880 Implied in Edgefield County, South Carolina Probate Records. Easley: Southern Historical Press.

LaRoche, C. and M. Blakey (1997) 'Seizing Intellectual Power: The Dialogue at the New York African Burial Ground.' *Historical Archaeology* 31(3):84–106.

Larsen, E. (1994) 'A Boarding House Madonna—Beyond the Aesthetics of a Portrait Created through Medicine Bottles.' *Historical Archaeology* 28(4):68–79.

Lavitt, W. (1983) *Toys.* New York: Alfred A. Knopf.

Layne, L. L. (2000) 'Baby Things as Fetishes? Memorial Goods, Simulacra, and the "Realness" Problem of Pregnancy Loss.' In H. Ragoné and F. W. Twine (eds.), *Ideologies and Technologies of Motherhood: Race, Class, Sexuality, Nationalism.* London: Routledge.

Leach, W. (1993) *Land of Desire: Merchants, Power, and the Rise of a New American Culture.* New York: Vintage Books.

Leavitt, J. W. (1986) *Brought to Bed: Childbearing in America 1750–1950.* Oxford: Oxford University Press.

Leavitt, J. W. and W. Walton (1984) 'Down to Death's Door: Women's Perceptions of Childbirth in America.' In J. W. Leavitt (ed.), *Women and Health in America.* Madison: University of Wisconsin Press.

Lehner, L. (1988) *Lehner's Encyclopedia of U.S. Marks of Potter, Porcelain and Clay.* Paducah: Schroeder Publishing.

Leone, M. P. (1995) 'A Historical Archaeology of Capitalism.' *American Anthropologist* 97:251–268.

Lewis, J. (1997) 'Mother's Love: The Construction of an Emotion in Nineteenth-Century America.' In R. Apple and J. Golden (eds.), *Mothers and Motherhood.* Columbus: Ohio State University Press.

Litoff, J. B. (1978) *American Midwives 1860 to the Present.* Westport: Greenwood Press.

Litt, J. S. (2000) *Medicalized Motherhood: Perspectives from the Lives of African-American and Jewish Women.* New Brunswick: Rutgers University Press.

Little, B. (2000) 'Compelling Images through Storytelling: Comment on "Imaginary, but by No Means Unimaginable: Storytelling, Science, and Historical Archaeology." ' *Historical Archaeology* 34(2):10–13.

Litwack, L. F. (1979) *Been in the Storm So Long: The Aftermath of Slavery.* New York: Vintage Books.

——— (1999) *Trouble in Mind: Black Southerners in the Age of Jim Crow.* New York: Vintage.

Loewenberg, B. J. and R. Bogin (eds.) (1976) *Black Women in Nineteenth-Century American Life: Their Words, Their Thoughts, Their Feelings.* College Station: Pennsylvania State University Press.

Logan, O. (as told to K. Clark) (1989) *Motherwit: An Alabama Midwife's Story.* New York: E. P. Dutton.

Lupton, D. and L. Barclay (1997) *Constructing Fatherhood: Discourses and Experiences.* London: Sage Publications.

MacCormack, C. and M. Strathern (eds.) (1980) *Nature, Culture, and Gender.* Cambridge: Cambridge University Press.

Magnolia Cemetery Records (n.d.) Block by block listing of internments. Records on file, Magnolia Cemetery Office, Mobile, Alabama.

Maher, V. (1992) 'Breast-Feeding in Cross-Cultural Perspective: Paradoxes and Proposals.' In V. Maher (ed.), *The Anthropology of Breast-Feeding: Natural Law or Social Construct.* London: Berg.

Majewski, T. (2000) ' "We Are All Story-Tellers": Comments on Storytelling, Science, and Historical Archaeology.' *Historical Archaeology* 34(2):17–19.

Majors, M. A. (1918) 'Analysis of a Difficult Problem.' *Half-Century Magazine.* January: 16–17.

Malone, A. P. (1992) *Sweet Chariot: Slave Family and Household Structure in Nineteenth-Century Louisiana.* Chapel Hill: University of North Carolina Press.

Martin, E. (2001) *Woman in the Body: A Cultural Analysis of Reproduction.* Boston: Beacon.

Martin, E. W. (1942) *The Standard of Living in 1860.* Chicago: University of Chicago Press.

Mathews, C. E. (1941) *Highlights of 75 Years in Mobile.* Mobile: Gill Printing and Stationary Company.

Mathews, H. (1992a) 'Doctors and Root Doctors: Patients Who Use Both.' In J. Kirkland, H. Mathews, C. W. Sullivan III, K. Baldwin (eds.), *Herbal and Magical Medicine: Traditional Healing Today.* Durham: Duke University Press.

———— (1992b) 'Killing the Medical Self-Help Tradition among African Americans: The Case of Lay Midwifery in North Carolina, 1912–1983.' In H. Baer and Y. Jones (eds.), *African Americans in the South.* Athens: University of Georgia Press.

Matzenger, G. (1888) Map of Mobile. Washington, D.C.: Library of Congress.

McMillen, S. G. (1990) *Motherhood in the Old South: Pregnancy, Childbirth, and Infant Rearing.* Baton Rouge: Louisiana State University Press.

McMurry, L. O. (1998) *To Keep the Waters Troubled: The Life of Ida B. Wells.* Oxford: Oxford University Press.

McPherson, J. M. (1982) *The Negro's Civil War.* New York: Ballantine Books.

Mehrer, M. W. (1995) *Cahokia Countryside: Household Archaeology, Settlement Patterns and Social Patterns.* Carbondale: Northern Illinois Press.

Meskell, L. (1999) *Archaeologies of Social Life.* Oxford: Blackwell.

———— (2000) 'Re-em(bed)ding Sex: Domesticity, Sexuality, and Ritual in New Kingdom Egypt.' In R. A. Schmidt and B. Voss (eds.), *Archaeologies of Sexuality.* London: Routledge.

Meyerowitz, J. (1994a) Introduction to J. Meyerowitz (ed.) *Not June Cleaver: Women and Gender in Postwar America, 1945–1960.* Philadelphia: Temple University Press.

———— (ed.) (1994b) *Not June Cleaver: Women and Gender in Postwar America, 1945–1960.* Philadelphia: Temple University Press.

Miles, D. and R. W. Miller (1986) *Price Guide to Pattern Glass.* Radnor, PA: Wallace-Homestead Books.

Millholland, Mrs. J. (1911) 'Talks about Women.' *Crisis* 2:29.

Mobile City Directory (1871) Mobile: George Matzenger, Printer.

———— (1885) Volume 20. Mobile: George Matzenger, Printer.

———— (1889) Volume 24. Mobile: George Matzenger, Printer.

———— (1892) Volume 27. Mobile: George Matzenger, Printer.

———— (1897) Volume 32. Mobile: George Matzenger, Printer.

———— (1899) Volume 34. Mobile: George Matzenger, Printer.

———— (1900) Volume 35. Mobile: George Matzenger, Printer.

———— (1901) Volume 36. Mobile: George Matzenger, Printer.

———— (1902) Volume 37. Mobile: J. Wiggins Co.

———— (1904) Mobile: R. L. Polk and Co., Publisher.

———— (1905) Mobile: R. L. Polk and Co., Publisher.

———— (1906) Mobile: R. L. Polk and Co., Publisher.

———— (1907) Mobile: R. L. Polk and Co., Publisher.

———— (1908) Mobile: R. L. Polk and Co., Publisher.

———— (1909) Mobile: R. L. Polk and Co., Publisher.

———— (1911) Mobile: R. L. Polk and Co., Publisher.

———— (1913) Mobile: R. L. Polk and Co., Publisher.

———— (1914) Mobile: R. L. Polk and Co., Publisher.

———— (1915) Mobile: R. L. Polk and Co., Publisher.

———— (1915) Mobile: R. L. Polk and Co., Publisher.

———— (1925) Mobile: R. L. Polk and Co., Publisher.

Mobile County Death Certificate [MCDC] (1884) Alabama Center for Health Statistics, Death Certificate for Marshall Perryman, May 19, 1884.

———— (1894a) Alabama Center for Health Statistics, Death Certificate for Frank Perryman, February 20, 1894.

———— (1894b) Alabama Center for Health Statistics, Death Certificate for Sally Cunningham, July 17, 1894.

———— (1917) Alabama Center for Health Statistics, Death Certificate for Lecretia [sic] Perryman, February 4, 1917.

Mobile Municipal Archive (1870–1925) Municipal Tax Books. Microfilm housed at Mobile Muncipal Archive, Mobile, Alabama.

———— (1881–1908) Municipal Tax Books, special back taxes. Microfilm housed at Mobile Municipal Archive, Mobile, Alabama.

Mohr, J. C. (1984) 'Patterns of Abortion and the Response of American Physicians, 1790–1930.' In J. W. Leavitt (ed.), *Women and Health in America*. Madison: University of Wisconsin Press.

Mongeau, B. (1985) 'The "Granny" Midwives: A Study of a Folk Institution in the Process of Social Disintegration.' Department of Sociology, University of North Carolina. Ann Arbor: University Microfilms.

Moore, J. and E. Scott (eds.) (1997) *Invisible People and Processes: Writing Gender and Childhood into European Archaeology*. London: Leicester University Press.

Morrison, T. (1987) *Beloved*. New York: Knopf.

Mullins, P. R. (1999) *Race and Affluence: An Archaeology of African America and Consumer Culture*. New York: Plenum.

Nebinger, A. (1870) 'Criminal Abortion: Its Extent and Prevention.' Reprinted in C. Rosenberg and C. Smith-Rosenberg (eds.), *Abortion in Nineteenth-Century America*. New York: Arno Press, 1973.

Nelson, S. (1997) *Gender in Archaeology: Analyzing Power and Prestige*. Walnut Creek, CA: Alta Mira.

Neverdon-Morton, C. (1989) *Afro-American Women of the South and the Advancement of the Race, 1895–1925*. Knoxville: University of Tennessee Press.

Noel-Hume, I. (1969) *Historical Archaeology*. New York: Knopf.

Noll, S. (1998) 'The Sterilization of Willie Mallory.' In M. Ladd-Taylor and L. Umansky (eds.), *"Bad" Mothers: The Politics of Blame in Twentieth-Century America*. New York: New York University Press.

Nordmann, C. (1990) 'Free Negroes in Mobile County, Alabama.' Department of History, University of Alabama. Ann Arbor: University Microfilms.

Norsigian, J. (1990) 'RU-486.' In M. G. Fried (ed.), *From Abortion to Reproductive Freedom: Transforming a Movement*. Boston: South End Press.

Northern, W. J (1909) 'Tuberculosis among Negroes.' *Journal of the Southern Medical Association* 6:407–419.

Northup, S. (1968) *Twelve Years a Slave*. Baton Rouge: Louisiana State University Press.

Oakley, A. (1984) *The Captured Womb: A History of the Medical Care of Pregnant Women*. Oxford: Basil Blackwell.

Orser, C. E., Jr. (1987) 'Plantation Status and Consumer Choice: A Materialist Framework for Historical Archaeology.' In S. Spencer-Wood (ed.), *Consumer Choice in Historical Archaeology*. New York: Plenum Press.

———— (1988) *The Material Basis of the Postbellum Tenant Plantation*. Athens: University of Georgia Press.

———— (1994) 'The Archaeology of Slave Religion in the Antebellum South.' *Cambridge Archaeological Journal* 4:33–45.

———— (1996) *A Historical Archaeology of the Modern World*. New York: Plenum Press.

———— (2001a) 'Race and the Archaeology of Identity in the Modern World.' In C. E. Orser (ed.), *Race and the Archaeology of Identity*. Salt Lake City: University of Utah Press.

———— (ed.) (2001b) *Race and the Archaeology of Identity*. Salt Lake City: University of Utah Press.

Ortner, S. (1972) ' "Is Female to Male as Nature Is to Culture?" ' *Feminist Studies* 1(2):5–31.

———— (1996) *Making Gender: The Politics and Erotics of Culture*. New York: Beacon.

Otto, J. S. (1984) *Cannon's Point Plantation 1794–1860: Living Conditions and Status Patterns in the Old South.* New York: Academic Press.

Parloa, M. (1910) *Home Economics: A Practical Guide in Every Branch of Housekeeping.* New York: Century.

PCMC (Probate Court of Mobile County) (1869) Title Transfer, Charles Gazzam to Marshall Perryman, May 11. Deed Book 25:502.

——— (1870) Bond for title. C. W. Gazzam to Marshall Perryman, May 17. Miscellaneous Book H:186–188.

——— (1873) Title Transfer. Charles W. Gazzam to Marshall Perryman, April 30. Deed book 31:411–413.

——— (1881) Title Transfer. Goldthwait to Perryman, June 1. Deed Book 44:507.

——— (1889) Title Transfer. Frank Perryman to Joseph Macrone. March 9, 1889. Deed Book 52:641.

——— (1891) Quit Claim, Joseph Macrone to Lucrecia Perryman. February 24, 1891. Deed Book 64:458–459.

——— (1922) Quit claims. Bates, DeVaughan and Baker to Susie Butler; Lyons to Butler; Lyons to Saunders; Lyons to Dorsey; Lyons to Douglas, December 21, 1922. Deed Book 271:630.

——— (1923a) Affidavit of Walter Perryman, February 17. Miscellaneous Book 26:322.

——— (1923b) Title transfer. Walter Perryman and wife to James S. Radcliff, February 19. Deed Book 196:553.

——— (1925) Title transfer. James S. Radcliff and wife to City of Mobile, July 30th. Deed Book 196:579.

——— (1936) Affidavit of Carolyn Saunders. Deed Book 271:630.

——— (n.d.) Manumissions: Index to manumissions in Mobile County.

Peiss, K. (1998) *Hope in a Jar: The Making of America's Beauty Culture.* New York: Metropolitan Books.

Perkins, L. (1983) 'The Impact of the "Cult of True Womanhood" on the Education of Black Women.' *Journal of Social Issues* 39(3):17–28.

Picone, M. (1998) 'Infanticide, the Spirits of Aborted Fetuses, and the Making of Motherhood in Japan.' In N. Scheper-Hughes and C. Sargent (eds.), *Small Wars: The Cultural Politics of Childhood.* Berkeley: University of California Press.

Pomeroy, H. S. (1891) 'Is Man Too Prolific? The So-Called Malthusian Idea.' Reprinted in C. Rosenberg and C. Rosenberg-Smith (eds.), *Abortion in Nineteenth-Century America.* New York: Arno Press, 1974.

Porter, L. E. (1917) 'Domestic Science: Nutritive Spring Breakfasts.' *Half-Century Magazine.* May: 13.

Potter, P. B. (1994) *Public Archaeology in Annapolis: A Critical Approach to History in Maryland's Ancient City.* Washington, D.C.: Smithsonian Institution Press.

Praetzellis, A. (1998) 'Introduction: Why Every Archaeologist Should Tell Stories Once in a While.' *Historical Archaeology* 32(1):1–3.

Praetzellis, A. and M. Praetzellis (1992) 'Faces and Facades: Victorian Ideology in Early Sacramento.' In A. Yentsch and M. Beaudry (eds.), *The Art and Mystery of Historical Archaeology.* Boca Raton: CRC Press.

——— (1998a) 'Archaeologists as Storytellers.' *Historical Archaeology* 32(1).

——— (1998b) 'A Connecticut Merchant in Chinadom: A Play in One Act.' *Historical Archaeology* 32(1):86–93.

——— (eds.) (1998c) *Historical Archaeology* 32(1). Special Issue.

Praetzellis, A., G. H. Ziesing, and M. Praetzellis (1997) *Tales of the Vasco. Los Vaqueros Final Report 5.* Rohnert Park: ASC, Sonoma State University Academic Foundation.

Praetzellis, M. (ed.) (1994) *West Oakland—A Place to Start From: Research Design and Treatment Plan, Cypress I-880 Replacement Project.* Rohnert Park, CA: Anthropological Studies Center (ASC), Sonoma State University Academic Foundation.

Ragoné, H. and F. W. Twine (eds.) (2000) *Ideologies and Technologies of Motherhood: Race, Class, Sexuality, Nationalism.* London: Routledge.

Rawick, G. (ed.) (1973) *Alabama and Indiana Narratives. Vol. 6 of The American Slave: A Composite Autobiography.* Westport: Greenwood Publishing.

——— (1974a) *North Carolina Narratives, Part 1 & 2. Vol. 11 of The American Slave: A Composite Autobiography.* Westport: Greenwood Publishing.

———— (1974b) *North Carolina Narratives, Part 4.* Vol. 11 of *The American Slave: A Composite Autobiography.* Westport: Greenwood Publishing.

———— (1974c) *The American Slave: A Composite Autobiography. Arkansas Narratives, Parts 1 & 2.* Westport: Greenwood Publishing.

———— (1977) Vol. 3 of *The American Slave: A Composite Autobiography, Supplement Series 1. Georgia Narratives, Part 1.* Westport: Greenwood Publishing.

———— (1979a) *Alabama, Arizona, Arkansas, District of Columbia, Florida, Georgia, Indiana, Kansas, Maryland, Nebraska, New York, North Carolina, Oklahoma, Rhode Island, South Carolina, Washington.* Vol. 1 of *The American Slave: A Composite Autobiography, Supplement Series 2.* Westport: Greenwood Press.

———— (1979b) *Texas.* Vol. 2 of *The American Slave: A Composite Autobiography, Supplement Series 2.* Westport: Greenwood Press.

Recknor, P. E. and S. A. Brighton (1999) ' "Free from All Vicious Habits": Archaeological Perspectives on Class Conflict and the Rhetoric of Temperance.' *Historical Archaeology* 33(1):63–86.

Reed, J. (1984) 'Doctors, Birth Control, and Social Values, 1830–1970.' In J. W. Leavitt (ed.), *Women and Health in America.* Madison: University of Wisconsin Press.

Rich, A. (1976) *Of Woman Born: Motherhood as Institution and Experience.* New York: W. W. Norton.

Richardson, M. (ed.) (1987) *Maria W. Stewart: America's First Black Woman Political Writer: Essays and Speeches.* Bloomington: Indiana University Press.

Riddle, J. M. (1997) *Eve's Herbs: A History of Contraception and Abortion in the West.* Cambridge: Harvard University Press.

Roberts, D. E. (1997) *Killing the Black Body: Race, Reproduction, and the Meaning of Liberty.* New York: Pantheon Books.

Roedrique, J. M. (1990) 'The Black Community and the Birth-Control Movement.' In E. C. DuBois and V. L. Ruiz (eds.), *Unequal Sisters: A Multicultural Reader in U.S. Women's History.* London: Routledge.

Rollins, J. (1985) *Between Women: Domestics and Their Employers.* Philadelphia: Temple University Press.

Rorabaugh, W. J. (1987) 'Beer, Lemonade, and Propriety in the Gilded Age.' In K. Grover (ed.), *Dining in America, 1850–1900.* Amherst: University of Massachusetts Press.

Rosaldo, R. and L. Lamphere (eds.) (1974) *Woman, Culture, and Society.* Stanford: Stanford University Press.

Ross, A. (1993) 'Health and Diet in Nineteenth-Century America: A Food Historian's Point of View.' *Historical Archaeology* 27(2):42–56.

Ross, L. J. (1997) 'African American Women and Abortion, 1800–1970.' In R. Apple and J. Golden (eds.), *Mothers and Motherhood: Readings in American History.* Columbus: University of Ohio Press.

Ruddick, S. (1980) 'Maternal Thinking.' *Feminist Studies* 6(2):342–367.

———— (1994) 'Thinking Mothers/Conceiving Birth.' In D. Bassin, M. Honey, and M. M. Kaplan (eds.), *Representations of Motherhood.* New Haven: Yale University Press.

Ryan, M. (1981) *Cradle of the Middle Class: The Family in Oneida Country, New York, 1790–1865.* London: Cambridge University Press.

Salmon, M. (1997) 'The Cultural Significance of Breast-Feeding and Infant Care in Early Modern England and America.' In R. Apple and J. Golden (eds.), *Mothers and Motherhood.* Columbus: Ohio State University Press.

Savitt, T. (1989) *Science and Medicine in the Old South.* Baton Rouge: Louisiana State University Press.

Savitt, T. and J. H. Young (eds.) (1988) *Disease and Distinctiveness in the Old South.* Knoxville: University of Tennessee Press.

Schaffer, R. (1991) 'The Health and Social Functions of Black Midwives on the Texas Barzos Bottom 1920–1985.' *Rural Sociology* 56(1):89–105.

Scheper-Hughes, N. (1992) *Death without Weeping: The Violence of Everyday Life in Brazil.* Berkeley: University of California Press.

Scheper-Hughes, N. and C. Sargent (1998a) 'The Cultural Politics of Childhood.' Introduction to N. Scheper-Hughes and C. Sargent (eds.), *Small Wars: The Cultural Politics of Childhood.* Berkeley: University of California Press.

———— (eds.) (1998b) *Small Wars: The Cultural Politics of Childhood.* Berkeley: University of California Press.

Schmidt, R. A. and B. L. Voss (eds.) (2000) *Archaeologies of Sexuality.* London: Routledge.

Scholten, C. M. (1984) 'On the Importance of the Obstetrick Art: Changing Customs of Childbirth in America, 1760–1825.' In J. W. Leavitt (ed.), *Women and Health in America.* Madison: University of Wisconsin Press.

Schroeder, J. J. (ed.) (1970) *1900 Sears, Roebuck Catalogue.* Northfield, IL: DBI Books.

———— (1971) *1908 Sears, Roebuck Catalogue.* Northfield: DBI Books.

Schulz, P., B. R. Rivers, M. M. Hales, C. A. Litzinger and E. A. McKee (1980) 'The Bottles of Old Sacramento: A Study of Nineteenth-Century Glass and Ceramic Retail Containers Part 1.' *California Archeological Reports No. 20.* Sacramento: State of California— Department of Parks and Recreation.

Schuyler, G. E. (1932) 'Quantity or Quality?' *Birth Control Review* 16(6):165–166.

Schwartz, M. J. (2000) *Born in Bondage: Growing Up Enslaved in the Antebellum South.* Cambridge: Harvard University Press.

Scott, E. M. (2001) 'Food and Social Relations at Nina Plantation.' *American Anthropologist* 103(3):671–691.

Scribner, C. M. (2001) 'Progress vs. Tradition in Mobile, 1900–1925.' In M. Thomason (ed.), *Mobile: The New History of Alabama's First City.* Tuscaloosa: University of Alabama Press.

Sears, Roebuck, and Company (1933) Fall Catalog. Oakland: Sears, Roebuck, and Company.

Seifert, D. (ed.) (1991) 'Gender in Historical Archaeology.' *Historical Archaeology* 25(4).

Seifert, D., E. B. O'Brien and J. Balicki (2000) 'Mary Ann Hall's First-Class House: The Archaeology of a Capital Brothel.' In R. Schmidt and B. Voss (eds.), *Archaeologies of Sexuality.* London: Routledge.

Sheridan, R. B. (1985) *Doctors and Slaves: A Medical and Demographic History of Slavery in the British West Indies, 1680–1834.* London: Cambridge University Press.

Smith, E. (1951) 'Nurse Midwife: Maude Callem Eases Pain of Birth, Life and Death.' *Life,* 3 July, 135–145.

Smith, M. C. and L. J. Holmes (1996) *Listen to Me Good.* Columbus: Ohio State University Press.

Smith, S. L. (1994) 'White Nurses, Black Midwives, and Public Health in Mississippi, 1920– 1950.' *Nursing History Review* 2:29–49.

———— (1995) *Sick and Tired of Being Sick and Tired: Black Women's Health Activism in America, 1890–1950.* Philadelphia: University of Pennsylvania Press.

Sofaer-Derevenski, J. (1994) 'Where Are the Children? Accessing Children in the Past.' *Archaeological Review from Cambridge* 13(2):8–20.

———— (ed.) (2000) *Children and Material Culture.* London: Routledge.

Solinger, R. (1994) ' "Extreme Danger": Women Abortionists and Their Clients before *Roe v. Wade.*' In J. Meyerowitz (ed.), *Not June Cleaver.* Philadelphia: Temple University Press.

Spector, J. (1991) 'What This Awl Means: Toward a Feminist Archaeology.' In J. Gero and M. Conkey (eds.) *Engendering Archaeology: Women and Prehistory.* Oxford: Basil Blackwell.

———— (1993) *What This Awl Means: Feminist Archaeology at a Wahpeton Dakota Village.* St. Paul: Minnesota Historical Society Press.

Spelman, E. V. (1988) *Inessential Woman: Problems of Exclusion in Feminist Thought.* Boston: Beacon Press.

Stack, C. B. (1974) *All Our Kin.* New York: Basic Books.

Stack, C. B. and L. M. Burton (1994) 'Kinscripts: Reflections of Family, Generation, and Culture.' In E. N. Glenn, G. Chang, and L. R. Forcey (eds.) *Mothering: Ideology, Experience, and Agency.* New York: Routledge.

Stage, S. (1997) 'Ellen Richards and the Social Significance of the Home Economics Movement.' In S. Stage and V. Vincenti (eds.), *Rethinking Home Economics: Women and the History of a Profession.* Ithaca: Cornell University Press.

Steckel, R. H. (1996) 'Women, Work, and Health under Plantation Slavery in the United States.' In D. Gaspar and D. C. Hine (eds.), *More Than Chattel.* Bloomington: University of Indiana Press.

Stine, L., M. A. Cabak and M. D. Groover (1996) 'Blue beads as African-American Cultural Symbols.' *Historical Archaeology* 30(3):49–75.

Strathern, M. (1992) *Reproducing the Future.* New York: Routledge.

Summersell, C. G. (1949) *Mobile: History of a Seaport Town.* Tuscaloosa: University of Alabama Press.

Susie, D. A. (1988) *In the Way of Our Grandmothers: A Cultural View of Twentieth-Century Midwifery in Florida.* Athens: University of Georgia Press.

Thompson, H. A. (1974) Magnolia Cemetery: A Collection of Records from the Gravestones of One of the Oldest Cemeteries in Mobile, Alabama, including the Confederate Rest, Dating from 1828 to 1971. New Orleans: Polyanthos.

Thompson, R. F. (1983) *Flash of the Spirit.* New York: Random House.

Tomes, N. (1997) 'Spreading the Germ Theory: Sanitary Science and Home Economics, 1880–1930.' In S. Stage and V. Vincenti (eds.), *Home Economics: Women and the History of a Profession.* Ithaca: Cornell University Press.

Toulouse, J. H. (1971) *Bottle Makers and Their Marks.* New York: Thomas Nelson.

Tringham, R. E. (1991) 'Households with Faces: The Challenge of Gender in Prehistoric Architectural Remains.' In J. Gero and M. Conkey (eds.), *Engendering Archaeology.* Oxford: Basil Blackwell.

Troxler, C. W. (1976) *The Loyalist Experience in North Carolina.* Chapel Hill: North Carolina Department of Cultural Resources.

Tucker, S. (1988) *Telling Memories among Southern Women: Domestic Workers and Their Employers in the Segregated South.* New York: Schocken.

Ulrich, L. T. (1991) *A Midwife's Tale: The Life of Martha Ballard, Based on Her Diary, 1785–1812.* New York: Vintage.

University of South Alabama (1994) *Index to Divorce Cases of the Thirteenth Judicial Circuit Court of Alabama 1816–1918.* Mobile: University of South Alabama Archive.

Van Blarcom, C. C. (1914) 'Midwives in America.' *American Journal of Public Health* 4(2):197–207.

Van De Warker, E. (1872) 'The Detection of Criminal Abortion and a Study of Foeticidal Drugs.' Reprinted in C. Rosenberg and C. Smith-Rosenberg (eds.), *Abortion in Nineteenth-Century America.* New York: Arno Press, 1974.

Wall, D. D. (1991) 'Sacred Dinners and Secular Teas: Constructing Domesticity in Mid-Nineteenth-Century New York.' *Historical Archaeology* 25(4):69–81.

—— (1994) *The Archaeology of Gender: Separating the Spheres in Urban America.* New York: Plenum Press.

—— (2000) 'Family Meals and Evening Parties: Constructing Domesticity in Nineteenth-Century Middle-Class New York.' In J. A. Delle, S. A. Mrozowski, and R. Paynter (eds.), *Lines That Divide.* Knoxville: University of Tennessee Press.

Warner, M. S. (1998) ' "The Best There Is of Us": Ceramics and Status in African American Annapolis.' In P.A. Shackel, P. R. Mullins, and M. S. Warner (eds.), *Annapolis Pasts: Historical Archaeology in Annapolis, Maryland.* Knoxville: University of Tennessee Press.

Washington, M. (1904) 'Social Improvement of the Plantation Woman.' *The Voice of the Negro* 1(6):288–294.

Webb, A. B. W. (1983) *Mistress of Evergreen: Rachel O'Conner's Legacy of Letters, 1823–1845.* Albany: State University of New York Press.

Wertz, R. W. and D. C. Wertz (1979) *Lying In: A History of Childbirth in America.* New York: Schocken Books.

Wheaton, T. R., Jr. and M. B. Reed (1990) 'James City, North Carolina: Archaeological and Historical Study of an African-American Urban Village.' *New South Associates Technical Report 6.* Stone Mountain, GA: New South Associates.

White, D. G. (1985) *Ar'n't I a Woman? Female Slaves in the Plantation South.* New York: W. W. Norton.

Wilk, R. (1997) *Household Ecology: Economic Change and Domestic Life among the Kekchi Maya in Belize.* Carbondale: Northern Illinois University Press.

Wilkie, L. A. (1996) 'Medicinal Teas and Patent Medicines: African-American Women's Consumer Choices and Ethnomedical Traditions at a Louisiana Plantation.' *Southeastern Archaeology* 15(2):119–131.

—— (1997) 'Secret and Sacred: Contextualizing the Artifacts of African-American Magic and Religion.' *Historical Archaeology* 31(4):81–106.

────── (2000a) *Creating Freedom: African-American Constructions of Identity at a Louisiana Plantation, 1845–1950.* Baton Rouge: Louisiana State University Press.

────── (2000b) 'Magical Passions: Sexuality and African-American Archaeology.' In R. A. Schmidt and B. Voss (eds.), *Archaeologies of Sexuality.* New York: Routledge.

────── (forthcoming) 'African-American Midwives: Gender and Generational Mediators.' In J. Galle and A. Young (eds.), *Engendering African-American Archaeology.* Knoxville: University of Tennessee Press.

Wilkie, L. A. and G. W. Shorter, Jr. (2001) 'Lucrecia's Well: An Archaeological Glimpse of an African-American Midwife's Household.' *University of South Alabama Archaeological Monograph 11.* Mobile: University of South Alabama Center for Archaeological Studies.

Williams, B. (1992) 'Of Straightening Combs, Sodium Hydroxide, and Potassium Hydroxide in Archaeological and Cultural-Anthropological Analyses of Ethnogenesis.' *American Antiquity* 57(4):608–612.

Williams, F. B. (1904a) 'The Club Movement among the Colored Women.' *The Voice of the Negro* 1(3):99–102.

────── (1904b) 'The Colored Girl.' *The Voice of the Negro* 1(5):184–185.

────── (1906) 'The Refining Influence of Art.' *The Voice of the Negro* March: 211–214.

Williams, J. W. (1912) 'Medical Education and the Midwife Problem in the United States.' *Journal of the American Medical Association* 58(1):1–7.

Williams, S. F. (1904) 'The Social Status of the Negro Woman.' *The Voice of the Negro* 1(7):298–300.

Williams, S. R. (1987) Introduction to K. Grover (ed.), *Dining in America, 1850–1900.* Amherst: University of Massachusetts Press.

Wong, S. C. (1994) 'Diverted Mothering: Representations of Caregivers of Color in the Age of "Multiculturalism." ' In E. N. Glenn, G. Chang, and L. R. Forcey (eds.), *Mothering: Ideology, Experience, and Agency.* New York: Routledge.

Wood, A. D. (1984) 'The Fashionable Diseases: Women's Complaints and Their Treatment in Nineteenth-Century America.' In J. W. Leavitt (ed.), *Women and Health in America.* Madison: University of Wisconsin Press.

Work, M. N. (1912) *Negro Year Book: Annual Encyclopedia of the Negro.* Nashville: Sunday School Union Print.

Wright, R. (ed.) (1996) *Gender and Archaeology.* Philadelphia: University of Pennsylvania Press.

Wurst, L. A. and R. Fitts (1999) Introduction: Why Confront Class? *Historical Archaeology* 33(1).

Yentsch, A. (1994) *A Chesapeake Family and Their Slaves.* Oxford: Oxford University Press.

Young, J. H. (1961) *The Toadstool Millionaire: A Social History of Patent Medicines in America before Regulation.* Princeton: Princeton University Press.

Index

abolitionist literature and portrayals of mothering, 55, 59, 69–70

abortion: archaeology of, xxvii, 161–170; chemical means of, 149, 150–153, 155–156, 158; during enslavement, 60, 154, 156; in Japan, 2; mechanical means of, 156–157; regulation of, 147, 149–150; midwives' role in, 147, 150, 153–155, 160–162, 169; pharmacists' role in, 150, 153; related to eugenics, 150, 157

abortifacients, 150–152, 153, 155–156, 159, 164, 165, 217

advertising, 150–152, 184, 196

African-American: archaeology of, xix, 9–10, 64, 68, 85, 108–109, 168, 161–162, 209; class identities within, 85–89, 122, 182; constructions of motherhood, 55, 56, 79–80, 81–82; ethnomedical traditions, xvii, 64, 68, 121, 129–130, 158–159, 161–162, 200, 215; family life, 82–83; historiography, 15–16, 17–18, 20, 31, 66; land ownership, 87–88; memories of enslavement, 60–74; midwives, 34–35, 119–142, 177–203; political movements, 80, 81–82, 180–183, 203, 216; stereotypes of, 55–59, 74, 197, 198

African Burial Ground, 8

African continuities, 125–126, 134, 138

afterbirth, 132–133, 135

agency, xx, xxviii, 219

alcoholic beverages: class associations, 100–101, 102; containers, 101–102, 126–127; medicinal uses, 126, 158, 188

"Allen's Lung Balsam", 185, 196

American Medical Association (AMA), xviii, 123, 162, 197

American Woman's Home (The Beecher and Stowe), 178–179

Annapolis, Maryland, 85, 168

anemia, 156

anesthesia, 148

Anthony, Susan B., 82

antiseptics, 186

Apple, Rima, 4, 196

archaeological dating, 41–45

archaeological excavation, xvii–xviii, 41–45

archaeological features, 12–13, 40–45, 89–90

archaeology: and fictive narrative, xxii–xxviii; and relationship to present, xxii; and study of class, 4, 7, 9, 86, 89, 209; and study of gender, xix, 4–5, 210–211; and study of mothering, 4, 6–8, 11–12, 46–48, 219; and study of race, xxiii, 8, 209

asafetida, 156, 159

A Voice from the South (Cooper), 81

axes, 133–134

babies: breast feeding, 65, 66–67, 162, 189–190, 194, 195; care, 129, 178, 182, 185, 189–190; introduction rituals for, 138; protection of, 6, 68, 123, 181–184; separation from mothers, 65–66

"bad mothers", 3, 12

Bahktin, Mikhail, xxv, xxviii

Bakongo cosmogram, 138

Ballard, Martha, xviii

beads, 68

Beausang, Elisabeth, 5

Beecher, Catherine, 178–179

beef tea, 129

beauty ideals, 109–112

"Bienville Pharmacy", 166, 167, 169

bioarchaeology, 8, 66–67

birth, 5–6, 11, 46, 60, 132–135

birth control, xxvii, 8, 60, 64–67, 147, 149, 150, 151, 157, 160, 161, 164

Birth Control Review, 157, 161

black political movements, 79, 80, 180–183, 203, 216

Blakey, Michael, 8, 61, 66–67